Reclaiming a Nation at Risk

The Battle for Your
Faith, Family, and Freedoms

D1602804

Pam Hafen

Reclaiming a Nation at Risk

*The Battle for Your
Faith, Family, and Freedoms*

By Brannon S. Howse

Bridgestone Multimedia Group
Chandler, Arizona 85226-2618

About the Author

As president of the American Family Policy Institute, Brannon Howse spends countless hours each year reading legislation and writing issue briefs in an effort to inform the American people about policies that affect the family — either positively or negatively. Some of his extensive research and knowledge on family and educational issues has been compiled in this and his first book, *Cradle to College: An Educational Abduction.*

Brannon also hosts his own national radio show, "The American Family Policy Update," which is now heard on over 125 stations each weekend. In addition, Brannon has been a featured speaker at Dr. D. James Kennedy's "Reclaiming America Conference," along with such notables as Alan Keyes, Cal Thomas, and Dr. Kennedy. He has also addressed the ACSI conference, which is the world's largest private school association, and spoken at numerous colleges and universities.

Due to his expertise in family issues, Brannon has been a guest on over 200 radio and television programs, including "Truths That Transform" with Dr. D. James Kennedy; "The G. Gordon Liddy Show," "The Michael Reagan Show," "Action Sixties," "Point of View," "Crosstalk," "Family News and Focus," "U.S.A. Radio News," "Standard News," and "The Phyllis Schlafly Show," to name a few.

As the Education Reporter for "The Michael Reagan Show," Brannon takes to the airwaves many times each year to inform Mr. Reagan's listeners of the latest attacks on educational freedom and parental authority and to give them proactive ways to be involved in the battle for faith, family, and freedoms.

In April and August, 1995, Brannon was asked to act as substitute host of Michael Reagan's program, which is the nation's third largest syndicated radio talk show. True to form, Brannon alerted Americans to the dangers of government education reform.

Acknowledgements

I would like to thank my wife Melissa for the love and support she gives me each and every day and for her commitment to faith, family, and freedoms.

A special thank you to my editor Val Cindric. Val was not only my editor for this book but for my last book as well. As long as Val agrees to continue to edit them, I will continue to write them.

I must acknowledge my agent Joyce Hart of Hartline Marketing. Joyce has been representing me since before my first book. I am very grateful for her knowledge, experience and commitment to me and the things of which I write and speak.

I also want to thank my publisher Bob Campbell Jr. for his passion and drive for excellence. His commitment to producing and publishing quality books, videos and teaching materials for today's family has made his company one of the largest family publishers in America.

I want to thak the following individuals who were in involved in proof reading, type setting and other pre-production business.

Paul Wilkenson
Carol Pomeroy
Patrick Conrad
Alan Christopherson
David Redding

Dedication

This book is dedicated to my father George Howse and to the thousands of other men like him in America who are committed to faith, family, and freedoms.

If only all men in America would instill into their children the values of hard work, leadership, perseverance, honesty, responsibility, and individualism that my father instilled into me by word and example — then we could, without a doubt, reclaim America.

I would also like to dedicate this book to a few other men who have and continue to be an example to me by their faithfulness and passion to reclaim America.

To Michael Reagan, host of America's third largest national radio program and the largest nationally syndicated nighttime show. Michael Reagan continues to lead the Reagan Revolution started by his father, President Ronald Reagan.

Michael believed me, my message, and my research enough to ask me to serve as his education reporter. I am honored to be a guest on his show many times each year to report to his listeners the latest government attack on educational freedom.

Michael also has bestowed on me the honor of hosting his national radio program on more than one occasion. The first time I hosted the Michael Reagan show was also my very first time to host any radio program. Thanks to Michael, who gave me my start, today I host my own national weekend radio program that can be heard on more than 100 stations.

To Steve Holly, a former history teacher turned pastor who has been a good and faithful friend for many years. His frequent long-distance phone calls — which he makes to check on me, encourage, and challenge me — are a shot in the arm each and every time.

To Dr. D. James Kennedy, author of countless books, pastor of a 6,000 member church, host of a national radio and television program, and, in my opinion, the greatest Christian statesman alive today.

Dr. Kennedy's commitment to the family, traditional values, and quality education has stood the test of time. He was politically incorrect long before most of today's conservative authors and talk show hosts were even born. It has been an honor and privilege to share the platform with him and to be a guest on his radio program several times.

To Geoffrey Botkin, one of America's most articulate journalists, who has been successful wearing many different hats in the nation's capital — business executive, political consultant, filmmaker, and author. But Geoffrey's greatest accomplishment by far has been at home, where he and his wife have created for their seven children the kind of culture our nation needs to recover. I have been in their home and can testify to their parenting and teaching success.

Contents

Foreword
by Michael Reagan

In February of 1994, I invited Brannon Howse to be a guest on my national radio program. Very rarely do we keep a guest on for a full hour, but Brannon's knowledge of his subject and the interest by my listeners led me to interview Brannon for a few minutes and then open up the phone lines for callers to ask him questions.

Shortly after this first encounter with Brannon, I asked my producer to invite him back on the program to give my listeners an update on certain educational bills he had read and was tracking through Congress. Brannon's passion and commitment to inform and equip Americans with the truth caused me to ask him to serve as the education reporter and consultant for "The Michael Reagan Show."

Brannon can be heard several times each year on my show reporting to my listeners the government's latest attempts to undermine parental authority and traditional education. In April and August of 1995 Brannon sat in for me as a guest host of "The Michael Reagan Show," reporting to my listeners much of what is in this book.

Many of you have become increasingly frustrated with our unresponsive, unwieldy government. More and more Americans want to do something to help save the dream of our Founding Fathers. In this book, Brannon provides information you need to affect your government's decision-making process — a process that is today being controlled too often by the desires and goals of the cultural elite.

Our Founding Fathers declared that it was a right of the people — not a small group of elitist — to exercise control over their own government. That ideal was expressed in 1774 by the Continental Congress. "The first grand right is that of the people having a share in their own government by their repre- sentatives chosen by themselves, and . . . being ruled by laws which they themselves approve, not edicts of men over whom they have no control."

The Founding Fathers left us with a system of government based upon the notion that the authority and the rights come from the people. Thomas Jefferson believed that all men are born with not only the right, but the responsibility to make sure his government is not becoming "destructive to these ends."

In the words of my father, Ronald Reagan, "Government does not solve problems; it subsidizes them." We cannot allow our governments to do what no government can morally or effectively do — become a substitute for individual responsi- bility, hard work, strong families, quality education, and per- sonal convictions.

America is still a great nation, but it is imperative that informed, thoughtful, and noble citizens take hold of the rud- der and navigate this nation out of the swirling waters of col- lectivism and rushing current of moral relativism.

We can reclaim this at-risk nation by reclaiming and defending our faith, family, and freedoms.

This book by Brannon Howse is well-researched and docu- mented and can be trusted and used to help you reclaim America in a positive, pro-active way. Begin reading and then begin defending.

Michael Reagan,
Host of the Nationally syndicated radio program,
"The Michael Reagan Show"

Introduction

$\mathbb{M}$any in our nation today believe and proclaim that we need to "re-invent America."

Does our country really need more change away from the traditions and moral absolutes that made it so great? Is change the answer, or does our nation just need restoration?

Many agents of change have for generations committed themselves to bringing about irreversible social, political, economic, and moral change. This is alarming when you realize that our nation is going down a path completely contradictory to what our founding fathers intended and what most Americans want.

The November 1994 elections indicated that many Americans are not happy with where we are headed as a nation. A large number of Americans want change — a change back to what made America great — individual responsibility and freedom. The American people in November 1994 were calling for a *smaller* federal government — not more government.

Much of what is being forced on this once great nation of ours is in complete and total violation of our Constitution and Bill of Rights.

Regardless of what the liberals say, our country was established and based on Judeo-Christian principals and standards. Today, over 200 years later, we are faced with a government who wants absolute control, a political system that is amuck with impropriety, and an educational system that has decided it no longer wants to teach, but rather wants to tell us how best to raise our children. No wonder we live in such troubling times. All that our founding fathers established for our great nation is slowly being chiseled away.

Someone has said, "If you don't learn from history, you are doomed to repeat it." We can certainly learn from history that great nations do fail and some even fall. America should take heed before history repeats itself.

The Greatest Nation on Earth

At one time, there was a great nation. In fact, it was the greatest nation on the face of the earth. Its power and influence were felt throughout the entire world.

Several key factors contributed to this nation's greatness: strong families, quality education, religious freedom, personal accountability, and small government.

What made this nation's families strong? History reveals it was the absolute respect given to the father as the head of the home. The culture imposed tremendous responsibility upon the father to be the leader of his household. In fact, fathers had the legal authority to discipline rebellious children.

Men who shrugged their responsibilities and leadership positions were despised and ridiculed by their peers. This kind of cultural respect and high expectation placed upon the fathers resulted in a nation comprised of strong family units.

Parents — not the government — were responsible for the education of their children. Home education greatly strengthened the relationships between parents and children by allowing the family to know each other on more than a casual basis. Parental control over education allowed parents to instill into their children personal accountability and religious values. The nation's heritage and culture were also emphasized. Home education and private schools controlled by parents were the only institutions of education this nation knew for more than 150 years.

Strong families combined with family-centered, religious education led to a strong nation. The strength of any nation rests in the strength of its families.

A Once Great Nation

The same factors that contributed to the rise of this great nation ultimately affected its downfall when strong families, quality education, and small government were compromised.

Due to pressure from some of the nation's cultural elite, day schools were started. These schools were free to all and funded by taxing all citizens, whether their children were educated in the schools of the cultural elite or not.

Years later the schools were taken over by the government, which created a centralized bureaucracy in its capitol. As conservatives had predicted years before, the schools of the cultural elite were a dismal failure - both academically and morally. From the standpoint of the schools' founders, however, they were accomplishing their objective — to create a citizenry that could be easily controlled.

The government schools also undermined traditional values and parental authority. As a result, respect for the father as the head of the home lessened as did the strength of the family. Eventually the father lost his legal authority, and the nation's families began to fall apart. The authority that once belonged to the father was taken by the city, state, and, eventually, the nation's oversized government.

Before long, the size, power, and control of government ballooned. To finance all the government's new responsibilities, which once belonged to the fathers, mothers, and local communities, taxes were greatly increased. This high tax burden placed upon the citizens led to declining national prosperity.

While the government allowed all forms of humanistic religion, one form of worship was despised by many government officials and the nation's court judges. They made it their goal to rid the nation of this religion's symbols and books in an effort to squelch the teachings of its Leader — who advocated personal freedom, individual opinion, creative expression, and true spiritual worship.

In the end, due to the lack of strong families, quality education, and religious freedom, and the increase in big government and high taxation, this weakened nation began to crumble from within.

What is the name of the once great nation? The United States of America. The facts are clear and the evidence is abundant.

To those who doubt my analysis of America's decline, I suggest you read this book from cover to cover.

Questions for a Nation At Risk

There is still time to reclaim America, but we must act now.

Many governmental programs being promoted and implemented by America's social engineers have resulted in the long arm of Washington subtly taking control and forcing societal change. This change includes the loss of many freedoms, a bigger government, the increase in taxes, the decline in quality education, and the weakening of the American family.

Is America on the verge of falling?

Newsweek magazine reported, in July 1995, that nearly half of America's citizens believe the United States won't exist in a hundred years. Unless there is a great revolution based on the mandate to roll back and downsize big government, unless we demand personal responsibility and integrity from everyone and every elected official, unless America returns to using its original moral compass, our days as a free and great nation are numbered.

Let me ask you:

• Were the November 1994 elections the beginning of a revolution?

• Can we stop the liberal agents of change and see a rebirth of America?

• Have the agents of change simply done too much damage?

• Do America's liberal elite have so much power and control outside of and over Congress that even a new Congress is no real long-term threat?

These are questions we will examine in an effort to stop

America's agents of change, preserve faith, family, and freedoms — and reclaim a nation at risk.

1

America's Schools Held Hostage

During the 1994 Minnesota State Fair, I was the guest on a live radio talk show being broadcast in front of a crowd of on-lookers.

A caller, who identified himself as an educator, phoned in and asked, "What are your qualifications, and why don't you just leave these matters to the educational experts?"

To this I replied, "Well, I have written a few books on the subject of education and spent untold hours studying today's educational system. Despite such credentials, my qualifications to discuss such issues rest in the fact that I am a tax-paying American.

"You ask, Why don't I just leave it up to the experts?" I continued. "This is exactly the attitude that is permeating our educational system today, and parents are sick of it. Parents are being lowered to the status of mere breeders, who give birth to their children, and are then supposed to turn them over to the educational experts."

"Well, let me tell you," I said, my voice rising indignantly. "It is the moms and dads all across this country who are fighting programs like Outcome-Based Education because they know it does not work. They have seen it fail in Virginia, Kentucky, Chicago, and Minnesota. It doesn't take a Ph.D. to realize that this program is a failure and should be dumped.

"Yet, it is the educational experts, like William Spady, William Glasser, and Secretary of Education Richard Riley," I said, "who are running around the country promoting what parents know — and have the data to prove — that OBE does not and *will not* work. The difference between a parent and a Ph.D. is that the parent has common-sense!"

With that statement, the assembled crowd, made up of many parents, cheered loudly.

When another guest on the radio talk show was asked about his background, he apologetically admitted that he had his Ph.D. in Education Administration.

Parents — Mere Breeders

During my state fair interview, I mentioned that parents are being lowered to the status of mere breeders. Why would I make such a statement? Because that is how educators describe parents.

Arizona Superintendent of Public Instruction, Carolyn Warner, proves my point when she says,

> Those who educate are more to be honored
> than those who bear the children. The latter
> gave them only life, the former teach them the
> art of living.[1]

Keep in mind, it is the experts who have gotten us where we are today. The downfall of America's educational system began when it went from no longer being controlled by mom and dad to a group of social engineers who did not respect parental authority or parental desires. Their only goal was and is to use the most powerful institution of all time for mass indoctrination.

Constitutional attorney, William Ball, hit the nail on the head when he said, "The nation's most important institution is the institution of education because it is the institution that affects all others."

As you read on, you will understand why this is true.

The Global Education Agenda

e aspect of the liberal's social engineering involves fit-
ti   nerica into the United Nations' global plan for educa-
tio.

As Vice-Chairman, and later Chairman, of the National
Governors Association, Bill Clinton helped develop the educational monster, Goals 2000 — America's version of a global
education agenda established by the World Conference on
Education for All.

This conference, sponsored by the Interagency
Commission on Education for All, consisted of the World
Bank, the United Nations Children's Fund, the United Nations
Development Programme, and the United Nations
Educational, Scientific and Cultural Organization.

The outcome of this conference, which was held in
Jomtien, Thailand, March 5-9, 1990, resulted in the World
Declaration on Education for All and Framework for Action to
Meet Basic Learning Needs.

Not long after he arrived in Washington, President Clinton
made sure that Goals 2000 was passed by Congress so he
could sign it into law in the spring of 1994.

Why is President Clinton pushing Goals 2000? Because it
puts the federal government in control of all 110,000 of
America's elementary and secondary public schools.

Paying for Goals 2000

How did Bill Clinton fund this massive federal takeover of
American education by our government? He had his friends at
the Department of Education and on Capitol Hill completely
re-write the Elementary and Secondary Act of 1965, (ESEA),
which is the largest bill for federal funding of public education
ever devised.

Originally designed to provide federal dollars to disadvantaged school children, this bill was seen by the federal government as an opportunity to meddle in local educational affairs.
As a result, very few of ESEA's millions went to poor children.
Since 1965, both advantaged and disadvantaged children have

State Senator Bill   1-817-939-3562
              Sims

suffered the debilitating effects of governmental interference.

The Elementary and Secondary Act of 1965 must be approved by Congress every five years. Bill Clinton had the 1994 version of ESEA completely re-written with an additional several hundred pages of strict federal controls over local education. He then enlarged the ESEA budget ($12.5 billion for one year alone) to fund his plan — Goals 2000.

Many of these controls were clearly unconstitutional, but congressmen were afraid to vote against something that started out to help disadvantaged children get a better education. To make it even harder for congressmen to vote against H.R. 6, the authors gave it this euphemistic title: "The Improving America's Schools Act of 1994."

H.R. 6 and S. 1513, which are the House and Senate numbers for the Elementary and Secondary Act of 1965, represents the taxpayers' money that funds Clinton's baby, Goals 2000.

This put the states and public schools in a bind. In order to receive a piece of the $12.5 billion of federal money allowed for by H.R. 6 and S. 1513, states and schools must comply completely with Goals 2000.

After H.R. 6 and S. 1513 passed the House and Senate, these bills went to conference where the Senate and House versions were merged into one bill, now known as simply H.R. 6. Once out of conference, H.R. 6 was again approved by the House and the Senate to become law.

H.R. 6 — The Stealth Takeover

Where does that leave America? With an educational system that will never be the same again. As a result of H.R. 6, our educational system will be drastically changed.

Research journalist, Geoffrey Botkin, explains the impact H.R. 6 will have on America's school systems:

> Even if Congress could repeal H.R. 6, American
> public education will never be the same.
> Americans are now aware that the mysterious
> educators at the top of public education are

bad boys with dishonorable intentions. They
betrayed a trust.

Stephen Arons, a nationally syndicated columnist, wrote in
February 1994 about "An Education Bill of Rights." He notes
that H.R. 6 and Goals 2000 will so greatly change the magni-
tude of power that the Federal Government has that in order
to protect our constitutional freedoms, and the future of education in our country, we must have an Education Bill of Rights.

Bob Holland, writing in the *Washington Times*, February 8,
1994, called H.R. 6 and Goals 2000 a "stealth takeover of education."

Why must there be this stealth takeover of education by
our federal government?

Thomas Toch, in the January 11, 1993, *U.S. News and World
Report*, answered this question in his article, "The Perfect
School":

> It is tremendously difficult to build national
> momentum behind a particular reform when
> 50 state legislatures, 50 state boards and more
> than 15,000 local school boards have veto
> power.

In other words, American's agents of change cannot
accomplish their determined agenda under the rules of a
democracy. After all, you the people may have a mind to veto
Goals 2000 at the state or local level. To keep that from happening, the agents of change must work behind the scenes to
take over America's educational system.

As far back as 1992, John Leo of *U.S. News and World
Report*, warned parents in his article, "Schools to Parents: Keep
Out." He told parents to "look for more stealth programs in
schools."[2]

One former U.S. Department of Education official has
called H.R. 6 "one of the most unconstitutional bills to ever
pass through Congress."

Goals 2000 — Unconstitutional?

What makes Goals 2000 and the funding package, H.R. 6, unconstitutional? Within the content of this chapter I will provide eleven reasons why Goals 2000 flies in the face of our constitutionally protected rights as Americans and as parents.

1. H.R. 6 grants unconstitutional powers to the National Education Standards and Improvement Council, established by Goals 2000.
This 20 member board will be based in Washington D.C. and act as a national school board. These 20 members are mostly appointed by the President and must be "professional teachers," which means members of the National Education Association.

Once this 20 member national school board is in place, you can say good-bye to local control, which will receive mere lip service because federal dollars will be driving the process.

Goals 2000 and H.R. 6 give the states the power to actually fire locally elected school board members unless they comply with the federal legislation.

Non-compliance to Goals 2000 and ESEA by any state or school district would mean that this state or school district would be subject to losing federal dollars allowed for by this legislation. Therefore, the Department of Education in any state has the power to remove dully elected school board members and replace them with individuals who will comply with the federal mandates in order to ensure the receipt of federal dollars for the state or school district.

2. Goals 2000 and ESEA violates the tenth amendment by taking the right of the people in each state to control their own educational system, according to the Bill of Rights, and gives it to the federal government.
The word "education" is not mentioned in the Constitution. Why? Because it is the right of the parents in each state — not the federal government.

3. H.R. 6 strives to "develop with parents for all children a school-parent compact that outlines how parents, the school and students will share responsibility for improved student achievement and the means by which the school and parents will build and develop a partnership."

The bill goes so far to say that the schools will pursue to "work with parents as equal partners."

I don't think most parents want their school to be equal with them when it comes to raising their children. Most Americans believe the school should act as the school and the parents should act as the parents.

I don't need the federal government to become "equal partners" with me in the raising of my child.

4. ESEA will allow for school-based clinics.

Why are these clinics unconstitutional? Because, as Geoffrey Botkin explains, they will "be given money and incredible powers, including latitude to administer super-secret exams, vaccines, contraceptives, abortion counseling and unlicensed psychological therapies to some children without parental consent."

To promote such intrusive programs, the agents of change must sugar coat and wrap them in legislation that appears to be good and noble. Otherwise, the American people would reject such programs for what they really are — social engineering.

Is Your Family "At Risk"?

5. Goals 2000 and ESEA will help fund a controversial and mandatory national program known as "Parents as Teachers."

This program involves the use of a "home educator," which is actually a high-sounding name for a low-level social worker who comes into your home to "evaluate" your family.

In a speech on the Senate floor, Tom Harkin made it clear how he feels about invading American homes with social workers.

> So early intervention programs, such as think-
> ing that education begins at birth and prepara-

tion begins before birth. . . . We know scientifi-
cally and medically that much of a child's brain
capacity is developed long before they begin
elementary school. . . . If you really want to
have an effective Head Start Program, let us get
these kids right after birth and start a Head
Start Program right then, and not wait until
they are four years old.[3]

This program should really be called "Teachers as
Parents." Why? Because it allows for a politically correct social
worker to come into your home to collect personal data on
your child/children and entire family.

This home educator receives a mere 30 hours of training —
less than a full work week — to become a "professional" on
how to teach parents to be parents. The process is made simple
by the use of 12 computer codes, which determine whether or
not your family is "at risk."

The ironic fact is that there is no computer code for "normal." As a result, every child and family will be found at risk.
Under this program any child can be removed from the home
by the government. Remember, this is all done in the name of
improving America's educational system.

The home educator uses 12 very vague codes to determine
whether or not your family is, "at risk." Every family, in one
way or another, is going to meet at least one of the "at risk"
codes. (For a complete list of the "at risk" codes, see my first
book Cradle to College.: An Educational Abduction.)

Some of these "at risk" codes include a parent who is ill,
overweight, tired, depressed or is moving to a new home,
given birth to the child's sibling, had a death in the family —
and several more shocking "at risk" situations.

Funded federally on a national basis through Goals 2000,
the "Parents as Teachers" program is currently a voluntary
program. On July 21, 1993, however, the deputy director of the
"Parents as Teachers" program, which is based in St. Louis,
testified before the U.S. Ways and Means House Committee
that she believed it was the right of every child to receive a
regularly scheduled home visit from a home educator.

What's so bad about that? Sure, there are children who are not being cared for properly and who are being abused and who need to be monitored. Yes, there are children who are in awful situations who need to be removed until the parents can clean up their act. In some cases, there are children who should never be returned to their parents because of the extreme neglect or abuse they have undergone.

If you study the "Parents as Teachers" program, however, you will see that its purpose is not to end child abuse or give help to parents who need to learn to love and care for their children.

This program is voluntary. What parent is going to volunteer for this program if they are mistreating their child? In fact, under the all inclusive "at risk" codes every parent reading this book would fall into the category of "at risk."

No Certificate — No Nothing

6. ESEA will aid in establishing a sort of high-tech report card or diploma called "The Certificate of Initial Mastery."

This certificate is supposed to indicate that the student has "mastered" the outcomes necessary for graduation. Without a certificate of mastery, a student will find it increasingly difficult to be accepted into a college, get a job, receive health care, obtain a drivers license, travel around the country, and even vote.

In 1994, Cottage Grove, Oregon graduated their fist class of unhappy students who earned their official certificates of initial mastery. Berit Kjos, author of *Under the Spell of Mother Earth*, explains the dangers behind this certificate in her monthly newsletter:

> The Oregon Education Act for the 21st Century
> (H.B. 3565) decreed that all tenth grade students
> must pass an outcome-based test to earn their
> Certificate of Initial Mastery. Those who fail —
> including home schoolers and students in
> Christian schools whose responses fail to reflect
> global values — will move on to special

Learning Centers. The pressure to conform to the new view of reality will be intense, since people can neither attend college nor be employed without the Certificate. The Oregon law parallels a federal School-to-Work law that has passed the House and Senate and is now law.[4]

The original Oregon bill states in Section 25:1, "By July 1, 1996, it shall be unlawful for an employer to employ any person under 18 years of age who has not obtained a Certificate of Initial Mastery."

While the final bill deleted the most objectionable statements, it "left the framework which could achieve the same results,"[5] according to Berit Kjos, who draws this frightening conclusion:

> Oregon's law matches the goals of the National Center on Education and the Economy, of which Hillary Clinton sits on the Board of Trustees, which recommends: "(1) all students achieve a Certificate of Initial Mastery, (2) Youth Centers for continued pursuit of the Certificate and (3) occupational certification programs" only for those who have their Certificates of Initial Mastery. "(4) The assessment standard would be the same for both adults and students."[6]

At this time Oregon and Massachusetts have mandated these cards by law, and Alabama, Arkansas, Pennsylvania, Kansas, West Virginia and Washington State are considering the initial Certificate of Mastery.

Bob Holland of the *Richmond Times Dispatch*, writing on June 16, 1993, describes how this card would affect students:

> With a Certificate of Initial Mastery in hand, students then would choose among college-prep, taking a job, or a technological certificate. Meanwhile, the Labor Department would set "voluntary" skill standards-almost surely the

precursor to sharptoothed mandates for entry
to virtually all occupations.

Mandating OBE

Two more reasons why Goals 2000 is unconstitutional
involve forcing OBE on schools, teachers, parents, and students.

*7. Goals 2000 and ESEA will mandate Outcome-Based
Education on every state in the union, by mandating opportunity to
learn standards.*
Outcome-Based Education operates on the principle of relativism — the belief that there are no right and wrong
answers. If this continues to be the foundation of not only our
educational system but also our society, there will be an ever-increasing moral, social, spiritual, and industrial decline in our
society.
We will discuss OBE more fully in the next chapter.

*8. H.R. 6 calls for the development of "educational technology"
that will involve the Department of Labor in assessing all students in
their efforts to attain OBE outcomes.*
The kind of technology that H.R. 6 calls for is basically a
computer on every child's desk that is hooked into a main
frame at the state Department of Education.
In 1989, an education supercomputer went on line to keep
an electronic micro-record of every child's failures. Many parents are concerned about the tracking of students who are not
sufficiently politically correct. Many OBE tests have already
measured and stored students' answers to political and religious questions.

Backing Away From the Basics

9. ESEA and Goals 2000 are unconstitutional because they discourage the teaching of the basics.
The original preamble of ESEA declared:

The disproven theory that children must first
learn basic skills before engaging in more com-
plex tasks continues to dominate strategies for
classroom instruction, resulting in emphasis on
repetitive drill and practice at the expense of
content rich instruction, accelerated curricula,
and effective teaching to high standards.

The common sense question would be, How can you reach
high standards without learning the basics?

The Elementary and Secondary Education Act (ESEA) is
full of negative references to "rote memorization" and "repetitive drill."

Catherine Barret, former president of the National
Education Association, or as *Forbes Magazine* recently called
them, the "national extortion association," was quoted in a
1973 issue of the *Saturday Review of Education* as saying:

Dramatic changes in the way we will raise our
children in the year 2000 are indicated, particularly in terms of schooling. . . . We need to recognize that the so-called "basic skills," which
currently represent nearly the total effort in elementary schools, will be taught in one-quarter
of the present school day. . . When this happens
— and it's near — the teacher can rise to his
true calling. More than a dispenser of information, the teacher will be a conveyor of values, a
philosopher. . . . We will be agents of change.

The agenda today is not education but indoctrination. As
someone has said, "Education today is planned failure, intellectual slavery, if you are not educated, you are easily controlled."

The negative references to rote-memorization in H.R. 6 will
eventually eliminate the teaching of phonics, spelling, math
facts, and other basic skills.

I have had numerous parents tell me that their child has
brought home worksheets that ask such stupid questions as,

"How do you feel about three times three?" Who cares? The correct answer is and always will be "nine," no matter how the child feels.

It has been documented in numerous places, including the *Washington Times*, that children in many schools are not made to memorize their multiplication tables but simply permitted to use a calculator.

While I was a guest on "The G. Gordon Liddy" radio talk show, I mentioned this rising trend.

With his normal wit and wisdom, Mr. Liddy asked, "What will these children do when the batteries in their calculators run down? Many of them will not even be able to read the instructions on how to replace the battery."

In a recent press release, U.S. Congressman Dick Army criticized H.R. 6:

> H.R. 6 represents the triumph of the idea, cur-
> rently popular in education circles, that teach-
> ing children the basics shackles their creative
> inner selves.

Such wording as found in ESEA will discourage the teaching of phonics as well as the multiplication tables.

The theory is: Why waste so much class time on repetitive drill and rote memorization teaching a child their multiplication tables when you can teach students how to use a calculator in 10 minutes. Without a doubt this would free up hours and hours of class time that would normally be spent on repetitive drill. The promoters of such action claim that this would allow for more time to be spent on "content rich instruction. "

My question would be, what is their definition of content rich instruction? Is it books like, *Heather has two Mommies*, *Daddy's Roommate* or *Gloria Goes to Gay Pride?* Or lessons in Yoga, condom use, or the life of Elvis?

Whole Language or Half Baked?

One of the most basic and successful methods of teaching reading — phonetically — has already been tossed aside by "enlightened" educators. "Whole Language" is now the instruction of choice for most public schools.

What is Whole Language?

An article in the January 1994 issue of *The Executive Educator*, "Rethinking Whole-Language," explains:

> The most basic principle of Whole Language, according to many laudatory books on the subject, is that illiterate people can best learn to read and write in precisely the same way they learned to speak. . . . To develop writing skills, children are encouraged to "invent" the spellings of words and the shapes of letters they need for their compositions. In short, Whole Language demands that instruction be directed unsystematic, and nonintensive.
>
> The second fundamental principle of Whole Language is that individual learners should be "empowered" to decide what written materials mean.

The article goes on to say, "Language never can communicate exactly what the author intended to convey."

In teaching kids to read, whole-language proponents utilize relativism, as the *Executive Educator* article reveals:

> The founders of Whole Language call reading a guessing game; in other words, the meaning of a written passage is generally anyone's guess. Whole language teachers urge students to use sentence context cues to guess at the identity of the various words they read. Students accordingly substitute, add, and omit words in sentences they read — as they see fit. . . .
>
> A student is at liberty to "reconstruct" the meaning of a reading selection in his or her own personal, idiosyncratic terms. Differing interpretations of the author's intended mean-

ing are encouraged. Whole-language advocates
dismiss concerns that such reading habits leave
students unprepared to examine an author's
ideas and expression critically.

You can imagine the results. Parents of children who have
experienced the Whole Language approach have been wondering why Johnny can't read, spell, sound out words, construct a
simple sentence, or analyze the meaning of story. Now they
know.

Forbes Magazine in their February 13, 1995 issue reported
the failure of the Whole Language approach:

Parents dislike Whole Language because it
downgrades accuracy — children are allowed
to approximate meanings — and also because
it seems not to work: San Diego schools, for
instance, found that the percentage of first-
graders scoring above the median on reading
test dropped by half after 18 months of Whole
Language instruction. And a study of two
schools by University of Georgia professor,
Stephen Stahl, shows that children at the school
using traditional instruction far outperformed
those at the Whole Language school.
Yet Whole Language is increasingly
inescapable: Many states have actually mandated its use. [7]

Educators, in an effort to bolster their argument for the
continued use of the Whole Language approach, have decided
that some readers are "genetically indisposed toward learning
phonics."

Pages and pages of undeniably accurate data are available
to school boards, administrators, and superintendents, proving
that students who read by phonics consistently test higher
than students who learn to read under Whole Language.
Despite these facts, Whole Language continues to be widely
used in America's schools.

The War Against "Hooked on Phonics"

As a result of Whole Language's failure to teach students how to read, grassroots phonic groups like the National Right to Read Foundation have sprung up.

The National Right to Read Foundation led the charge in helping Gateway products, the producer of "Hooked on Phonics," fight off the federal government. The Federal Trade Commission in early 1995 not only attacked Gateway Products but also home education and basic skills.

The Federal Trade Commission claimed that Gateway Products had been making "misleading claims about the ability of its 'Hooked on Phonics' program to teach users . . . including those with learning disabilities . . . to read."

The FTC complaint filed against Gateway Products also claimed that reading cannot be taught "in a home setting without a teacher or tutor."

Bob Sweet, the president of the National Right to Read, said in a press release that this charge was "insupportable, arrogant, and perhaps dangerous. The tens of thousands of home-schooled students, including Abraham Lincoln, would strongly disagree."

The problem with the FTC complaint and the FTC ruling, which was finally made, may have an impact on all commercial providers and consumers of home-based education products. The FTC ruling could eventually aid in making it difficult for millions of children to benefit from having access to a home-based phonics program unless it is being purchased and used by a licensed teacher or tutor.

Why did the FTC go after Gateway Products and "Hooked on Phonics"? Because they are the largest producer of a home-based phonics program. The inaccurate attacks of the FTC and the news program, "Dateline NBC," have greatly hurt Gateway Products to the point that their future is unknown.

Who will be next? Our government obviously has it out for anyone or any company that would seek to profit from creating and selling materials that teach and reinforce basic skills. If these materials can be used in the home by parents, the attacks are even more aggressive.

Inventive Spelling?

Carol Innerst, in the September 7, 1994, *Washington Times* wrote about Laurie Andrew, a Westport mother of seven, who became concerned when "she ran into 'inventive' spelling — a teaching method that aims to build self-esteem by encouraging children to write without any heed for proper spelling."[8]

Laurie Andrews was quoted as saying, "A middle-school principal told me that in our society, with the advent of computers and spell check, it's not as important that children know how to spell correctly."[9]

When Laurie Andrews and her husband questioned "inventive" spelling at a parents night, they were told, "With invented spelling you're never wrong. When Mrs. Andrews complained about uncorrected spelling on her fourth-grader's papers, she was told that it's important for her child to feel good about her creativity and that the spelling will come later."[10]

When Mrs. Andrews began to question what was going on at her children's school, a school official told her that she was "part of the problem." This outraged Mrs. Andrews to the point that she ran for school board in Westport, Massachusetts and won — despite being called a "religious radical" and a part of the "religious right."

Although Mrs. Andrews became a member of the Westport school board, she and her husband have pulled their children out of public schools and enrolled them in a local private school. Why? Because, as Mrs. Andrews told the superintendent, "My kids are not guinea pigs. They have one chance at an education. I can't sacrifice them for your theories."[11]

Some would claim that if the Andrews children are not attending the local public school, then Mrs. Andrew has no business being on the local school board.

As a taxpaying American, Mrs. Andrews and anyone else, has every right to run for this public office — as does any citizen, whether or not they have school-age children or any children at all. If the public disapproves, then they can vote Mrs. Andrews off the school board the next time she is up for re-election.

Bribing the States

10. H.R. 6 will give the Secretary of Education unconstitutional powers.

Let me give you several reasons why these powers are unconstitutional:

A. The Secretary has the power under ESEA to "withhold funds" from a state until the state submits an educational plan that meets the approval of the U.S. Secretary of Education.

This is nothing less than federal control.

At the time this book went to press, the Department of Education had approved plans submitted by Kentucky, Utah, and Oregon, making them the first Goals 2000 recognized states in the union.

Ohio and Massachusetts have also submitted statewide improvement plans. The remaining states are either not participating or are still in the process of developing their plans. According to H.R. 6, those states that refuse to develop their plans will be punished.

In Idaho, State Superintendent Ann Fox campaigned on pulling out of Goals 2000. Although elected by the people to do just that, Ms. Fox has been prohibited by the state school board in a vote of 7 to 1 from returning the Goals 2000 money, which the state received in order to assist them in developing their state plan.

In Virginia, the state board of education has voted to apply for Goals 2000 funding, but Governor Allen continues to stick to his promise of not accepting Goals 2000 money. Governor Allen believes the program allows the federal government to be too intrusive in the educational process of his state.

Virginia's attorney general has ruled that both the board of education and the governor would have to be in agreement in order to participate in Goals 2000. Virginia's participation could eventually be decided in the courts.

Montana has become the first state to officially opt out of Goals 2000. The state legislature voted in April to bar the state's office of public instruction from using the Goals 2000 money it had applied for. This decision was made by the state legislature despite the fact that the state's governor and super-intendent supported the states involvement in Goals 2000.

South Dakota has recently applied for Goals 2000 funding, and Wyoming will also submit an application for Goals 2000 funding but not without receiving some assurances in writing.

Wyoming is submitting its Goals 2000 application with a resolution requesting written assurance from the United States Secretary of Education, Richard Riley, "that there will be no federal mandates for curriculum, assessment, or teaching methodology and that Wyoming may withdraw at any time."

All this means that — at the time of press — the only states vowing *not* to participate in Goals 2000 are New Hampshire, Virginia, and Montana.

B. *If after two years, "a state does not have challenging content and performance standards," the Secretary of Education can force onto this state the standards, or outcomes, of another state.*

According to H.R. 6, the states can be sued into compliance by the Secretary, and the state "shall not be immune under the 11th amendment from such action."

What is H.R. 6 really saying? "Sorry the 11th amendment does not apply in this situation because we say so."

C. *If a local school district does not comply with this federal leg-islation, the state can be forced by the federal government to fire school board members and even the district superintendent in order to gain compliance to H.R. 6 and Goals 2000 so the state and district can receive federal dollars.*

The federal government is putting major pressure on the states to comply with this legislation. In turn the states are putting tremendous pressure on the districts.

In the *Washington Times*, February 8, 1994, syndicated columnist Bob Holland in writing about this "stealth takeover of education" by the federal government, further comments:

> The Clintons' complex scheme for restructuring
> elementary and secondary education would
> write into federal law a "corrective action" pro-
> vision that would oblige states to oust local

school board members and superintendents if they were deemed to be falling short of the new federally prescribed outcome-based standards.

Some states are being encouraged by H.R. 6 to completely take over local districts, firing dully elected officials and "decreasing decision making authority at the school level," in order to bring about compliance, so the state can receive its federal dollars.

Good-Bye to Home and Private Schools?

D. *Section 9401 in H.R. 6 is entitled "Waivers of Statutory and Regulatory Requirements."*
This section declares,

> The Secretary may waive any requirement of this Act or of the General Education Provisions Act, or of the regulations issued under such Acts, for a State educational agency, Indian tribe, or other agency, organization, or institution that receives funds under a program authorized by this Act from the Department and that requests such a waiver if, the Secretary determines that such requirements impede the ability of the State educational agency or other recipient to achieve more effectively the purpose of this Act.

What does this mean? In my opinion, and in that of many credible colleagues, we believe that certain "requirements" of this Act, if they get in the way of any "recipient" or state educational agency or other agency, which "receives funds from a program authorized by this Act from the Department," then the U. S. Secretary of Education may waive that requirement. In other words, they could make null and void the "Home School Private School Freedom Amendment" or Section 432 of the "General Education Provision Act."

The General Education Provision Act is crucial to the autonomy of local school districts. If the provision is abandoned as the "Waivers" act quoted above decrees, schools would be subject to federal takeover.

Section 432 of the General Education Provision Act forbids any department, agency, officer, or employee of the U.S. to exercise any direction, supervision, or control over the curriculum program of instruction, administration, or personnel of any educational institution, school, or school system.

H.R. 6 declares that the U.S. Secretary may waive these requirements.

Suppose the Department of Education in Illinois receives federal dollars from H.R. 6, which they will. Once they are on board with the agenda of Goals 2000 and H.R. 6, the state educrats may decide to come into private or home schools and offer some kind of service or administer a test, examination, or evaluation.

Is that legal? Not according to the "Home School Private School Freedom Amendment."

According to H.R. 6, however, the U.S. Secretary of Education has the right to offer a waiver to the Illinois Secretary of Education if he feels it would help to "achieve more effectively the purpose of this Act." Such vague wording leaves various interpretations, leaving home schooling parents at the mercy of the state's discretion.

Many deny this would ever happen because Section 9508 in H.R. 6, which is the "Home School Private School Freedom Amendment," states: "Nothing in this Act shall be construed to permit, allow, encourage, or authorize any federal control over any aspect of any private, religious, or home school."

That is all well and good, but if a test or a service is defined as a "requirement" of this Act, then it can be waived. This is not the sort of loose wording we want left to the discretion of a federal judge to interpret during a court case.

The best answer to this problem is to have the "Home School Private School Freedom Amendment" added to Subsection C, "Waivers Not Authorized," found in Section 9401 of H.R. 6. This would close any loop hole no matter how big or how small, whether this wording was deliberate or not.

Sections 438 and 439, known as the Hatch Act and Buckley Act, protect student privacy and protect the federal funding of programs that involve personality and psychological testing in our schools. Since these Acts were seen to be important enough to include in Subsection C, "Waivers Not Authorized," why not add Section 432 of GEPA and the "Home School Private School Freedom Amendment?"

If Section 432 of GEPA and the Home School Private School Freedom Amendment were included in the list of waivers not authorized, then they would be protected from being swept away by the U.S. Secretary of Education at will.

Filling in the Blanks

My last reason for considering H.R. 6 to be unconstitutional is:

11. The wording of H.R. 6 is so vague that it is open to massive interpretation.

Research Journalist Geoffrey Botkin has said, "H.R. 6 is a masterpiece of flexible language and creative new terminology that can mean almost anything government lawyers want it to mean."

Botkin goes on describe "the most dangerous parts of the bill" as the "regulations" suggested in the bill for later development. H.R. 6 creates many policies the details of which, according to the bill, "shall be developed."

Liberal legislators want to pass a bill that has not even been completely written, with the flexibility to fill in the blanks later.

Just what do they have in mind? Are their plans so corrupt and evil that if they put them in writing for all to see, the bill may not pass because of public outrage?

Why do we find ourselves in this situation? Because we did not heed the words of President Eisenhower or President Reagan, who both warned us of the importance of not loosing local control over education.

In the *New York Herald Tribune* on February 9, 1955, President Eisenhower is quoted as saying:

A distinguishing characteristic of our nation —
and a great strength — is the development of
our institutions within the concept of individual
worth and dignity. Our schools are among the
guardians of that principle. Consequently . . .
and deliberately their control and support
throughout our history have been — and are —
a state and local responsibility. . . . Thus was
established a fundamental element of the
American public school system — local direction by boards of education responsible immediately to the parents of children. Diffusion of
authority among tens of thousands of school
districts is a safeguard against centralized control and abuse of the educational system that
must be maintained. We believe that to take
away the responsibility of communities and
states in educating our children is to undermine
not only a basic element of our freedoms but a
basic right of our citizens.[12]

On February 5, 1976, the *Los Angeles Times* published an
article titled, "Teachers Group Seeks National System Like
Hitler's for U.S. Schools, Reagan Says." Ronald Reagan was
quoted as saying that the NEA wants:

A federal educational system, a national school
system, so that little Willie's mother would not
be able to go down and see the principal or
even the school board. She'd actually have to
take her case up to Congress in Washington. I
believe this is the road to disaster and the end
of academic freedom.

Eighteen years later, Ronald Reagan's words came true
when Goals 2000 became law in April 1994 and H.R. 6 passed
Congress in September 1994.
America's schools are now held hostage.

Notes

[1] Laura Rogers in "In Loco Parentis: The Brave New Family in Missouri," *Freedom Report*, February 1993, p. 15.

[2] John Leo, "Schools to Parents: Keep Out," *U.S. News and World Report*, October 5, 1992, p. 33.

[3] *Congressional Record* (Senate), February 2, 1994, S623, and S624.

[4] Berit Kjos, *Monthly Newsletter*

[5] Ibid.

[6] "Americas Choice: High Skills or Low Wages," *National Center on Education and the Economy Report*, June 1990, p. 71-72.

[7] Peter Brimelow and Leslie Spencer, "Comeuppance," *Forbes Magazine*, February 13, 1995, p. 124.

[8] Carol Innerst, "Parents Rebel as Outcomes Replace Three R's," *The Washington Times*, September 7, 1994.

[9] Ibid.

[10] Ibid.

[11] Ibid.

[12] Dr. Dennis Cuddy, *Chronology of Education with Quotable Quotes*, (Pro Family Forum, Inc. Highland City, Fl. 1993), p.31.

2

The Rising Tide
of Mediocrity

J orge Rodriquez, the meanest, orneriest bandit on the Texas-Mexico border, would often slip across the line, raid the banks of South Texas, and steal them blind. Before authorities could catch him, he would race back into Mexico and hide out. No matter how hard the law tried, they could never catch him.

Finally, the Texans got fed up with this nonsense and decided to put the toughest Texas Ranger they had on the case. After only a few days of searching, the Ranger found the bandit in a dingy, dusty saloon south of the border.

He bolted into the bar, pulled both guns, and yelled, "Okay, stick'em up, Jorge; you're under arrest! I know you've got the money."

Suddenly a little guy over in the corner butted in. "Wait, wait. Just a minute, Senor," he said. "Jorge does not speak English. He's my amigo, so I'll translate for you."

The Ranger explained, "Look, we know he's the bandit we've been looking for. We know he's taken thousands and thousands of dollars. We want it back now. Either he pays up, or I'll fill him full of holes. You tell him that!"

"Okay, okay! I'll tell him. I'll tell him."

So the little fellow turned to Jorge and repeated in Spanish everything the Ranger had said. The Texas Ranger, not knowing a word of the language, waited for the bandit's reply.

Jorge listened to his friend, frowned, and responded in Spanish, "Okay, they got me. Tell him to go down to the well just south of town, count four stones down from the top of the well, then pull out the one loose stone. All the money I have stolen is hidden behind the stone."

Then the clever little translator turned to the Texas Ranger and translated with a shrug, "Jorge says, 'Go ahead, you big mouth; go ahead and shoot 'cause I'm not telling you where the money is.'"

What is the moral of this story? People can get hurt when the truth is not told.

Children all across American are being hurt today because the truth has not been told about the "education reform" movement. The basis of this movement is Outcome-Based Education, and I want to tell you the truth before your child gets hurt.

Mediocrity At Its Best

All Americans should be concerned about the future of our children — regardless of our age or political party. Why? Because ultimately the way we educate our children affects all of us.

As Abraham Lincoln so wisely said, "The philosophy of education in one generation, will be the philosophy of government in the next."

Aristotle also wrote, "All who have meditated on the art of governing mankind, are convinced that the fate of empires depends on the education of youth." The quality of the future of our nation depends on how well we educate our children.

The National Commission on Excellence in Education declared in 1983 that the United States was a nation at risk. The report stated:

> The educational foundations of our society are presently being eroded by a rising tide of mediocrity that threatens our very future as a nation and a people.

Have America's students improved since that report was written in 1983? No!

According to the *Education Reporter* July of 91, "Fewer than one in seven students in grades four, eight, and twelve can do mathematics at or above their grade level. More than that are two or more grade levels behind."

In the 1992 International Test Comparison in science, American students ranked thirteenth, answering only 67 percent of the questions correctly. This score placed the U.S. behind countries such as Korea, Taiwan, the Soviet Union, Slovenia, Israel, Canada, and France.

One reason for this rising tide of mediocrity is the implementation of programs that promote mediocrity instead of excellence. Outcome-Based Education is one such program.

After years of "experimentation," the jury is in on OBE. Outcome-Based Education is a complete failure. While it is impossible to receive a failing grade under OBE, that is exactly what OBE is getting from parents all across the country.

Let me share with you some of the new information we have uncovered since the release of my first book, *Cradle to College*.

The Ever-Widening Gap

When it comes to promoting and modeling excellence, particularly in our industry, our country has had a very rich heritage. America is the home of some of the world's largest companies such as 3M, Cargill, Pillsbury, General Mills, ATT, Microsoft, and many more large and small businesses that pursue excellence every day in every way.

But what about our schools? Are they pursing excellence today in the classroom so our students can pursue excellence tomorrow in the work place?

Not according to a 1992 report prepared by the International Center for Leadership in Education, which stated:

> The skills necessary for the work place are
> changing at a rate four to five times faster than

curriculum and organizational structure in
schools, leaving a gap between what students
learn and what will be expected of them in the
work place.[1]

Outcome-Based Education widens this gap and gives rise
to an ever-increasing acceptance in mediocrity. If allowed to
continue, OBE will flood our nation with uneducated, unqualified adults who will find themselves unable to compete for
jobs in our world's growing technologically advanced marketplace.

Employers are already facing the dilemma posed by
underqualified job seekers, as this report on "Business and
Reform" indicates:

Motorola found that an appalling four-fifths of
those seeking employment could not pass a test
of seventh-grade English and fifth-grade math.
New York telephone had 117,000 job applicants
in 1988, but could find only 2,100 who could
pass the company's employment test.[2]

Is this the trend we want to perpetuate in our nation? Of
course not. Yet, the United States Department of Education
has already embarked on a course that has proven to be nothing less than a total and complete failure for many states.

When Is "Not Yet"?

The February 5, 1994 *Washington Times* reported that
Kentucky, which had embarked on a massive Outcome-Based
Education plan in 1990, spent more than $1 billion of addition-
al tax money on the changeover. Yet, Kentucky Commissioner
of Education Thomas Boysen said last October that test scores
show "no clear difference between schools that have been
deeply involved in reform efforts and others that have made
no changes."

The July 28, 1993 *Richmond Times Dispatch* reported that

Outcome-Based Education has been a financial and education-al failure for Rochester, New York. In 1987, Rochester spent $4,253 per pupil in local tax dollars. By 1991, that figure had risen to $5501 per pupil, and tens of millions more were being pumped in by the state, private corporations, and foundations.

What impact did OBE have in Rochester?

• In 1987, 23% of Rochester's pupils earned the New York State Regents' Diploma, the most rigorous offered. By 1991, only 18% did.

• In 1991 more than 70% of the freshmen at Wilson Magnet School, generally considered Rochester's best, flunked the state's basic math test.

• The percentage of third-graders passing the state reading exam fell from 81 to 79 during the reform's first four years. The goal had been a 90% passing rate by 1991, according to *U.S. News and World Report*, May 25, 1992.

Chicago schools used Outcome-Based Education for ten years but finally dumped OBE after the program dropped their test scores to the 25th percentile,[3] not to mention the millions of dollars they spent to obtain these results.

In South Washington County, Minnesota, two high schools and two junior high schools service approximately 5,000 students. In 1992, under OBE, these four schools had 15,510 incompletes.[4] That's three incompletes for every student.

No one seemed to mind — especially the students — since incompletes have no ill effect on a student's grade point average. The end results are grade inflation and misleading class rankings. How can that be? Because many schools have done away with the traditional grading scale of A, B, C, D, and F and have opted for giving out an "I" for Incomplete or a "NY" for Not Yet.

In a special report on education by the *Washington Times* in September 1994, Leonard Gahm, a Maryland father, is quoted as being troubled over the plans afoot in his district to eliminate the traditional A-through-F grading system. What reason did the district give for this radical switch from traditional scoring? "So no child suffers the trauma of failing."

After speaking at a banquet for a North Carolina political action group in September 1994, a mother and father approached me.

"We were confused when our son recently brought home a test with the grade of F+," they said and explained how they had handled the situation.

Unable to contain their curiosity as well as their anger, these parents called their son's teacher and asked, "What is an F+?"

The teacher responded, "It is just a point or so from being a D-."

Now there is a grade to be proud of!

"Why wasn't he given the old-fashioned F?" the parents wanted to know.

The teacher explained her reasoning. "I felt it was important that your child know that he just barely received an F. That's why I gave him an F+."

It did not matter that their son had deserved the F. The teacher just wanted to make sure his "feelings" weren't hurt!

Solving the OBE Mystery

Many parents and taxpayers are asking, "What exactly is Outcome-Based Education?"

Many who ask this question, however, never receive a consistent or understandable answer — especially from OBE's proponents. For some reason they like to maintain an ambiguous air of mystery about this radical educational approach. Why? Because they know if parents ever really understand what OBE is, there will be a national outcry against it.

I want to give you unclouded facts so you can decide for yourself the merits or demerits of OBE.

Behind every method of teaching is a philosophy of education on which it is based. Outcome-Based Education's foundation is supported by two predominate tenants:

1. The belief that all students can learn and learn well.
2. The idea that equality should mean equality of outcomes rather than equality of opportunity.

In order for the outcomes to be based on equality, the standard must be lowered to ensure that all students, regardless of their ability, can reach the set standard. For example, if you want everyone to slam dunk, you have to lower the basket.

When Mastery Learning, the foundation stone of OBE, received negative reviews from parents, an attempt was made to disguise it. (For more information on Mastery Learning read my first book, *Cradle to College, Stopping the Educational Abduction of America's Children*. See Chapter 12 to order.)

William Spady, one of OBE's most well-known gurus, devised a cover-up and encouraged educators to do away with the old terminology of Mastery Learning and instead refer to it as Outcome-Based Education. This is how William Spady told educators to implement this deception:

> I pleaded with the group not to use the name "mastery learning" in the network's new name because the word "mastery" had already been destroyed. I argued that we had about five years before they destroyed the term "outcomes," but at least we could get a start.[5]

At a conference sponsored by the Free World Research in Des Moines, Iowa in February 1994, Dr. William Coulson, who was a longtime colleague of Dr. Carl Rogers, quoted Rogers as saying, "Change the name of [the reform policy] as fast as necessary to stay ahead of the critics."

Now that OBE has been unmasked, the spin doctors of the educational elite are out in full force using at least 21 different names to disguise Outcome-Based Education.

Hiding OBE has become for many educators a full time endeavor. To keep parents and the public confused, OBE proponents cloak their educational approach in different terms. Here is a list of their most common terminology:

Mastery Learning
Results Oriented
Total Quality Management
Quality Schools

Essential Schools
Transformational Education
Reformed Education, Restructured Education
Competency Based Education
Break the Mold 21st Century Schools
Mission 2000
Vision 2000
Exit Based Teaching
High Standards
Skills 2000
Performance Based Learning
High Level Learning
Mastery Teaching
Formative Testing
Correctives Teaching
Extensions Learning
Summative Evaluations
Credentialing Curriculum
Advancement Teaching
Results-Based Curriculum

While I was in Columbus, Ohio, in the fall of 94, speaking
for a teachers convention, a teacher informed me that in his
public school, teachers had been informed to no longer refer to
the standards they were using as "outcomes."

Five years must be up. I wonder what name they will
come up with next.

Why Socialism Never Works

Outcome-based-education as we know it today is nothing
less than the promotion of socialism. It is the old theory that
no one can be better than anyone else. Instead of re-distribut-
ing wealth, Outcome-Based Education re-distributes grades.

The concept of socialism has been tried many times and
has proven to be a complete and total failure. Why then are we
teaching America's children the philosophy of socialism in and
through education?

The former Soviet Union may never recover from the years

of socialism that kept it from becoming prosperous and advanced. Countless other societies have tried without success to make socialism a productive system by which to live, teach, and govern.

Socialism, however, will never create success because it is based on the false belief of equality. Everything and everyone cannot be equal. Whenever government tries to equalize salaries or the standard of living or education, productivity takes a nose-dive.

Few people realize that socialism's bent for failure was proved in America's first colony established by the Pilgrims.

When the Mayflower set sail on August 1, 1620, it carried 102 passengers, including 40 Pilgrims led by William Bradford. On the journey, Bradford set up an agreement, or contract, that established just and equal laws for all members of their community irrespective of their religious beliefs.

Where did the revolutionary ideas expressed in the Mayflower Compact come from? The Bible. The Pilgrims were completely steeped in the lessons of the Old and New Testaments and looked to the ancient Israelites as their example. Because of the biblical precedents set forth in Scripture, they never doubted that their experiment would work.

During the first winter, half the Pilgrims — including Bradford's wife — died of either starvation, sickness, or exposure. When spring finally came, Indians taught the settlers how to plant corn, fish for cod, and skin beavers for coats.

Life improved for the Pilgrims, but they did not yet prosper. Why not?

The original contract the Pilgrims entered into with their merchant-sponsors in London called for everything they produced to go into a common store, and each member of the community was entitled to one common share. All of the land they cleared and the houses they built belonged to the community as well.

Bradford, who had become the new governor of the colony, recognized that this form of collectivism was as costly and destructive to the Pilgrims as that first harsh winter, which had taken so many lives. He decided to take bold action and assigned a plot of land to each family to work and manage, thus unleashing the power of the marketplace.

Long before Karl Marx was even born, the Pilgrims had discovered and experimented with what could only be described as socialism. "What Bradford and his community found was that the most creative and industrious people had no incentive to work any harder than anyone else, unless they could utilize the power of personal motivation!"[6]

Writing about the experiences of the Pilgrims, Bradford noted,

> By taking away property, and bringing community into a common wealth, would make them happy and flourishing — as if they were wiser than God. . . . For this community [so far as it was] found to breed much confusion and discontent, and retard much employment that would have been to their benefit and comfort. For young men that were most able and fit for labor and service did repine that they should spend their time and strength to work for other men's wives and children without any recompense . . . that was thought injustice.[7]

If socialism and the myth of equality — the belief that everyone must be the same — has proven to be a detriment to any and every society that has governed by it, why do we permit this philosophy to be taught in America's schools?

No Right Answers

The fantasy-world mentality of socialism sets a dangerous precedent for any child who attends public school. Why? Because OBE never permits a child to fail.

Children are robbed of the valuable lessons of determination and persistence learned from failure. Failure can be used to teach children to dig in and double or even triple their efforts in order to reach a set goal. The real world is not going to slow down and let these children catch-up.

William Glasser, one of OBE's national promoters, wrote in

his book, *Schools Without Failure:*

> We have to let students know there are no right
> answers, and we have to let them see that there
> are many alternatives to certainty and right
> answers.[8]

William Glasser takes his cues directly from one of the most notorious agents of change ever to be involved in the American educational system, Benjamin Bloom. In his book, *Taxonomy of Educational Objectives*, Bloom calls for the "thorough-going through and reorganization of attitudes and values."[9]

Why? Because Bloom believed and taught that the highest form of intelligence has been reached when a individual no longer believes in right or wrong.

In his book, *All Our Children Learning*, Bloom openly discloses what he believes is the ultimate goal of education. "The purpose of education and the schools is to change the thoughts, feelings and actions of students."[10] Bloom goes on to write:

> The curriculum may be thought of as a plan for
> changing students' behavior and as the actual
> set of learning experiences in which students,
> teachers, and materials interact to produce the
> change in students.[11]

In other words, Bloom was espousing corrective thought control.

What kind of change does Bloom desire to create in students? That students question everything taught to them — except of course what he would teach them — and to base their beliefs on no set moral absolutes. Remember, Bloom believes that the highest form of intelligence occurs when one no longer believes in right or wrong.

An Elite Group of Thinkers

What is Bloom's final objective? To change the students into exactly what he is — a humanist and an elitist. Bloom's goal is to tear down any and every authority figure that a child would have, and then replace those authority figures with a new authority figure — the state group consensus.

How does Bloom plan to do this? By making students believe that they have been subjected to superior thought that is beyond the ability of most people, particularly the child's parents, to understand. Students are fed a line that goes something like this:

"Do not expect to be understood by your parents, pastor, or even some of your friends. You are part of an elite group of thinkers. If you truly want to be an intellectual thinker, you have to be a liberal thinker. You can't believe in the old standard of right or wrong. You must decide for yourself what is right and what is wrong based on your own feelings, beliefs, and ideas. It is okay to challenge and question the things your parents or society have taught you. That is all part of becoming part of a rare group of leaders and achievers."

Am I over-stating the case? No, as Bloom's own words prove:

> The careful observer of the classroom can see that the wise teacher as well as the psychological theorist use cognitive behavior and the achievement of cognitive goals to attain affective goals. . . . [A] large part of what we call "good teaching" is the teacher's ability to attain affective objectives through challenging the student's fixed beliefs.[12]

And where does the student Bloom is talking about acquire his "fixed beliefs"? That's right, more than likely from his parents.

Most of us would respond, "All the more reason why those fixed beliefs should remain fixed, instead of being torn down and replaced by some liberal, socialist, humanist, elitist educrat like Benjamin Bloom, William Spady, or William Glasser."

OBE for Every School in America

What if I told you that your federal tax dollars have been used to purposely promote Outcome-Based Education? The fact is, such funding has been going on for years.

In a letter to former U.S. Secretary of Education Terrel Bell, dated July 27, 1984, the then Utah State Superintendent of Public Instruction, G. Leland Burningham, wrote:

> I am forwarding this letter to accompany the proposal which you recommended Bill Spady and I prepare in connection with Outcome-Based Education. This proposal centers around the detailed process by which we will work together to implement Outcome-Based Education using research verified programs. This will make it possible to put Outcome-Based Education in place, not only in Utah, but in all schools of the nation.[13]

G. Leland Burningham and William Spady, Director of the Far West Laboratory, applied for a grant from the U.S. Department of Education totaling $152,530. The grant was approved, and the Far West Laboratory received the funds.

Our federal tax dollars were used to "make it possible to put Outcome-Based Education in place, not only in Utah, but in all schools of the nation."

Did you notice that this grant was approved by U.S. Secretary of Education Terrel Bell in 1984? That is right, President Ronald Reagan's Secretary of Education aided in the promotion of Outcome-Based Education.

As one of Ronald Reagan's fans and as a friend of and education consultant for Michael Reagan's national radio show, I was disappointed to discover this information. My first reaction was to overlook this fact and not include it in this book. Why? Because I believe with all my heart that President

Ronald Reagan was one of America's greatest presidents.

So why did I include this information about this beloved President?

The Weak Link

First, because as a researcher, I owe it to you to always do my best to provide the most accurate data I can.

Secondly, I want you to remember that no matter who controls the White House or the Congress, you and I must always stay involved and be alert. There is never an excuse for becoming apathetic.

Thirdly, I want to use this as an opportunity to make a point about the Department of Education.

I know for a fact that if President Ronald Reagan had known for himself about this grant and the true meaning of Outcome-Based Education, he would have objected.

It is easy to sit on the outside and criticize others. Until you have been on the inside, fighting day after day to defend faith, family, and freedoms, you can not imagine what a difficult job it is.

The President cannot run every governmental department himself, so he appoints experienced and qualified people to head various departments. Despite even the best intentions, no administration is perfect or selects the right person for each job. Many appointees obtain positions in conservative administrations even though they lack a true conservative ideology.

It must also be pointed out that for decades career bureaucrats have been in charge of the Department of Education, and such was the case during the Reagan administration. The political appointees come and go with each administration, but many others at the DOE remain year after year.

With almost 6,000 employees, the Department of Education is staffed with some career employees who hate and despise the traditional values that you and I hold dear. Under a conservative administration such agents of change may not vocalize their feelings loudly, but they will work just as hard if not harder for their liberal agenda.

I have experienced this kind of undermining firsthand. In

my research of educational issues, I am in contact with the aides of many U.S. senators and congressmen. Many of these aides hold powerful positions within the offices of these elected officials, yet their ideology is often much less conservative than their bosses'. In most cases, the congressman or senator has no idea that his aid holds opposing viewpoints to his.

I have been confronted with aides who, due to ignorance or lack of true conservatism have refused to brief their bosses about an item on which the congressman or senator needed to take action. When this happens, we must resort to plan B, alert the public, and cause the phones and fax machines to start ringing. A significant number of phone calls and faxes will get the attention of the lawmaker without the help of his aide.

Despite how conservative a president or lawmaker may be, the chain is only as strong as its weakest link. We need to stay alert and involved working to replace the weak links — or at least letting them know we are keeping tabs on them.

Danger! Competition Ahead!

At a 1995 high school graduation ceremony in Pennsylvania, no mention was made of the students with the highest grade point averages nor were these two students asked to give a valedictory and salutatory address. Instead, the administration permitted any graduating seniors to submit essays on a series of topics. From those, the five best essays were chosen, and those students addressed the families and students at the graduation ceremony.

When a visiting relative asked about this unusual approach, an administration official replied that they felt it was "unfair to honor one or two students above the others."

This seems to be the trend among "more progressive" school districts. During a recent trip to San Antonio, I was informed that a Texas school had dispensed with honoring the valedictorian and salutatorian because "it creates too much competition among the students."

I had no idea that the practice of honoring the valedictorian and salutatorian was so dangerous! What about those students who go to schools where such barbaric behavior is still occurring?

The intense competition may damage them for life. In fact, the stress, tension, and disappointment of those who do not achieve the status of valedictorian or salutatorian could be so crushing that they never dare compete or strive for excellence again because of the horrible memory of having not succeeded. We could forever be damaging the self-esteem of thousands and thousands of American students each and every year.

What kind of society is America if we deliberately harm the egos of our nation's greatest resources, our children?

Rush Limbaugh has said, "With competitiveness being stigmatized, it's no wonder American students have lost their drive."

Could that be why we have hundreds of thousands of individuals on welfare today? The fear of failure is so great because of the over-emphasis on competition and the relentless pressure to be better than the next guy, such competition makes many afraid to even try. Such discrimination must stop.

Believe it or not, some educators would actually agree with such psycho-babel. I am sorry to say that this is the point to which the philosophy of Outcome-Based Education has brought us in America today.

Aiming at Nothing

One mother who is also a substitute teacher in her daughter's public school said she had had enough. "I have applied for a position at a Christian school, and I am enrolling Jennifer there, too."

When asked why, she replied, "Everything in public school is done in groups," she said. "There is no emphasis on individuality or the idea of taking pride in your own work. As a result, the kids who do no work get the same recognition and grade as those in their group who did most of the work."

Students involved in Outcome-Based Education are spared from "dangerous" competition. Instead, they are often given the freedom to study at a rate, place, and time that is most convenient and effective for them — and they progress only as fast as their personal ability permits.

That sounds nice, but in the real world if there are no standards and competition, there is no progress.

Competition makes for better cars, better restaurants, and even better students. We must not lower the standard of education in order to guarantee success for everyone. Such a philosophy is not based on the reality of the real world in which our children must be prepared to survive. Instead, such thinking hinders and punishes the achievers, those who want to strive for excellence. We need to keep the standard high and encourage every student to do his or her best.

Most assuredly, not every child can or should be expected to reach the same standard. Yet, it is imperative to the advancement of a progressive, civilized, and capitalist society that every child be encouraged to do his or her best to meet the highest possible standard.

The ultimate emphasis should not be on whether or not every child reached the highest possible standard, but did each and every child strive to do their best, reaching their highest potential by using the set standard as a target? After all, if you aim at nothing, you will be sure to hit it.

The real world is not going to slow down and let every child catch-up. Your child's boss is not likely going to let him do a project over and over again until he gets it right.

Many of today's jobs require the ability to be accurate and reach a specific and precise goal or objective. When your child does his job incorrectly, his boss is not going to care if he almost did it right or if he was close to having the right answer.

When "Close" Is Not Good Enough

In life there is usually a right answer and a wrong answer, and being accurate can mean the difference between a job well done or possibly loosing your job. In some situations an inaccuracy can mean the difference between life and death. Even being 99.9 percent correct can cause major confusion in some situations.

In fact, someone has catalogued a sampling of mistakes

that would result if every person were 99.9 percent right:

- Two million documents would be lost by the IRS.
- In the next 60 minutes, 22,000 checks would be deducted from the wrong bank accounts.
- Telecommunication services would misplace 1,314 phone calls every minute.
- 12 babies would be given to the wrong parents every day.
- In the next 12 months, 2,488,200 books would be shipped with the wrong cover.
- One of three sections would be missing from 3,056 copies of tomorrow's Wall Street Journal.
- There would be 291 pacemaker operations performed incorrectly this year.
- Incorrect cardholder information would appear on the magnetic strips of 880,000 credit cards in circulation.
- Over the next 12 months, 20,000 incorrect drug procedures would be written.
- Some $762 million would be spent in the next 12 months on tapes and compact discs that will not play.

The proof is clear. We must teach America's students the importance of meeting high standards, which are based on cognitive and moral absolutes. This is a must, not a luxury.

As someone who flies on a regular basis, I would not want to fly with a pilot who had been trained under the belief that he can attempt a landing over and over again until he got it right. In most cases, that pilot has only one chance to do it right, anything less than excellence could mean the lives of hundreds of people.

At the same time, I do not want to be flying with a navigator who was taught math under the OBE philosophy of "How do you feel about three times three?" as I saw on one worksheet. Math is not based on feeling but on fact.

Dr. Leland Miles wrote in his book, *Phi Delta Kappan*, "There are young navigators who died in China because they could not add, subtract, divide, and multiply two and three digit figures without making a mistake; and a mistake in the air of one degree means that your airplane will miss its home base by 60 miles."

If you want to talk about a dangerous ideology, then the ideology of OBE should be on the top of your list. Such a mentality has the potential to destroy what made America great, which is capitalism, competition, and the pursuit of excellence. The opposite has become the basis of OBE — mediocrity, laziness, procrastination, and most assuredly, socialism.

Outcome-Based Basketball

The following illustration was sent to me by a school administrator in Forest City, Iowa. The author is unknown.

Outcome-Based Basketball

To: All high school principals
From: The district superintendent
Re: The new rules for basketball

All varsity and junior varsity basketball teams must use Outcome-Based Basketball beginning next season. To ensure that all teams feel successful, we will not keep score. It is more important that the team learn the process and finish the game at the skill level determined by the coach rather than be winners.

To make sure everyone meets all the outcomes, poor players must be given more practice time and coaching. No scores will be kept, and no winners will be announced. During games, anyone who fails to make goals, double dribbles, fouls, or displays an uncooperative attitude toward the process, will be re-mediated during time-outs. The better players must

sit on the bench and help coach the others
until they demonstrate the right moves, or
engage in enrichment activities such as playing
tag. These games will last much longer, so be
prepared to stay.

All teams will complete 12 games and will
receive the same trophy. No records will be
kept, no statistics will be needed, nor will we
need any play-offs, all star teams, or recognition banquets. Trophies will be meaningless,
but everyone will get one.

Psycho-behavioral basketball experts feel
that this will increase the self-esteem of every
player, who will feel great about his/her
accomplishments. We discourage playing any
games against teams that don't have the same
regulations. It would be unfair competition to
play against teams that emphasize excellence
and winning. The peer pressure of not being
part of our group should be sufficient motivation to conform the "traditional" team to the
Outcome-Based Basketball Model.

This is Outcome-Based basketball, where
excellence is relative, everyone is equal, everyone feels great about his/her performance, and
all players work to their highest potential so
long as it does not exceed the skill level determined by the coach.

How foolish! Outcome-Based Basketball would prove to be
a complete failure, accomplishing nothing positive and only
wasting everyone's time and money.

To make matters worse, it would inculcate into players the
philosophies, character traits, and habits that would only harm
and render them unprepared and unqualified should they
desire to compete in the real world of college or professional
basketball.

Just as Outcome-Based Basketball would be a complete
and total failure, Outcome-Based Education has proven to be

the same. Those who disagree, only need to review the overwhelming facts that have been collected from many credible sources and compiled into this book.

Just Say, "No!"

"Outcome-Based Education has no future in Pennsylvania." At least that's what Eugene Hickok, Pennsylvania's Education Secretary, recently told a group of Pittsburgh businessmen.

According to the newspaper reporter, "the remark provoked an outburst of loud applause from an otherwise restrained audience."

Hickok explained that Governor Ridge wants to make OBE optional for local school boards to implement or reject as they see fit.

Many state governors are realizing that OBE does not work and that it is not fair to force it on the states and the local school districts.

While he was Virginia governor, L. Douglas Wilder "shelved a state OBE plan called the Common Core of Learning."[14]

Current Republican Governor George Allen is so opposed to OBE that "he may not apply for federal funds under Goals 2000."[15]

Governor Allen has made a wise decision. Why? Because in order to receive federal dollars under Goals 2000 each and every state must develop "opportunity to learn standards" which is OBE, making Goals 2000 a gross violation of the tenth amendment.

When it comes to receiving the massive dollars allotted to states under Goals 2000 and H.R. 6, more of our nation's governors should have the courage and character to just say, "No!"

According to the *Washington Times*, however, "Parents in Prince William and Fairfax counties [Virginia] say OBE is alive and well, and educators continue to implement it at the school level."[16]

Sounds to me like Governor Allen's Secretary of Education

needs to lay down the law to superintendents across the state, and, if necessary, give some of those liberal social engineers a pink slip. There is nothing more elitist than for local school officials to continue to force a program when the owners, i.e., the taxpaying public, does not desire it. This is another example of the "we know better than you" attitude that oozes from today's educational system.

Educators in a rush to jump on the latest bandwagon fail to realize that traditional education (the three R's) is also outcome-based in the true sense of the phrase. Students must meet set requirements in order to receive a passing grade in a subject or to move to the next grade level.

Now there's a novel idea!

A Big, Fat, Red "F"

To determine the difference between OBE and traditional education we must ask ourselves:

What outcomes are we looking for?

Do we want a student who has a firm foundation in the three R's who enjoys competing with himself and with others, gets all the facts in order to make an informed decision, is independent, and strives for excellence? Or do we want a student who whines when challenged, can't think for himself, expects others to lead him, goes with the flow and doesn't make waves, and is content to settle for something less than the best?

Phyllis Schlafly writing in the *Washington Times*, February 5, 1994, made this observation:

> Parents don't send their children to school to study self-esteem or to engage in gab sessions with drug abusers, HIV victims and people who are thinking about suicide. Parents send their children to school to be taught reading, writing, mathematics, history, geography and science.

Carol Innerst wrote in the *Washington Times* about Laurie

Andrews, a Westport, Massachusetts mother of two whose "6-year-old came home and described how to make and sniff crack cocaine and how it kills a person. School officials said she learned this from another child, but Mrs. Andrews saw the teachers' guide where it instructed the teacher to describe it. 'You can't trust the schools anymore,' she said."[17]

Outcome-Based Education is a poor choice for our nation for several reasons:

1. OBE lowers the standard of education by lowering the standard of academic achievement.

2. OBE infringes on parental authority by teaching and imposing values under the guise of outcomes.

3. OBE takes away parental control at the local level due to the state and federal governments' over-involvement with pre-set outcomes.

4. OBE has proven to be a very expensive endeavor lacking positive results.

How expensive is OBE?

Federal and state spending for public elementary and secondary education rose from $75.9 billion in the 1984-85 school year to $128.1 billion in the 1991-92 school year.[18]

What do we have to show for it? Some 90 million Americans can barely read.

By contrast, consider kids who are home schooled by parents who donate their time to teach and spend their own money for text books and other educational supplies. How do those home-taught students compare to the government's heavily subsidized pupils?

A recent survey conducted by the Riverside Publishing Company, using the Iowa Tests of Basic Skills, found that the average home schooler outperformed 79% of his peers in reading and did better than 73% in mathematics and language. In addition, 54.7% of home schoolers attained individual scores in the top 25% of the population while only 20.4 % were in the bottom 50%, and only 6.7 % in the bottom quarter. These results were based on 16,000 home-taught students from all 50 states.

Why do Christian and private schools consistently turn out a much superior student on far less money? Because money and learning have little in common. In fact, most research shows little or no relationship between the amount of spending on education and student performance.

So why does the government continue to throw money at a sinking ship?

Nakedly Political

The Carnegie Foundation summed up the goal and result of Outcome-Based Education when they said, "The age of individualism is closing, and a new age of collectivism is emerging, with an enlargement of the functions of government."

Collectivism can be replaced with the word "socialism" — what's yours is mine. In this age of socialism or collectivism, governments and their functions are getting bigger.

Forbes Magazine, in their February 13, 1995 issue, reported:

> Judged by letters and calls to *Forbes*, no aspect of current education policy has aroused more intense grassroots parental concern than OBE. It particularly alarms parents because it downgrades content matter in favor of nebulous "outcomes" like "thinking skill," "group learning," and associated educrat gobble-dygook."

Forbes went on to say that OBE is not "educational at all, but in the American context today nakedly political. Conservative and religious parents suspect that their values are under attack. They are probably right."

Those concerned parents *are* right, and this chapter and this book clearly presents the evidence to back up such a claim.

Under Outcome-Based Education it is impossible for a student to fail. America's informed parents and taxpayers, however, have graded OBE the traditional way and given it a big, fat, red "F" — for failure!

Notes

1 W.R. Daggett, "Preparing Students for the 1990's and Beyond," International Center for Leadership in Education, January 1992.

2 Robert Morrison, "Business and Reform: A Golden Opportunity," Family Policy Volume 4, Number 5, p.5.

3 "The Blumenfeld Education Letter," April 1993, Vol. 8, No. 4.

4 C.P. Yecke, St. Paul Pioneer Press June 1992.

5 Ron Brandt, "On Outcome-Based Education: A Conversation with BIll Spady," *Educational Leadership*, December 1992/January 1993, p. 68.

6 Rush Limbaugh, *See, I Told You So*, (New York, New York: Simon & Schuster, 1993, 1994), p. 78-80.

7 Ibid;,

8 Dr. Dennis Cuddy, *Chronology of Education with Quotable Quotes*, (Highland City, FL: Pro Family Forum, Inc., 1993), p. 43.

9 Benjamin Bloom, *Taxonomy of Educational Objectives*, 1964, page 85.

10 Benjamin S. Bloom, *All Our Children Learning: A Primer for Parents, Teachers, and Other Educators* (New York: McGraw-Hill Book Company, 1981), p. 180.

11 Ibid.

12 Ibid., p. 54.

13 I was first alerted to this fact by Charlotte T. Iserbyt in her booklet, "Back to Basics or OBE Skinnerian International Curriculum," p. 11. For more information on this grant you can order it from your Congressman. The grant application number is No. 84:122B and is titled "Excellence in Instructional Delivery Systems: Research and Dissemination of Exemplary Outcome-based Education Programs." "Appendix A" of the grant application titled "Excellence in Our Schools — Making It Happen."

14 Carol Innerst, "Parents Rebel as 'Outcomes' Replace Three R's," *The Washington Times*, September 7, 1994.

15 Ibid.

16 Ibid.

17 Ibid.

[18] Rush Limbaugh, "When A Means Average: Our Schools Are Failing," *Family Circle Magazine*, May 16, 1995, p. 146.

3

The National
Extortion Association

America has gone through many years of disturbing change — much of which has not been positive. As a nation, we have moved far away from that which our founding fathers had envisioned. In fact, many of our great leaders warned us about the kind of change that would be prescribed and urged us to resist.

Much of the negative changes in our nation have come at the hands of many agents of change: the American Civil Liberties Union (ACLU), the National Education Association (NEA), the National Organization of Women (NOW), Planned Parenthood, and People for the American Way.

How much influence and power have these radical organizations had over our nation's most powerful lawmakers and leaders?

Who started these organizations and for what purpose?

What are their true goals and plans?

How has America changed under the influence of these agents of change?

To answer this last question, allow me to quote from my first book *Cradle to College: An Educational Abduction.*

America the Way It Used to Be

Let's imagine we have been transported back to 1955. For a few moments try to visualize this post-war period and its culture, people, and values.

Those of us who were not alive then can use images from television re-runs like "Leave It To Beaver," "Father Knows Best," "Dennis the Menace," "I Love Lucy," and "Ozzie and Harriet," to aid our imaginations. That, my friends, despite what the critics say, is how the 1950s really were.

Do you have a feel for the times? Most people don't bother to lock their doors, and kids roam freely up and down the streets without fear of abduction or drive-by shootings.

On school days, children walk to the local school instead of riding a bus to a consolidated facility miles from their homes. After the teacher begins the day by reading a Psalm, the class says the Lord's Prayer out loud and then repeats the Pledge of Allegiance to the flag. On the wall, the Ten Commandments are posted beside a picture of the Good Shepherd holding a tender, young lamb.

At the high school, most students are grade conscious, and those who have no plans for college study for a trade at the "technical" school. After graduation, some choose a career in the armed forces as a way of serving their country. There are few high school "dropouts," but even they are able to find jobs at the local factories.

Television is a relatively new invention, and most programs revolve around American family life. In fact, an entire family can watch almost any sitcom — or go to the movies together — without fear of being assaulted by filthy curse words, bedroom scenes, or bloody violence.

Teenage pregnancy and babies out of wedlock — even divorce — all are rare occurrences. Hardly anyone has even heard of the word "abortion," and birth control devices are discussed only between a married couple and their doctor.

Sure, the kids may call somebody a "queer" but few have ever met a homosexual. Guys open the doors for their dates, and only "loose" girls call boys on the phone. Most young people get married, have children, and raise a family with the same values they learned as children.

Back to the Present

Now imagine we jump back to 1995. All the doors are locked and security systems and window bars are a necessity in most cities. Kids never go anywhere alone, and nearly every milk container portrays the sad faces of missing children.

School children rise before the crack of dawn to catch their bus to the racially mixed school on the other side of town. At the back of the bus, the older kids smoke and discuss their sexual exploits from the night before.

After passing through a metal detector, the students straggle into their classrooms where the teacher begins the day with a few choice profanities. Prayer is merely a joke since it was banned long before these kids started kindergarten. In fact, the last "nerd" who brought a paperback New Testament to school was suspended for three days and threatened with expulsion if he did it again.

Down the hall at the school "health clinic," a "nurse" begins her day by handing out condoms to a few girls — for some reason the boys never request them. Outside the clinic office, a lonely, depressed teenage girl waits for the dismissal slip that will get her out of classes for the day. She'll be going for her abortion appointment at "Women's Reproductive Services" — arranged by the school nurse and without the girl's parents' permission, of course.

When the bell rings, kids rush out of classrooms and into the hallways, pushing and shoving. The less aggressive students hide in doorways for fear of being punched or stabbed. No one dares enter the restrooms unless they want to smoke or do drugs.

During the next class, the students gather into groups to finish the "projects" they've been working on for weeks. Most are laughing and talking while the teacher tries to maintain order. In the back, several serious students discuss how they will ever get accepted into college since they aren't graded on academic subjects but merely rated on vague "outcomes."

Over at the elementary school, first graders open their reading books to find the ugly face of a scary witch staring back at them from the pages. After a brief discussion on why the witch likes to boil young children in her cauldron, the teacher reads the class a story about a little girl who doesn't have a daddy and whose mommy likes to be affectionate with a woman named Janet.

That evening, the kids watch TV or a rented video in the family room with mom and dad. Amidst a stream of profanity, blasphemy, nudity, and suggestive sexual jokes, they all laugh together without embarrassment. Some stay up to enjoy the late night talk shows, where comedians ridicule every tradition of American Society — especially marriage and the church. No one is exempt from their mockery — except liberals and the "politically correct" — and it's open season on everyone from conservatives like Dan Qualye to religious leaders like Pope John Paul.

If you were to go from 1955 to 1995 overnight, you would realize how low our culture has sunk in the last 40 years. You would wonder, How did we get to this point? Why did we let it happen?

Let's face it, if the trends continue, our nation will become more and more pagan, depraved, violent, and ignorant. Although the way things are today didn't happen overnight, we still cannot deny the tragic consequences. Like the frog being boiled in the pot, the fire has been turned up so slowly that many of us do not even realize that the American value system is on the verge of extinction.[1]

This scenario is based on fact. All the examples given, have and are occurring in homes, schools, and neighborhoods all across the nation.

One of the most powerful organizations today aiding in bringing about such devastating change to our educational system — and ultimately our nation — is the National Education Association.

The Worm in the Apple

In the June 7, 1993 issue of *Forbes Magazine*, Peter Brimelow and Leslie Spencer wrote an article titled, "The National Extortion Association?"

What has the National Education Association done to deserve such criticism? The more accurate question may be, What hasn't the NEA done?

The NEA is the nation's largest union and the world's largest educational organization.

> The 2.1 million-member National Education Association — which some years ago passed the Teamsters to become the country's biggest union — is the worm in the American education apple.[2]

Begun in 1857 at the hands of 43 leaders under the name, National Teachers Association, it was first based in Philadelphia. In 1870, the National Teachers Association merged with the National Association of School Superintendents and the American Normal School Association to form what is now called the National Education Association.

The NEA, in 1922, moved its headquarters from Philadelphia to Washington D.C., where it is based today.

> The NEA was totally recast as a labor union in the 1960s largely by a little known, tightly knit clique who still control it. This is the 'Michigan Mafia,' including Terry Herndon, Keith Geiger and Don Cameron, who all began their NEA careers importing labor union methods into Michigan schools.[3]

One of NEA's formative leaders, John Dewey, an avowed humanist socialist, was made honorary president of the NEA in 1932. In 1933, Dewey co-authored the *Humanist Manifesto*.

John Dewey, who traveled to Russia in the 1930s to help organize and implement the Marxist educational system there, today is known in America as the "Father of Progressive Education." In 1935, Dewey became the President of the League of Industrial Democracy, which was originally called the Intercollegiate Socialist Society.

What does this tell us about the National Education Association? That it is an organization founded and functioning on the philosophies of elitism, socialism, and communism.

When Is a Socialist a Marxist?

Do you think calling them a communist organization smacks of McCarthyism? I don't. Especially when there is little difference between a socialist, a communist, and a Marxist.

A communist is a socialist who is in a hurry. A Marxist is a communist who has a gun. And the foundation of communism and Marxism is socialism.

Webster's Dictionary backs up this claim by stating that socialism is, "a stage of society in Marxist theory transitional between capitalism and communism."

Webster's defines Marxism as, "a theory and practice of socialism," and communism as, "a doctrine based on revolutionary Marxian socialism and Marxism-Leninism that is the official ideology of the U.S.S.R."

Anyone who endorses and promotes the philosophies of socialism is, in fact, endorsing and promoting the foundation of communism and ultimately Marxism.

In the December 1933 *NEA Journal,* editor Joy Elmer Morgan wrote an editorial calling for government control of corporations. The government control of corporations is called "fascism."

How does Webster's dictionary define fascism? As "a political philosophy, movement, or regime that exalts nation and often race above the individual and that stands for a centralized autocratic government headed by a dictatorial leader."

We have only to study the words and writings of NEA's leaders to be convinced of their socialist/communist leanings, as the following documented material makes clear.

On June 29, 1938, the *New York Herald Tribune* published a story on the NEA Convention being held in New York City and reported the following:

> Dr. Goodwin Watson, Professor of Education at
> Teachers College, Columbia University, begged

the teachers of the nation to use their profession to indoctrinate children to overthrow "conservative reactionaries" directing American government and industry. . . . (He) declared that Soviet Russia was one of the most notable international achievements of our generation.

Has the NEA Changed?

"That was 1938," you say. Surely, the NEA has changed since then. Has it?

To answer that question, let me list some of the dozens of resolutions — that had nothing to do with education — approved by members at the National Education Association annual convention held the weekend of July 4 , 1995.

According to columnist Cal Thomas, who cites information from *Education Reporter*, the 1995 NEA convention adopted:[4]

• Five resolutions indicating the NEA's antagonism toward parents who make private or home school choices.
• At least 15 resolutions dealing with the sexual orientation issue. ("These were crafted by the NEA's Gay and Lesbian Caucus.")
• The feminist agenda
• The environmental rights agenda
• Ratification of the U.N. Treaty on the Rights of the Child
• A change in the purpose of Thanksgiving to replace giving thanks to God with a celebration of "diversity."

Sounds to me like the NEA is still trying to "indoctrinate children to overthrow 'conservative reactionaries.'" Looks like nothing has changed in over 57 years after all.

In fact, today the organization is worse than ever.

Why has the NEA earned the unfavorable title of being the "National Extortion Association"?

The article in *Forbes Magazine*, provided several telling examples.

Apparently, the California Education Association, the state

branch of the NEA, offered a signature collecting firm $400,000 dollars to turn down the job of collecting the signatures needed to have the school voucher proposition included on the ballot.

I'd call that extortion. Wouldn't you?

Forbes also reported that the NEA members blocked people from being able to get up to the table in a shopping mall to sign the petition that would put the measure on the ballot. Union members had also reportedly attempted to sabotage the petition with fake names.

Eventually Proposition 174, school vouchers, made it on the California ballot in November 1993 but lost after the NEA spent over $10 million to defeat it. The successful battle fought by the NEA shows just how powerful they are.

But the NEA may have done Californians a favor.

Although I am in favor of the concept behind vouchers and parental control, I would discourage any private school from accepting government dollars in any form. Why? Let me give you an example.

If your state approves a voucher system and your local private school decides to participate, student enrollment at the school will rise dramatically. As a result, more teachers and staff will be hired and facilities expanded to meet larger class sizes.

Suppose, two years after the voucher system was enacted, the state begins to put demands on private schools receiving state voucher dollars. Officials insist that private schools use the state's approved tests and curriculum — which is really Outcome-Based Education.

What will your local private school do? Turn down the money by no longer accepting vouchers? What about the parents who depend on that money to supplement their children's tuition at the private school? Without this subsidized tuition, how will the school pay for teachers' salaries and the mortgage on the new facilities?

The private school will have no choice but to continue to accept state voucher money along with state intrusion. Before long, the private school loses its identity and becomes just another government public school. Could that be why some liberals are now supporting the voucher system?

Government money — state or federal — always comes with strings attached. My advice? "When in doubt, do without."

Instead of getting trapped in the voucher Catch 22, I suggest we lobby our elected officials to increase dramatically the deduction for minor dependents.

Promoting the Global Agenda

In 1940, a California Senate Committee was assembled to investigate how various foundations were using their resources to promote certain philosophies and control teacher training. The committee discovered that the Rockefeller Foundation had spent millions of dollars rewriting current history books and creating new history books that undermined patriotism and a free enterprise system.

The California committee was shocked to discover that the curriculum, which was funded by the Rockefellers and promoted by the NEA, taught socialist ideas.

The committee stated:

> It is difficult to believe that the Rockefeller Foundation and the National Education Association could have supported these textbooks. But the fact is that the Rockefellers financed them and the NEA promoted them very widely.[5]

Why would the NEA promote the removal of traditional history from our schools? If children do not know where they came from, they will not know where they are headed.

Karl Marx said, "Take away the heritage of a people and they are easily persuaded."

Another reason many educators do not teach traditional history is because their goal is not to create a U.S. citizen but a global citizen. The new global citizen must be taught to respect and have allegiance for the promoter of the global agenda, the United Nations.

The NEA has actively promoted the United Nations and its global education plan. The United States version is called Goals 2000.

In the January 1946, *NEA Journal,* editor Joy Elmer Morgan wrote an editorial entitled, "The Teacher and World Government," which stated:

> In the struggle to establish an adequate world government, the teacher . . . can do much to prepare the hearts and minds of children for global understanding and cooperation. . . . At the very top of all the agencies which will assure the coming of world government must stand the school, the teacher, and the organized profession.[6]

The next year, in October 1947, the *NEA Journal* published at article titled, "On the Waging of Peace," by NEA official William Carr, who wrote:

> As you teach about the United Nations, lay the ground for a stronger United Nations by developing in your students a sense of world community. The United Nations should be transformed into a limited world government. The psychological foundations for wider loyalties must be laid. . . . Teach about the various proposals that have been made for strengthening the United Nations and the establishment of world law. Teach those attitudes which will result ultimately in the creation of a world citizenship and world government. . . . We cannot directly teach loyalty to a society that does not yet exist, but we can and should teach those skills and attitudes which will help to create a society in which world citizenship is possible"[7]

Some teachers are following William Carr's advice to the letter.

A Model U.N.

In Woodbury, Minnesota, the Junior world history class at our local high school spends an entire semester putting together a "Model U.N." Each student studies the country they will represent, and then in January, the class takes over Woodbury's City Hall Chambers and acts out a mock U.N.

I was also shocked to discover this is not something new; it has been taking place every January for the past 16 years.

According to Susan Travis, the instructor and advisor for this United Nations project, the goal is to give students a taste of what life is like at the U.N. The students are graded on oral participation, lobbying, and coalition-building.

I wonder if the students are told about the waste and mismanagement of U.S. tax dollars that occurs by U.N. representatives and officials of other governments? The United States provides the funds for a large percentage of the U.N.'s budget. In addition, the recent debacle in Bosnia has highlighted the U.N.'s inability to make and implement even the most basic decisions.

Instead of glorifying this inept, bungling institution, teachers should inform students of the U.N.'s true purpose — that the U.N. was started by a group of globalist socialists who saw this organization as a limited form of a world government that would prepare the way for a real one-world government.

Is there any doubt that the NEA was founded on, and continues to promote socialism and ultimately communism, Marxism, and fascism?

Most Americans are completely unaware that a powerful organization, which has no respect for parental authority, teaching basic skills, true American history, or competition, is controlling their child's educational system.

So what is the purpose of the NEA if it not to establish educational policies?

A Major Political Force

The NEA's ultimate goal, according to their own leaders, is to become a powerful political force in America to bring about great social change. The NEA desires to control every teaching institution and every teacher in the nation. Along the way to accomplishing their goals, the NEA desires to stifle those who oppose them and force out traditional teachers.

In 1967, Sam Lambert, executive secretary of the NEA, said,

> The NEA will become a political power second to no other special interest group. . . . NEA will have more and more to say about how a teacher is educated, whether he should be admitted to the profession, and whether he should stay in the profession.[8]

In 1974, then NEA president Helen Wise spoke at an NEA political fund-raiser saying, "We must reorder Congressional priorities by reordering Congress. We must defeat those who oppose our goals."[9]

In an editorial titled, "The Uses of Teacher Power," from the 1975 November-December NEA journal, *Today's Education*, then NEA president John Ryor wrote, "We must become the foremost political power in the nation."[10]

Were they successful? Yes. By the 1970s, the NEA was able to convince President Jimmy Carter to establish the Department of Education and make the Secretary of Education a cabinet position.

Cal Thomas has said, "Record levels of cash have been flowing into education since the Department of Education was established 25 years ago by Jimmy Carter as a payoff to the National Education Association for that lobby's political support." [11]

All this political maneuvering by the NEA is done under the guise of being a teachers union that is concerned about American teachers and students.

The NEA is not at all interested in representing teachers. It is clear from statements made by NEA leaders that they do not represent teachers but their own political agenda. In fact, the NEA has found itself doing and endorsing issues that many of their members oppose.

The Day I Met NEA's President

While sitting in the Memphis airport on November 18, 1994, waiting to board a plane to San Antonio, a man walked by whom I immediately recognized as Keith Geiger, president of the National Education Association .

At the time, I couldn't help but remember a quote from an article I had read about him in *Forbes Magazine* 's June 7, 1993 issue:

> Keith Geiger's style may be more polished now than in his salad days as president of the NEA's Michigan Education Association affiliate, when he astonished Walsh College economics professor Harry C. Veryser by gesticulating obscenely at him during an in-studio radio debate. "He flipped me the finger when school choice came up," remembers Veryser, who jokes that the union's ruthless and insatiable drive for power and perquisites should earn it a new name: the National Extortion Association.

With a wry grin, I said, "Hello, Keith Geiger."

He smiled and seemed pleased that I had recognized him. I think he expected me to be an NEA member who was going to sing the praises of his leadership and the organization.

Very politely Mr. Geiger asked, "And who are you?"

I said, "I am Brannon Howse, author of the book, *Cradle to College, Stopping the Educational Abduction of America's Children.*"

His response to this revelation was, "Oh, brother."

I proceeded to tell Mr. Geiger that I had seen him on "This Week with David Brinkley," August 29, 1993. "I appreciated your honesty," I said, "when you admitted that the main purpose of the NEA was not to represent teachers."

Mr. Geiger responded quickly by saying, "That's not what I said! I said, the main purpose of the NEA is not only to represent teachers."

I told Mr. Geiger that I had the show on video tape and had replayed it several times, but that I would view the program once again.

Later, after reading the transcript of the program provided by Journal Graphics, I discovered that Mr. Geiger's actual statement was, "No, no, I'm telling you, that the sole purpose of this union is not to protect teachers' jobs."

After discovering we were both headed for San Antonio, Mr. Geiger asked what was I going to be doing in San Antonio.

I said, "I am speaking at a conference on education. Why are you going to San Antonio?"

Geiger replied, "Well, I am going to the same conference, and when you are done speaking, I am going to get up and tell the truth!"

To this we both laughed.

Since, in actuality, I was the featured and only speaker for this evening conference on education, I took it upon myself to extend him a serious invitation to come to the seminar and have a friendly debate or round table discussion. Of course, my request was denied.

During our visit in the airport, a women approached the two of us and said with great surprise, "Brannon!"

Mr. Geiger obviously knowing who she was said, "Do you two know each other?"

"Oh sure," I replied. "I debated Judy for three hours on radio last summer at the Minnesota State Fair."

Judy was and is at this time, the president of the Minnesota Education Association.

We were having a regular convention right there in the Memphis airport. However, I was quickly out-numbered as I realized that a few more NEA state presidents were standing and sitting nearby, all waiting to board the same plane.

Even though there is little that Mr. Geiger and I would ever agree on, it was for the most part a very delightful brief meeting.

Mr. Geiger must be more polished now than a few years back because he did not flip me the finger. In fact, he smiled and even shook my hand when we departed.

Teacher Salaries and NEA Dues

On August 29, 1993, Wisconsin State Representative Polly Williams appeared on "This Week With David Brinkley" to promote the concept of school choice and vouchers. The anti-school choice guest was the President of the National Education Association, Keith Geiger.

The following statements from the transcript of this news program proves the NEA's first and foremost responsibility is not to represent teachers despite what they tell their teachers under the guise of a teachers union.

> *Ms. Williams:* I'm here to protect the lives of our children. We have two different purposes here.
>
> *Mr. Geiger:* I'm a parent, Polly. I'm a parent as well as a teacher.
>
> *Ms. Williams:* Yes, but you also have a job that says you have to look out for teachers' jobs.
>
> *Mr. Geiger:* No, I don't. No, I don't.
>
> *Sam Donaldson:* You don't?
>
> *Ms. Williams:* You are here to protect teachers from any kind of excess —
>
> *Sam Donaldson:* Well, if I were a member of your union and you weren't looking after my job, I'd try to oust you.
>
> *Mr. Geiger:* No, no, I'm telling you that the sole purpose of this union is not to protect teachers' jobs.

The NEA portrays itself as a defender and supporter of teachers in order to attract members and thus make larger sums of money to fund its aggressive agenda. Why do you think the NEA pushes for higher teacher salaries? Because it will increase membership dues, thus creating more money for the NEA, as *Forbes Magazine* reported in its June 7, 1993 issue:

> Regardless of its needs, NEA dues are a fixed proportion of the average teacher's salary.

> Thus, just as real estate agents have a vested
> interest in rising property prices, so does the
> NEA have a direct institutional interest in
> teacher salary increases.

Although teachers pay their yearly dues to the NEA to have someone looking out for their best interest, they are being robbed by those they trust to protect them.

Former U.S. Secretary of Education in the Bush Administration, Lamar Alexander, has said, "They [the NEA] consistently advocate proposals that are against the interest of their members."[12]

Why is that? Because the main purpose of the NEA is *not* to represent teachers.

Teachers — NEA's Pawns

The NEA also makes large sums of money off selling life insurance to its members. "Federal government filings show that the NEA has been receiving about $10 million a year, 30% of the premium members pay for NEA-marketed Prudential life insurance."[13]

What does that mean? That the NEA charges its members about 30% more than the insurance actually costs and pockets the profit.

Teachers in Michigan are offered insurance through the Michigan Education Special Services Association (MESSA), "a 200-plus-staff, $370 million (revenues) subsidiary of the Michigan Education Association. Messa Sells Blue Cross and Blue Shield teacher health insurance to school districts."[14]

Teachers receive insurance through Messa even though the insurance "cost some $1,000 more per head than the state employee health plan."[15]

Why is this allowed to continue?

Forbes Magazine reported that "the cost is just bargained into contracts under the threat of strikes and passed on to tax-payers."

What does the Michigan Education Association receive in return? *Forbes Magazine* reports that "the subsidiary is immensely valuable."

> Apart from paying the MEA an annual fee of
> some $1.5 million, Michigan Education Special
> Services Association (Messa), buys computer
> and other services from the MEA's for-profit
> Michigan Education Data Network Association
> at a cost of over $8 million in fiscal 1992. Messa
> may well be subsidizing the MEA in other
> ways: All three operations are so integrated
> that they share the same switchboard, and
> Messa carries MEA workers on its payroll."[16]

Do you see what is happening here? The Michigan
Education Association uses Messa (Michigan Education
Special Services Association) as its health care provider,
despite the fact that the insurance is about $1,000 per person
more expensive than the plan offered by the state of Michigan.
The added cost does not matter to the teacher's union because
the added cost is bargained into contracts. If the cost is not
covered in the teacher's contracts, the MEA has the teachers
threaten to strike.

Who gets stuck holding the bag so that the Michigan
Education Association, the state branch of the NEA, can make
big money? The taxpayer.

The cost of the expensive insurance offered by Messa is
paid for by the taxpayer as part of the teachers' total contract
package. If the taxpayers refuse to pay for the expensive insurance, the teachers threaten to strike.

This falls into the category of extortion.

The MEA is making big money off the taxpayers, using
teachers and children as their pawns.

Forbes Magazine was correct when they called the NEA the
National Extortion Association.

But this is just the tip of the iceberg.

Conveyors of Values?

In 1970, the then-president of the NEA, George Fischer,
told NEA representatives during an assembly.

> A good deal of work has been done to begin to
> bring about uniform certification controlled by
> the unified profession in each state. . . . With
> these new laws, we will finally realize our 113-
> year-old dream of controlling who enters, who
> stays, and who leaves the profession. Once this
> is done, we can also control the teacher training
> institutions.[17]

By controlling teacher training institutions, the NEA can
control what kind of teacher enters the profession. If the NEA
had its way, our nation's colleges and universities would be
using cookie cutters to create American teachers.

Under the NEA's uniform certification, every teacher leaving the training institutions and entering the profession will be
an anti-American socialist with the goal of becoming "an agent
of change." The goal of every teacher under NEA control
would be interested in indoctrination not education.

I quoted earlier the shocking statement made by former
NEA president, Catherine Barrett in the February 10, 1973
issue of the *Saturday Review of Education.* Her words make clear
the objective of this powerful organization:

> Dramatic changes in the way we will raise our
> children in the year 2000 are indicated, particu-
> larly in terms of schooling. . . . When this hap-
> pens — and it's near — the teacher can rise to
> his true calling. More than a dispenser of infor-
> mation, the teacher will be a conveyor of val-
> ues, a philosopher. . . . We will be agents of
> change.

Education is not the goal of the NEA — it is indoctrination.
The teacher no longer teaches skills; he is now a philosopher
who conveys "values." Is that why parents send their children
to school? To be subjected to philosophical meandering all day
long and indoctrinated by the humanistic "values" of godless
educators?

Just Change the Test

Aren't kids supposed to be attending school to receive an education? Not according to the NEA, who considers giving letter grades to students another archaic practice.

In 1969, the *NEA Journal* published an article by Sidney Simon, who wrote, "The grading system is the most destructive, demeaning, and pointless thing in education."

Why does the NEA condemn letter grades? Because grades only serve to highlight and prove the total failure of our educational system under NEA's control.

As long as there is a system of letter grades, the American people can determine whether their tax dollars are being used for what they were intended — the educating of children.

When SAT scores are low, and students across the nation are not excelling academically in large enough numbers, Americans begin to protest. The protesting turns into investigating, and the investigating produces the reason for low SAT scores and the increasing number of uneducated American children.

What do educators plan do to raise SAT scores? Teach more subject matter to prepare students for the SAT? No. That would fly in the face of their agenda.

Instead, they just change the test.

The Associated Press recently reported, "Big Improvement Made by High School Grads in 1995 SAT Tests."[18] Although scores had increased by a few points, the article noted that in 1994, "the name of the examination was changed to the Scholastic Assessment Test from Scholastic Aptitude Test."

Other changes were also made. The 1995 test was "greatly modified" and students were permitted to use calculators. They were also given 15 more minutes to solve problems on each test.

At 428, the overall 1995 verbal score was the highest since 1988. A great improvement? Not exactly.

> The 1995 mark is quite a comedown from the late 1960s and early 1970s when students consistently scored in the 450-460 range, and it's a

breathtaking drop from several decades ago
when the average was 500.[19]

Not to worry. Next year a new "re-centered" SAT scoring
system goes into effect "that could increase marks by up to 100
points." Wow!

How do critics view these changes in the SAT test and the
new method of scoring? "As a ploy to improve the image of
the nation's school system — just as 'grade inflation' trends
have students earning more A's and B's than ever."[20]

Why is the educational system, controlled by the NEA,
deliberately not educating children — and instead merely inflat-
ing grades and changing tests? The answer may surprise you.

In order to educate America's students, teachers must concentrate the majority of their class time on teaching basic skills.
The NEA does not want teachers to concentrate on teaching
basic skills. Why? Because they want most of the school day to
be spent on brainwashing.

Why would educators buy into this guaranteed prescription for educational failure? The answer takes us back once
again to the philosophy of the NEA who consider failure to be
success.

Education today is planned failure, which results in intellectual slavery. If you are not educated, you can be easily controlled.

Tap Dancers and Security Guards?

What does the NEA think about traditional teachers who
went to college and obtained a teaching degree in order to
impart true cognitive, academic knowledge to their students?
Not much.

In 1971, the NEA publication, *Schools for the 70's and
Beyond: A Call to Action*, the NEA declares:

> Teachers who conform to the traditional insti-
> tutional mode are out of place. They might find
> fulfillment as tap-dancers, or guards in maxi-
> mum security prisons or proprietors of reduc-

ing salons, or agents of the Federal Bureau of
Investigation — but they damage teaching,
children, and themselves by staying in the
classroom.

This is a slap in the face to the many outstanding teachers
who are gifted in the art of teaching — Adela Jones.

As a geometry teacher in Georgetown, Delaware, Adela
Jones refused to grade on a curve or use grade inflation or
implement Outcome-Based Education. Instead, Adela taught
her classes using a high standard of expectation — after all
geometry is a college track course. As far as she was concerned
there was one right answer in math, and her students must be
graded and judged on the absolute standard of right or wrong,
correct or incorrect.

As a result, Adela's classes had the highest failure rate of
any teacher in the school. (Remember, no one is supposed to
fail in OBE.) Administrators told her she needed to bring her
failure rate in line with the other teachers. When she refused to
play the numbers game simply to please her liberal administrator, Adela was fired.

On two different days, Adela's students walked out of
school to protest her firing with signs and banners. One sign
read, "It was not Adela Jones' fault that I failed!"

When the story was covered by "Dateline NBC," only one
student went on camera to discuss her in a negative way, and
even he said that between geometry class and soccer, he could
not keep up his grades.

The dismissal case went to court where the judge learned
about Adela's commitment to her students. Often on duty
from 7:00 a.m. to 7:00 p.m., she was happy to give extra
instruction to any student who asked for help. In addition, she
conducted a pre-test study group for those who wanted to participate. Students were also allowed to call Adela at home if
they needed help in the evenings with their homework.

Due to public support, the judge told the local school
board either to reinstate Adela Jones or he would. I guess all
the kids in geometry class will have to meet Adela's high standards, including soccer players.

The Bible explicitly lists "teaching" as a God-given gift. No wonder many excellent teachers are leaving the profession. And those who aren't leaving are sending their own children to private schools.

What Do Teachers Know that You Don't?

While a guest on "This Week with David Brinkley", August 29, 1993, NEA president Keith Geiger admitted, under pressure from George Will, that many public school teachers do not send their children to public schools, but to private schools.

> *George Will:* Mr. Geiger, . . . about 50 percent of urban area public school teachers with school-age children send their children to private schools. What do they know that we ought to know?
>
> *Keith Geiger:* It's about 40 percent.
>
> *George Will:* Okay, 40 percent send their children to private schools. What do they know that we should know?
>
> *Keith Geiger:* Look, I don't know what they know that you should know, but I do know that a public school teacher has an option to send his or her child to whatever school. . . .

The President of the NEA publicly admits what many have known for some time. Many teachers are not happy with the condition of the public school system.

In Milwaukee, Wisconsin, the Center for Education Reform showed that 33 percent of public school teachers send their own children to private schools. Why? Because "nearly half of Milwaukee students don't graduate from high school, and those who do have a D-minus average."[21]

If 30%-40% of America's public school teachers are so dissatisfied with the condition of the public school system that they refuse to put their own children through it, what does that tell you?

What's Good for the Goose . . .

George Will and Wisconsin Democratic State
Representative Polly Williams, appearing on "This Week With
David Brinkley," August 29, 1993, questioned NEA President
Keith Geiger about President and Mrs. Clinton's decision to
send their daughter, Chelsea, to a private, religious school.

George Will: Yours is the largest union in the
country.

Mr. Geiger: Right.

George Will: You give pots of money to the
Democratic party. You send the largest
group of delegates to the Democratic convention.

Mr. Geiger: Right.

George Will: You elect a democratic President.
Given the choice of any public school in the
city of Washington, he chose a private
school. What's that tell you?

Mr. Geiger: That tells me that he decided that,
for his daughter, he needed to have her in a
school where she wasn't going to be the
issue of the school, and the school he chose
for her to go to is already the school of many
famous people in D.C. ,and she wasn't as
stand-out-. . . .

Polly Williams: Exactly. And those people who
legislate, that says low-income families . . .
the low-income families can't do exactly.
You're saying . . . those children [who] were
born to families with money have the privilege of having a good education. But those
who were born to families such as mine —
you don't deserve it because you don't have
money. Remember, the President's money
comes from the public dole. He takes public
dollars and puts it into a private school. If
he can do it, what is wrong with the average

parent doing the same thing? Taking their
public dollar and putting it where they think
their child can be best educated.?

Rep. Polly Williams makes a very good point. The
hypocrisy from the liberals and the NEA is immense.

When I debated the president of the Minnesota Education
Association, the state branch of the NEA, on WCCO-AM for
three hours in September 1994, the hypocrisy came shining
through. During the debate, the MEA president, in referring to
school vouchers, said, "Public dollars should be used for public education."

I responded by asking, "Why is it okay for President
Clinton to take his salary as President, which comes from public money, and put it toward private education for his daughter? What's good for the goose is good for the gander."

I never received an answer to that question.

The Battle for Turner School

According to *The Wall Street Journal*, "one of the most
important education reform battles in the country" is being
waged in a town just outside of Pittsburgh.[22] The outcome will
determine who has the right to run the schools — "school
boards elected by parents and other members of the community or teachers' unions dedicated to preserving the status quo."

In this working-class, mostly black community,
Wilkinsburg's district reflects the problems faced by many
inner city schools — violence, gangs, and a high drop-out
rate. With a population of 21,000, the Wilkinsburg district had
only 60 in the high school graduating class. Last year, only
one senior scored above the national average on the SAT tests,
and only three seniors this year have grade-point averages
above a C.

Is money the problem? No. The city has the highest tax
rate in the area and spends $8,800 per child a year — that's
$3,000 above the national average! In addition, the district
employs 141 teachers for 1,900 children — a ratio of 13 students per teacher.

In 1993, parents — outraged over high taxes and poor student performance — replaced former school board members with new members dedicated to real reform. For starters, the new board invited the teacher's union and outside groups to submit proposals to restructure the 400-student Turner Elementary School. Five outside groups submitted detailed proposals.

What did the NEA teachers do? Nothing. In fact, they refused to submit a plan and declared the entire process illegal. When they realized the school board was not intimidated by such tactics, the union eventually presented a hastily devised, sketchy plan.

After evaluating all the proposals, the school board signed a five-year contract with Alternative Public Schools, a Nashville, Tennessee company, to manage Turner Elementary. APS's annual cost per student came to only $5,400 a year, and teacher pay will be linked to student performance. APS also planned to extend the school year to 212 days instead of the state's mandated 180 and provide programs for students before and after school.

What did the local NEA do about the school board's decision? The union did everything possible to prevent the APS takeover, including bringing in NEA president Keith Geiger for a rally and finally taking the school board to court. A local judge issued an injunction to block the APS program and found the board's members in contempt. Fortunately, the state Supreme Court overturned the local judge's decision, and — for now — APS is operating the Turner school.

Before the start of classes on Sept. 5, 1995, the newly hired APS teachers went door-to-door in Wilkinsburg meeting parents and students. The response from the community was overwhelming as people began to realize that these teachers were out to "earn" their paycheck and provide a better product in return.

The court battle is not yet over, but an important message has been sent to union teachers and administrators by these courageous school board members. As a result, school districts across the nation will be watching to see what happens in Wilkinsburg, Pennsylvania.

Why is the struggle over Turner School so important?
Because, as Professor John McLaughlin of St. Cloud University
in Minnesota says, it "will decide who controls public education, the local school board or the teachers' union."

America's Most Powerful Interest Group

The NEA, however, wants to control more than just a local
school like Turner Elementary.

The NEA's main objective has always been to assume
national political power and control much more than education. Their planned takeover has not happened overnight, nor
has their agenda been hidden. As far back as November 14,
1984, U.S. Senator Steve Symms wrote the following letter
expressing his concern over the NEA.

> I am writing you today to alert you to a
> radical Big Labor takeover of the schools in
> your community. The National Education
> Association (NEA) — a union second only to
> the teamsters in size and power [today the
> NEA is the largest] — is about to seize control
> of public education in America. Unless you and
> I take immediate action on this emergency situ-
> ation, the NEA will succeed in pushing legisla-
> tion through Congress that will force compul-
> sory unionization on every public school in the
> country. This is not an idle threat. It is just one
> part of the NEA's Legislative Program for the
> 98th Congress, adopted at its July 1982
> Convention in Los Angeles.
>   Further, the NEA has publicly boasted of its
> plan to seize control of the agencies and boards
> that decide who is allowed to teach and what is
> to be taught. . . . The NEA has become the most
> powerful special interest group in the U.S.
> Their lobbying has brought about a 17-fold
> increase in federal education spending in the
> last 20 years.

> In 1982, their contributions of $1,183,215
> and their army of "volunteer" campaign work-
> ers helped elect 222 Congressmen — a majority
> of the House of Representatives. But instead of
> using its influence to improve the quality of
> American education, the NEA has presided
> over the virtual crumbling of our nation's
> schools.[23]

Earlier I gave you a quote by NEA's executive secretary
Sam Lambert who, in 1967, said that the NEA would become
the most powerful special interest group. Guess what? As U.S.
Senator Steve Symms indicated in 1984, that is actually what
the NEA has become, "the most powerful interest group in the
U.S."

What does the NEA — the most powerful union and special interest group in the U.S. — plan to do with all this
power?

The NEA has many goals. Among them are these reported
by several conservative organizations:

• The NEA strongly supports hiring of homosexual teachers.

• The NEA believes that union contracts with local school
boards should require *all* teachers to pay dues or fees to the
union.

• The NEA is opposed to merit pay for teachers.

• The NEA is opposed to voluntary prayer in schools.

• The NEA opposes tuition tax credit legislation — i.e.,
school vouchers.

• The NEA is opposed to the use of school facilities after
school for voluntary religious meetings.

• The NEA opposes any effort to amend the Constitution
requiring a balancing of the federal budget.

• The NEA favors socialized medicine

• The NEA spent millions of dollars in 1992 to elect Bill
Clinton President and supported other liberal candidates for
Congress.

Bill Clinton's Partners

In return for their support, Bill Clinton told the NEA candidate screening panel in December 1991, "If I become President, you'll be my partners. I won't forget who brought me to the White House."[24]

Clinton kept his promise, and in 1993 while addressing the NEA delegates Clinton thanked the NEA for "the gift of our assistant secretary." Clinton was making reference to former NEA staffer Sharon Robinson who became the U.S. Assistant Secretary of Education for the Office of Educational Research and Improvement.

Clinton went on to say,

> I believe that the president of this organization
> [Keith Geiger] would say we have had the
> partnership I promised in the campaign in
> 1992, and we will continue to have it. . . . You
> and I are joined in a common cause, and I
> believe we will succeed.

Any common cause that involves the NEA and Bill and Hillary Clinton, or anyone of the like, sends up red flags.

Although the Clintons will probably come and go, the damage that he and the NEA will have done to America's educational system in the four years of his administration through their partnership will forever be felt in some form or another.

Bill Bennett, the former U.S. Secretary of Education, made this comment regarding the NEA, "You're looking at the absolute heart and center of the Democratic Party."[25]

Why did he say that? Because it is the truth. Just look at these statistics:

> In 1992 one in eight delegates to the
> Democratic National Convention were mem-
> bers of the NEA. According to the NEA, their
> members have been the largest single bloc of
> delegates to attend the Democratic
> Conventions since 1976.[26]

In partnership with Bill Clinton, the NEA continues to push for these major objectives:

- Increased federal funding and NEA control of primary and secondary education.
- Goals 2000 and H.R. 6
- School-Based Clinics with contraceptive services and abortion referrals in public schools.

In March 1991, the NEA publication titled, *Today*, published an interview conducted by Stephanie Weiss with the president of Planned Parenthood, Faye Wattleton. In the article, Wattleton says that she supports "comprehensive sexuality education" beginning "well before . . . kindergarten age."

Does that give you an idea of where they want to take America?

Limiting Parental Authority

What else is on the NEA agenda?

- The NEA wants major restrictions and requirements placed upon home schoolers.

In 1988, the NEA adopted Resolution C-34, which said:

> The National Education Association believes that home-school programs cannot provide the child with a comprehensive education experience. The Association believes that, if parental preference home-school study occurs, students enrolled must meet all state requirements. Instruction should be by persons who are licensed by the appropriate state educational licensure agency, and a curriculum approved by the state Department of Education should be used.

If the NEA has its way, parents would have to get a teach-

ers license in order to home-school their children. Parents
would also have to meet state requirements, which would
mean using Outcome-Based Education if their state required it.

In 1993, the same resolution quotes above, C-34, was once
again adopted — this time as Resolution B-58.

Why would the NEA oppose home schooling? Because it is
part of their overall agenda to limit parental authority.

In the NEA's annual edition publication, *Today's Education
1983-1984*, the NEA made it clear how it feels about parental
authority:

> The National Education Association believes
> that communications between certified person-
> nel and students must be legally privileged. It
> urges its affiliates to aid in seeking legislation
> that provides this privilege and protects both
> educators and students.

At the same time, the NEA would be highly opposed to
communications between a parent and a child being legally
privileged. The NEA wants teachers to be able to know exactly
what is going on in your home, but they don't want you, the
parent, knowing what is going on behind the doors of the
guidance counselor's or school psychologist's office.

Not Without a Price

After reading this highly documented chapter on the NEA,
I trust you will be encouraged to get involved and fight
aggressively for your child's education and ultimately for the
future of our nation. After all, the NEA is organized, committed, and very serious about their cause.

Just how serious is the NEA? In 1971, in an NEA brochure
titled, "Commission on Professional Rights and
Responsibilities" (no. 163-04940-71), the following challenge
was issued.

> Gather information about the various individu-
> als and groups who criticize or oppose educa-

tion, and make resumes of their activities.

If the NEA or any of its members were watching you and making resumes of your activities, could they even fill up a page? If you were put on trial for being a conservative American who believes in and holds dear faith, family, and freedoms, would there be enough evidence to convict you? If not, why not?

Anything that is worth fighting for comes at a price.

Should you take up the challenge to get more seriously involved in the fight for faith, family, and freedoms? It may require sacrifice. You may be required to sacrifice time, energy, possibly finances, and even your reputation. You could come under some serious personal attacks for your commitment to truth.

The personal attacks could be in the form of negative letters, threatening phone calls, one-sided and mean-spirited articles in your local paper. You may even come face to face with someone who expresses great hostility toward you for your strong stand and opposition.

Such attacks do not necessarily have to come from the NEA or any of its members. Yet, I dare say, the NEA along with other organizations — including the media — make it clear how they feel and what they think of conservative Americans.

If you attend church and have personal religious convictions, you might even be labeled part of the "religious right" — even if you have never said anything about religion or made your case from a religious foundation.

Just be forewarned, if you take up the challenge given in this book, which is to be committed to defending faith, family, and freedoms, it will more than likely not come without a price.

Notes

[1] Brannon S. Howse, *Cradle to College,* (Greenforest, AR: New Leaf Press, 1993) p. 201-204

[2] Peter Brimelow and Leslie Spencer, "The National Extortion Association," *Forbes Magazine,* June 7, 1993, p. 74.

[3] Ibid., p. 79.

[4] Cal Thomas, "School Choice: Puts Parents in Charge," *Greensburg Tribune Review,* Aug. 20, 1995.

[5] Gary Kah, *En Route To Global Occupation,* (Lafayette, LA: Huntington House, 1992), p.60.

[6] Dennis Laurence Cuddy, PH.D. *The Grab for Power,* (Marlborough, NH: Plymouth Rock Foundation, 1993) p. 6.

[7] Ibid., p. 7.

[8] Ibid., p. 12

[9] Ibid., p. 16.

[10] Ibid., p. 17.

[11] Cal Thomas, "Goals 2000 is Reason to Flee Public Schools."

[12] Brimelow and Spencer, p. 83.

[13] Ibid., p. 81.

[14] Ibid., p. 82.

[15] Ibid., p. 82.

[16] Ibid., p. 82.

[17] Ibid., p.13.

[18] Associated Press, "Big Improvement Made By High School Grads," *Greensburg Tribune Review,* August 24, 1995.

[19] Ibid.

[20] Ibid.

[21] Cal Thomas, "School Choice: Puts Parents in Charge," *Greensburg Tribune Review,* Aug. 20, 1995

[22] "Showdown in Wilkinsburg," *Greensburg Tribune Review,* Sept. 3, 1995, reprinted from *The Wall Street Journal.*

[23] Cuddy, p. 21.

[24] Brimelow and Spencer, p. 79.

[25] Ibid., p. 74.

[26] Ibid.

4

The Academic
Madhouse

When Bill Clinton was governor of Arkansas, he appointed his wife chairman of the state Education Standards Committee.[1]

At the time, Mrs. Clinton admitted that she did not come to the table with a lot of experience.

But no matter.

Two months after Hillary became Chairman of the Education Standards Committee in Arkansas, the committee released its first report, which stated opening page:

> Every child in Arkansas is entitled to attend a
> school that meets these minimum standards
> regardless of the location of the school district.[2]

To determine whether Hillary's standards were being met, the committee developed a state-administered Minimum Placement Test. This powerful tool for "educational reform" was mandated to be given to students in their third, sixth, and eighth grade years.

The MPT, however, did not solely test cognitive, academic facts. Hillary, like all good social engineers, prefers to test attitudes, values, feelings, and emotions — with the state determining what is the right or wrong answer.

In an effort to exercise control over local school districts, the committee mandated that 85% of the students taking the MPT in each district, pass the test, or the state could take over the district.

In 1990, John Jacob Cannell of Friends for Education, an industry watch dog, said he received "a lot of letters from Arkansas teachers who didn't feel right about cheating."[3]

Why would teachers make such a statement? Because school administrators were asking teachers to play with the test scores so that the district would not loose control to the state. I guess Arkansas' students weren't politically correct enough to meet Hillary's minimum standards.

What about academically? How did Arkansas students fair under the iron hand of Hillary? Not well. In 1992, results provided these statistics:

> . . . 57 percent of all freshman entering
> Arkansas colleges had to be given remedial
> classes in reading, writing, or math. Over the
> past ten years, the number of students
> enrolling in Arkansas colleges has increased by
> 32 percent, but the graduation rate has
> increased by only 13 percent. The trouble
> extends to the lower grade levels as well. In
> May 1991, a record 22 percent of the Little Rock
> School District's eighth-graders failed the
> state's Minimum Performance Test.[4]

I wonder, What would the results have been if these were "maximum" standards?

New Standards or Old Tricks?

As the First Lady, Hillary is now on the governing board of the New Standards Project (NSP), located at the University of Pittsburgh's Learning Research and Development Center.

What is the purpose of the New Standards Project? To destroy the current testing system and replace it "with an ungraded OBE curriculum approach allowing pupils to take a group of test as many times as they need to pass it."[5]

That's right, under OBE a student can take a test as many times a necessary in order to pass.

The NSP has stated boldly that their aim is nothing less than "to develop a radically new approach to the assessment of students' progress that would drive fundamental changes in what is taught and learned."

In other words, read, writing, and arithmetic — the three R's — must be changed so Hillary and her friends can determine "what is taught" to children.

In a 1992 article in *Educational Leadership* magazine, Hillary and Ira Magaziner (the same Ira Magaziner who tried to push through national health care) were interviewed.

Hillary rationalized her plan under the guise of national industrial policy, noting that if America is to compete in the global economy, we must promote "world class standards" in our educational system.

What Hillary does not mention is that "the key components of the Hillary Plan are found in Outcome-Based Education."[6]

Robert Holland of the *Richmond Times Dispatch*, who also writes occasionally for the *Washington Times*, has written numerous articles on the educational reform movement.

Holland writes:

> There would be one standard for all American students, to be met at or around age 16. States would be responsible for ensuring that virtually all students passed this common world class test.[7]

Such a system would establish the Certificate of Initial Mastery. Without such a certificate, a student cannot get a job — or much else for that matter.

The Key Players

Under Goals 2000, the Department of Education, the Department of Labor, and the Department of Health and

Human Services, will be the key players in this massive federal takeover of education.

While sitting in the Senate gallery on February 2, 1994, my findings were confirmed by Senator Tom Harkin of Iowa who rose to endorse the passage of Goals 2000.

Senator Harkin said, "I also want to thank Secretary of Labor, Robert Reich, again for all of his help, all of them for their outstanding leadership in developing this legislation."[8]

Senator Harkin went on to say,

> I recall the first hearing held by the Labor and Human Resources Committee on this piece of legislation. For the first time, two Cabinet Secretaries sat down at a committee hearing and testified together, the Secretary of Labor and the Secretary of Education. I remember saying that we were missing the third leg of that stool because HHS Secretary Donna Shalala was not present. The chairman assured me she would have been, but there was a scheduling problem and she could not be there.[9]

It is clear that the Departments of Labor, Education, and Health and Human Services are the major social engineers who have helped to write Goals 2000 and H.R. 6. As a result, America's parents, students, and school districts must now bow before not only the new national school board known as the National Education Standards and Improvement Council, but also the National Education Goals Panel, which is set up in the executive branch.

These agents of change have orchestrated a major hijacking of America's educational system.

The National Goals Panel and the National Standards and Improvement Council will work with the Department of Labor and the Secretary's Commission on Achieving Necessary Skills — also referred to as SCANS — and the other two departments and their secretaries to carry out the objectives of Goals 2000 and HR 6. Together they will develop the national testing and curriculum that Goals 2000 funds.

What will this national curriculum look like? In my first book, *Cradle to College,* I predicted that if Goals 2000 were to become law, it would drastically affect education. This was my warning:

> Believe me, this national curriculum will be less about academic achievement or cognitive knowledge and more about attitudes and values — and it most certainly will not be the Judeo-Christian values upon which this country was founded.[10]

Goals 2000 did become law, and my prediction was correct.

Thinks Purposefully?

How will the national testing that Goals 2000 and H.R. 6 proposes be administered? Using Outcome-Based Education.

The basis of such programs and testing will be not be the testing of cognitive academic facts, but about evaluating each student's attitudes, values, feelings, and emotions. In other words, the kind of early childhood intervention programs and testing that Goals 2000 is calling for will be Outcome-Based Education tests that evaluate a child's worldview.

Where do these "outcomes," which have caused such great alarm among parents, come from?

Research journalist Geoffrey Botkin answers that question in his documentary on H.R. 6 and Outcome-Based Education entitled, *Certain Failure.*

> Parents need to understand that Transformational OBE "outcomes" are not what any parent would come up with. They are not even what any self-respecting teacher would come up with. Transformational OBE outcomes were set by the U.S. Department of Labor. They represent exactly what big-government and global government advocates would

> like to achieve. . . . OBE outcomes are "atti-
> tudes" the government wants every citizen to
> have about politics, government orders, and
> individuality.[11]

Do not be fooled when your local educators say, "We are not copying the outcomes of any other state, we are coming up with our own outcomes."

Bologna! The outcomes being used today in each and every state look almost identical. Are we supposed to believe that this is just by chance? It is not by chance at all. Via Goals 2000 and H.R. 6, the development — and eventually the main- taining — of chosen *national* outcomes are being carved in stone.

Why are the outcomes in one state similar to the outcomes in another? Charlotte Iserbyt explains in her booklet, "Back to Basics Reform or OBE — Skinnerian International Curriculum?":

> Although local citizens are assured *their* goals
> and objectives were determined *locally*, evi-
> dence proves otherwise. Federally-funded
> *Course Goals Collection* has been disseminated to
> school districts across the nation over the past
> ten years by the U.S. Department of
> Education's Northwest Regional Educational
> Laboratory. According to the price list for this
> collection, 70,000 copies are currently in use
> throughout the United States, a fact which is
> highly significant, since there are only 16,000
> school districts in the nation. The collection
> consists of 14 volumes with 15,000 goals cover-
> ing every major subject taught in the public
> schools from kindergarten through grade
> twelve.[12]

What are some of the outcomes or standards on which each student is evaluated?

In Pennsylvania, parents were shocked to find that "thinks

purposefully" was one outcome their children were expected to achieve. Parents were even more angry when they discovered that "thinks purposefully" includes, "adapts quickly to change."[13] How is such an ambiguous outcome evaluated? By testing for rapid emotional and behavioral change "without protest."

You can see why this outcome would be important to the social engineers whose chief goal is to change your child's beliefs and attitudes to those deemed politically and socially correct.

The "Self-Directed Learner"

Other OBE outcomes being used in districts across the country include:

- Effective communicator.
- Productive group participant.
- Analyzes patterns and functional relationships in order to solve problems and determine cause/effect relationships.
- Applies data handling and measurement techniques to solve problems and justify conclusions.
- Applies multiple methods of inquiry in order to plan and conduct research.
- Draw conclusions and communicate findings.
- Understands the past and continues development of societies and cultures in human history.
- Applies informed decision-making processes to promote healthy lifestyles, social well-being, and stewardship of the environment.
- Self-directed learner.

What is a "self-directed learner"? *The Washington Times* on September 7, 1994, reported the following as the "pupil outcomes" sought in Kentucky's OBE plan under the heading, "Self-Directed Learner":

- Establish goals for improving and maintaining self-esteem. Plan, implement and record accomplishments.

• Identify and analyze stressful situations in your life.
• Interview a graduate from a substance-abuse program; create a case study of his/her drug history.

Is this how you want your child spending his school day? How will such "outcomes" prepare him for college and/or future employment — unless, of course, he plans to be a government social worker?

Under Goals 2000, eventually, every state and school district that wants to receive funds from this federal legislation, will be subject to a national test to determine whether or not the students in each state or district are achieving the mandated outcomes.

State assessments are being modeled after the National Assessment for Educational Progress (NAEP). That means, even if the federal Department of Education were completely abolished, everything is now in place at the state levels for Goals 2000 to be implemented and evaluated.

Would Rush Graduate?

Educational Researcher, Carol Pomeroy, describes how dangerous such a system can be — no matter who is in control — when the basis for pass or fail, graduating or not graduating, receiving a diploma, (now called a Certificate of Initial Mastery), getting a job or going on to college is all based on having the correct worldview as defined by the individuals in charge.

Pomeroy explains:

> Let me give you an example of how this could work. Suppose Bill Clinton were the teacher assessing his student Rush Limbaugh. He is assessing him on how he would deal with the budget deficit under the outcome, "understands the effective management of resources in a household, business, community, and government." Next, Bill assesses Rush on how he would deal with the environment

under outcome, "understands the stewardship
for the environment." Finally, Bill assesses
Rush on his recognition of the proper attitudes
and behaviors for a healthy family life, and
healthy sexuality under the outcome, "applies
informed decision making processes to promote the well-being of the individual and society."

Do you think that Rush will be considered
a successful student and would he graduate?
Could he get a job? Will this still be a free
country?[14]

Although humorous, this is a very dangerous scenario that
is being designed and implemented even now.

Creatures of the State

As I traveled the country speaking about Outcome-Based
Education, the popular response by many conservatives was,
"We agree, OBE is a bad thing, but if the outcomes were devel-
oped by people like us, it could be good."
Wrong!
"If it is morally wrong for the *state* to mandate one worldview, it is equally wrong for the *state* to mandate any other
worldview."[15]
The parents — or the private school — can teach any
worldview they choose, that is their constitutional right.
The public school, however, according to the U.S. Supreme
Court decision, *Wisconsin v. Yoder* (406 U.S. 205, 1972) is not to
impose or teach values that conflict with that of the child's
parents. The ruling specifically said, "Any conflict between
public schooling and a family's basic and sincerely held values
interferes with the family's First Amendment Rights."
This idea is stated even more emphatically in the decision,
Pierce v. Society of Sisters (1925):

Fundamental . . . liberty . . . excludes any general power of the state to standardize its chil-

dren. . . . The child is not the mere creature of
the state; those who nurture him . . . have the
right . . . to recognize and prepare him for
additional obligations.

Some of our lawmakers need to review not only the U.S.
Constitution, but also some of these U.S. Supreme Court rulings. Instead of reviewing and complying with the U.S.
Constitution, some lawmakers are working to keep it from
being the emphasis of today's civic and government classes.

Hatred for Traditional History

On October 20, 1994, the *Wallstreet Journal* published an
article by Lynne Cheney, wife of former Secretary of Defense,
Dick Cheney, titled, "The End of History." In her article
Cheney describes the new national standards for history that
have been developed:

> Imagine an outline for the teaching of
> American history in which George Washington
> makes only a fleeting appearance and is never
> described as our first president. Or in which
> the foundings of the Sierra Club and the
> National Organization For Women are consid-
> ered noteworthy events, but the first gathering
> of the U.S. Congress is not.
> This is, in fact, the version of history set
> forth in the soon-to-be-released National
> Standards for United States History. If these
> standards are approved by the National
> Education Standards and Improvement
> Council — part of the bureaucracy created by
> the Clinton administration's Goals 2000 Act —
> students across the country, from grades five to
> 12, may begin to learn their history according
> to them. . . .
> The general drift of the document becomes
> apparent when one realizes that not a single

one of the 31 standards mentions the
Constitution.

And just exactly what will American students learn if not
the U.S. Constitution?
Cheney goes on to give a detailed list of the most mentioned topics or individuals.

Counting how many times different subjects are mentioned in the document yields
telling results. One of the most often mentioned subjects, with 19 references, is McCarthy
and McCarthyism. The Ku Klux Klan gets its
fair share too, with 17.
As for individuals, Harriet Tubman, an
African American who helped rescue slaves by
way of the underground railroad, is mentioned
six times. Two white males who were contem-
poraries of Tubman, Ulysses S. Grant and
Robert E. Lee, get one and zero mentions,
respectively. Alexander Graham Bell, Thomas
Edison, Albert Einstein, Jonas Salk and the
Wright brothers make no appearance at all.

The midnight ride of Paul Revere also went unmentioned
and Lincoln's "Gettysburg Address" is only mentioned once.
Yet, the American Federation of Labor is mentioned nine
times.
America has not always done everything right, but maybe
that is because America was founded and led by men — and
men make mistakes. However, if you judged America and its
founders, great statesmen, and leaders by the new national
standards for history, you would consider them some of the
most self-serving, oppressive, vile tyrants who ever lived.
This new version of U.S. history would make any student
wonder how America as a nation — and Americans as a people — have managed to exist and survive for over 200 years.
The new National Standards mentions Henry Clay only
once while Daniel Webster doesn't even get a footnote.

Students are, however, encouraged to analyze — what they really mean is "criticize" — presidential candidate Patrick Buchanan's speech at the 1992 Republican Convention.

Cheney writes in her article published in the *Wallstreet Journal* on October 20, 1994, "The only congressional leader I could find actually quoted in the document was Tip O' Neill, calling Ronald Reagan "a cheerleader for selfishness."

Why would so-called "educators" stoop so low as to reveal their personal, liberal bias?

Cheney provides the answer when she quotes one member of the National Council for History Standards — the group that oversaw the drafting of the standards — as saying, "Those who were 'pursuing the revisionist agenda' no longer bothered to conceal their 'great hatred for traditional history.'"

Cheney concludes her article by saying, "We are a better people than the National Standards indicate, and our children deserve to know it."

Karl Marx once said, "Take away the heritage of a people and they are easily persuaded."

The question is: What are our children being persuaded to believe? Socialism? Without a doubt that is where the "revisionists" plan to take us.

I for one, however, won't go along without a fight, kicking and screaming all the way!

The Contest for Cultural Supremacy

The national standards for all other subjects are yet to come. If the national standards for history are any indication, those to follow will not be any better.

In fact, Cheney wrote in her article that the standards for world history, "by all accounts, the sessions leading to their development were even more contentious than those that produced the U.S. standards. The main battle was over the emphasis that would be given to Western civilization."

SCANS (The Secretaries Commission on Achieving Necessary Skills), which helped develop the new national standards for history, has another card up their sleeve. They plan to replace report cards with student resumes, which would include teacher ratings of pupils' personal qualities.

This new national test, developed in conjunction with SCANS, the National Education Goals Panel and the National Education Standards and Improvement Council will test more than academics. It will also be testing "self-esteem and sociability."[16]

Why are Washington educrats going to such great measures to control everything American students learn?

Brooks Alexander provides the answer:

> In the ideological contest for cultural supremacy, education is the prime target; it influences the most people in the most pervasive way at the most impressionable age. No other social institution has anything close to the same potential for mass indoctrination."[17]

Adolf Hitler also knew that power of education. He said, "Let me control the textbooks and I will control the country."[18]

The Teacher's Business

John Dewey, the so-called "father of modern education," was the honorary president of the National Education Association in 1932 and co-author of the 1933 *Humanist Manifesto*. In addition, he was president of the League for Industrial Democracy in 1935, formally known as the Intercollegiate Socialist Society, which Dewey helped found.

What does this humanist, socialist with communist leanings have to say about educating children? John Dewey explains in his own words:

> I believe the true center of correlation on the school subjects is not science, nor literature, nor history, nor geography, but the child's social activities. . . . I believe that the school is primarily a social institution. . . . The teacher's business is simply to determine, on the basis of larger experience and riper wisdom, how the

> discipline of life shall come to the child. . . . All
> the questions of the grading of the child and
> his promotion should be determined by refer-
> ence to the same standard. Examinations are of
> use only so far as they test the child's fitness
> for social life.[19]

Didn't Dewey attend a school where he was graded on his academic achievements? Isn't that where he learned to be articulate and to develop the ability to communicate his thoughts properly on paper so other people could understand him? Surely, he had a good education. Why, then, did he seek to deprive America's generations after him of a logical, systematic approach to learning that would enable them to become scholars like Dewey — only, hopefully, with more wisdom?

Why Johnny Can't Write

Unfortunately, Dewey's lopsided view of the world took root in American education, and decades later his ideas were still being espoused by wanabee philosophers of education. Sidney B. Simon's one of the pioneers of values clarification courses wrote an article in *Today's Education,* the NEA Journal, April 1969, titled "Down With Grades."

Simon parrots Dewey in his opinion of grades:

> For me, the grading system is the most destruc-
> tive, demeaning, and pointless thing in educa-
> tion. . . . In all candor, the only justification for
> grades is that they allow certain administrative
> conveniences. . . . Certainly, grades don't
> advance learning. . . . What our students get
> out of a course boils down to a single grade, a
> crude letter of the alphabet. Let's face up to
> what grades do to all of us, and banish from
> the land the cry? "Whatjaget?"[20]

Once again, I must ask: How did Mr. Simon develop his

writing and thinking skills to the point where he could be quoted in a national magazine on education? Surely grades must have advanced his learning, in spite of his ideas to the contrary. Without grades, I doubt that Mr. Simon would have been motivated to put two full complete sentences together much less write a complete magazine article.

That, however, is what seems to be goal of some educators. Columnist George F. Will, citing author Heather MacDonald, notes:

> More and more schools refuse, on the basis of various political and ethical and intellectual theories, to teach writing. [MacDonald's] essay, "Why Johnny Can't Write," . . . is a hair-raising peek into what she calls "one over-looked corner of the academic mad-house."[21]

What is the substance of the intellectual theories proposed by those cloistered away in the ivy league halls of academia? George Will explains:

> . . . many teachers now consider the traditional idea of teaching to be intellectually suspect and morally offensive because it is tainted by the authoritarian idea that there are defensible standards and by the inegalitarian idea that some people do things better than others.[22]

In an effort by academians not to offend anyone, no one is learning anything. All that matters is the "thought process." Facts and right answers are secondary — or even considered unimportant.

Rush Limbaugh writes about the lunacy of this kind of thinking:

> Instead of D or F grades, there is an L grade - for "learning." An L grade tells the parent: "Your child isn't doing so hot, but go easy on him — he's trying." What responsible par-

> ent would tolerate this type of mediocrity?
> A school system that invokes such a relax-
> ation in standards is not truly interested in its
> students' learning, but in a paternalism that
> seems to permeate our culture. . . . With com-
> petitiveness being stigmatized, it's no wonder
> American students have lost their drive.[23]

Could this actually be the intended purpose of those who
control America's educational system — to create students
who have "lost their drive" and are mediocre in their accomplishments?

Putty in Their Hands

Every day there is a new attack on the constitutional rights
of Americans. To make matters worse, the actual document
itself is under assault.

In 1987, President Ronald Reagan introduced the National
Bicentennial Competition on the Constitution and the Bill of
Rights. As the nation's largest and most successful program of
its kind, this competition is devoted to teaching and encouraging in students a commitment to the fundamental principles
and values of our constitutional democracy.

More than 70,000 teachers and more than six million elementary, middle, and high school students have been involved
in this program.

On April 19, 1993, Senator Christopher Dodd of New
Jersey offered Senate bill S. 881, which was intended to
"amend the Elementary and Secondary Education Act of 1965
(H.R. 6) to re-authorize and make certain technical corrections
in the Civic Education Program, and for other purposes."[24]

What did Senator Dodd want to correct? He sought to
strike the words "about the Constitution and the Bill of
Rights" from President Reagan's program and insert "in civics
and government."

Such an amendment would change the entire purpose of
the National Bicentennial Competition. Instead of being
required to teach "about the Constitution and the Bill of

Rights" in order to receive the federal dollars allotted by this program, states and districts could receive federal dollars if they simply taught "civics and government."

The question I have is: What will the "civics and government" lessons be based upon? It is our U.S. Constitution and Bill of Rights that makes our civics and government unique. Without these two important documents, instructors could be teaching the civics and government of North Korea.

Eventually, the majority of Senator Dodd's bill was rolled into H.R. 6. Senator Dodd, however, was unable to accomplish the striking of "about the Constitution and Bill of Rights." He did manage to have his "in civics and government" added.

States and districts that were once required to teach specifically "about the Constitution and Bill of Rights" can now instead teach "in civics and government" and still receive the federal dollars allowed for by the National Bicentennial Competition on the Constitution and the Bill of Rights.

Why would a U.S. Senator want to offer a bill that would do anything less than encourage the aggressive teaching of the Constitution — the very document he has vowed to uphold and defend?

Sad to say, but there are elected officials who do not respect our U.S. Constitution and Bill of Rights. In fact, for many of these national "agents of change," the Constitution is a constant burr in their saddle. They long to silence the loud voices of modern American patriots who — when their rights are being trampled — proclaim, "That is unconstitutional!"

One way to silence the opposition is to avoid teaching the tenets of the U.S. Constitution to the next generation. If the next generation of Americans is ignorant of our Constitution, they will not demand that its principles be followed and enforced.

No wonder the educrats have joined forces with liberal politicians in Washington. They have a common agenda — to maintain power by keeping America's masses in intellectual slavery. They know that the uneducated, are more easily controlled. That is the reason for the "planned failure" of America's schools — to create an illiterate underclass and keep them uninformed by feeding them lies and dribble from

Washington and the mainstream media.

It is shocking to realize, but the education establishment, liberal politicians, and the mainstream media have joined forces to mold an illiterate and uninformed underclass that — they hope — will become putty in their hands.

The Globalist Agenda

Why would a group of "elitists" want to control the people of America? Could it be that they have a higher purpose in mind? One that reaches beyond the shores of "the land of the free and the home of the brave"?

To answer these questions, consider the reason for the promotion of the "new world order" by politicians, educators, and the media. Could it be that the U.S. Constitution and Bill of Rights stands in the way of their goal to turn America's youth into global citizens?

In the 1970s, the United Nations commissioned a study titled, "Development of Education Technology in Central and Eastern Europe" (Unesco Ed. 77/ws/133 original: English:). This report showed the results of Outcome-Based Education technology in Hungry, Czechoslovakia, Finland, Bulgaria, and Greece.

The OBE system was developed in Hungry with U.N. guidance and promoted by the United Nations as the system that every member nation must adopt to prepare all students everywhere to be proper global citizens. The report stressed the importance of a centralized national and international curriculum, national testing, teacher retraining and monitoring, comprehensive OBE, and the elimination of local control of curriculum.

The report also stated plainly that it is essential for teachers to acquire information constantly by using computer-aided teaching and a pedagogical data bank.

The United Nations has already developed an international education plan which includes an international curriculum, and the United States has bought into the U.N. plan. What is the name of America's implementation of the U.N. plan? Goals 2000.

Theodore Sizer, one of the guru's of Outcome-Based Education has said, "We want to move away from nationalism toward the concept of world family."

I am not the only American to express my concern over the assault on the U.S. Constitution and the attempt to teach the globalist agenda.

Over 40 years ago, on March 20, 1952 in the Congressional Record, U.S. Senator William Jenner expressed his concern over the attack on our Constitution and the attempt to mold our children into global citizens versus U.S. citizens.

Senator Jenner is recorded as saying,

> I want to make one thing clear. This war against our Constitution is not being fought way off in Madagascar or in Mandalay. It is being fought here — in our schools, our colleges, our churches, our women's clubs. It is being fought with our money, channeled through the State Department. It is being fought twenty-four hours a day — while we remain asleep.
>
> How many of you Senators know what the U.N. is doing to change the teaching of the children in your own hometown? The UN is at work there, every day and night, changing the teachers, changing the teaching materials, changing the very words and tones — changing all the essential ideas which we imagine our schools are teaching to our young folks.
>
> How in the name of heaven are we to sit here, approve these programs, appropriate our own peoples' money — for such outrageous "orientation" of our own children, and of the men and women who teach our children, in this nation's schools?

Senator Jenner knew that the United Nations, as far back as the 1950s, was very active in its globalist agenda.

Do not forget that our entire U.S. educational system is

today under the federal legislation called Goals 2000 —
America's version of a global education agenda established by
the World Conference on Education for All. This conference
was sponsored by the United Nations in Thailand, March 5-9,
1990.

The agents of change are very busy people who do not
appreciate or love the principles and foundations that made
this country great. Many of these individuals still loath the
contributions made to this country by one of its greatest
Presidents, Ronald Reagan. Why? Because President Reagan
stood for and believed in all that made America great —
including the Constitution and Bill of Rights.

Notes

1 "Mrs. Clinton's Czarist Past," *The Wallstreet Journal*, April, 1993.

2 Ibid.

3 Ibid.

4 Ibid.

5 Robert Holland, "School Restructuring by Hillary," *Richmond Times Dispatch,* June 16, 1993.

6 Ibid.

7 Ibid.

8 Congressional Record — Senate S, 623, February 2, 1994.

9 Ibid. S 623-624

10 Brannon S. Howse, *Cradle to College,* (Green Forest, AK: New Leaf Press, 1993), p.20.

11 Geoffrey Botkin, "Certain Failure Part I," 1994.

12 Charlotte Iserbyt, "Back to Basics Reform or...OBE Skinnerian International Curriculum?" p. 37.

13 Carol Pomeroy, "Education According to Corporate Fascism," title of a speech delivered on March 3, 1995 at Northwestern College for "Day Set Apart for Women 1995."

14 Ibid.

15 Ibid.

16 Robert Holland, "Test-Makers Seek to Impose Radically New Structure on Schools," *Richmond Times Dispatch*, June 2, 1993.

17 Brooks Alexander, "The Rise of Cosmic Humanism: What is Religion?" *SCP Journal* (Vol. 5, Winter 1981-82), p.4.

18 Dr. James Dobson and Gary Bauer, *Children at Risk* (Dallas, Tx: Word Publishing, 1990) p. 179.

19 Dr. Dennis Cuddy, *Chronology of Education with Quotable Quotes,* (Highland City, FL: Pro Family Forum, Inc. 1993), p. 9.

20 Ibid.

21 George F. Will, "School Reforms Adopted in 1960s Foster Student Regression in 1990s," *Greensburg Tribune Review,* July 2, 1995.

22 Ibid.

23 Rush Limbaugh, "When A Means Average: Our Schools Are Failing," *Family Circle*, May 16, 1995, p. 146.
24 Senate Bill, S. 881, first page.

5

Cheap and
Easily Controlled

As if Goals 2000, H.R. 6 were not bad enough, another legislative bill was signed into law May 4, 1994.

This latest effort to control America's students has the socialist-sounding name, the School-To-Work Opportunities Act — and it means exactly what is says. Unless you submit to their idea of "school," you won't work — or go to college or trade school or anything else.

Within the next few years, American students will no longer be receiving high school diplomas. Instead, they will be graduating with government certified and recognized diplomas called "certificates."

In Oregon, where the concept was first tried and implemented, students receive a "Certificate of Initial Mastery" followed by the "Certificate of Advanced Mastery."

These new certificates are supposed to indicate that the student has "mastered" the outcomes necessary for graduation. In the future, students who do not possess these certificates could find it hard to get a job, receive health care, get a drivers license, travel around the country, and even vote.

Bob Holland of the *Richmond Times Dispatch*, June 16, 1993, explains the danger of such a certificate:

With a Certificate of Initial Mastery in hand,
students then would choose among college-
prep, taking a job, or a technological certificate.
Meanwhile, the Labor Department would set
"voluntary" skill standards — almost surely
the precursor to sharptoothed mandates — for
entry to virtually all occupations.

Oregon's Education Act for the 21st Century, also known
as H.B. 3565 or the Katz Bill (after the lawmaker who sponsored the bill) went into effect on July 1, 1991.

Lamar Alexander, former U.S. Secretary of Education in
the Bush Administration and 1996 Presidential candidate said,
"Oregon has taken a pioneering step, and America will be
watching and waiting."

Hillary Rodham Clinton, who has been a member of the
National Standards Project and a board member of the Board
of the National Center on Education and the Economy, has
also praised the Oregon bill.

Education Week, May 15, 1991, quoted Hillary Rodham
Clinton as saying:

It is the most ambitious effort to take a look at
the employment and training recommenda-
tions of the report. . . . Every state that's working on this will develop a response based on
that state's needs and profile . . . but what happens in Oregon and New York and Washington
will influence the deliberations in other states.

In spite of Hillary's accolades, Oregon's Education Act for
the 21st Century has been a complete and total failure.

The social engineers believed that if the bill was successful
in Oregon it should be implemented nationally. It failed. As a
result, the social engineers proclaimed Oregon's Education Act
a success.

How can that be? Remember, to the agents of change, failure is success because education is planned failure, resulting
in intellectual slavery. Students who are not educated can be
easily controlled.

Succeeding to Fail

Oregon's Cottage Grove High School was the first school to give out the certificates in the spring of 1994.

Citizens for Academic Excellence, an organization committed to repealing the Oregon Act, has reported that Cottage Grove High School completed the first Oregon pilot program for the Certificate of Initial Mastery (CIM) with these devastating results:

> They experienced over a 20% drop-out rate. Approximately 219 students started as freshman, and only 175 remained two years later. Out of the 175 who remained only 74 passed, 101 kids failed. 49 of those 101 kids went on to an "alternative learning site" were they will remain until they have met all the 12 Outcome-Based Education standards required by the state.
>
> Students cannot receive their Certificates of Initial Mastery until they have met all 12 outcomes. The remaining 51 students stayed in the school to receive the Certificate of Initial Mastery. As of December 1994, those 101 students were still working for their Certificates of Initial Mastery, meaning, that those 101 students were still failing the state program.
>
> Students were held back for such flimsy reasons as not having enough "seat time," not doing acceptable community service and expressing discontent with the program. Individual students found their SAT scores took a severe drop.
>
> Cottage Grove student Amber Davis said her SAT's went from 93rd percentile as an eighth grader to 70th percentile at the end of her sophomore year.[1]

After 1997, Oregon students will not receive a traditional academic diploma. Instead, by age 16, at the end of their sophomore year, each student ideally will have met the 12 state outcomes and receive a Certificate of Initial Mastery. With the certificate in hand, the student will choose from one of six career directions and will ideally spend the next two years pursuing their Certificate of Advanced Mastery. Part of this training includes community service work and job shadowing.

If the student fails to meet the required 12 state outcomes, he cannot receive his Certificate of Initial Mastery and must repeat the year until the 12 outcomes are met. The teacher may choose to allow the student to go on but require the student to repeat the work while going through their 11th grade.

Once the 12 outcomes are met, then the student would receive his Certificate of Initial Mastery, which lists the 12 outcomes.

Jay Tennison, whose mother has assisted me in tracking Jay through Cottage Grove High School, provided me with a copy of her son's Certificate of Initial Mastery. This is a list of the 12 outcomes Jay had to reach before he could receive his certificate.

1. Involved citizen
2. Quality producer
3. Self-directed learner
4. Constructive thinker
5. Effective communicator
6. Collaborative contributor
7. Quantify
8. Apply math/science
9. Understand Diversity
10. Deliberate on public issues
11. Interpret human experience
12. Understand positive health habits

And how are these ambiguous "outcomes" to be graded?

The students in Oregon under this Oregon bill can only receive an A, B, or "IP" for "in progress." No failing grades are given.

Students who receive too many IP's or who fall into the states "at risk" group are moved into one of the states "alternative learning sites" where they will be aided in reaching the 12 state outcomes.

Students with behavior problems or who display a dislike for the program can be moved over to an "alternative learning site." Students will stay in the "alternative learning site" until their behavior or attitude improves or until they reach the 12 outcomes depending on why they were sent to the "alternative learning site."

A student could conceivably be 21 years old and still be in the "alternative learning site" trying to meet the 12 state outcomes in order to receive his Certificate of Initial Mastery.

The Certificate of Initial Mastery is really an Outcome-Based Education diploma.

Creating a "Managed" Work Force

I have good reason to believe that children will be encouraged to choose their career tracks based on their economic background and worldview. Those who fit into the agenda of the "elite" will be encouraged to become the doctors, attorneys, social workers, teachers, etc. Those who do not fit into the agenda of the "elite ruling class" will become part of a poorly educated but easily controlled work force.

Based upon the child's Outcome-Based Education portfolio, specially trained counselors will help students choose the most "acceptable" career.

Why do I believe this will happen? I have first-hand reports from parents whose children are being encouraged to go into fields that are of no interest to the student.

One mother in Rochester, Minnesota told me her daughter wanted to be an accountant yet the school counselor told her that she was not qualified. The counselor gave the student a list of careers for which he felt the girl was qualified and included the suggestion she become a hair dresser.

The students in Oregon may choose from six career tracks — but not one of these career tracks is college bound.

If Jay Tennison wants to attend the college of his choice,

his mother and father must pay for him to go to school during the summer or hire a private teacher to ensure that Jay receives the credits he needs.

A recently passed state law now requires colleges in Oregon to accept any students who possess the Certificates of Initial Mastery and Certificates of Advanced Mastery. As of yet, however, Jay Tennison and some of his classmates have not been able to find a college outside of Oregon that will accept students who possess the certificates.

Why is such a ridiculous program being tried in Oregon? And if the program has failed, why did the School-to-Work Opportunities Act, (a federal mandated version of the Oregon bill to be implemented nationally) become law on May 4, 1994?

Thomas Stict, president of Applied Behavioral and Cognitive Sciences, Inc. in San Diego, California and a member of the U.S. Department of Labor's SCANS (Secretary's Commission on Achieving Necessary Skills) answered that question when he testified before the 101st Congress:

> Many companies have moved operations to places with cheap relatively poorly educated labor. What may be crucial, they say, is the dependability of a labor force and how well it can be managed and trained — not its general educational level, although a small cadre of highly educated creative people is essential to innovation and growth.[2]

"Managed and trained" — I get it! The social engineers want a cheap work force they can easily control.

Who are the others — the "small cadre of highly educated creative people . . . essential to innovation and growth" that Thomas Stict refers to? The elite ruling class, of course.

Big Names — Huge Agenda

The Department of Education and the Department of Labor through Goals 2000, H.R. 6, and the School-to-Work

Opportunities Act is developing a work force to fit into the global, new world order "work force."

Where and when did such a concept get hatched?

In 1992 while Clinton was President-elect, a private board based out of Rochester, New York — known as the National Center on Education and the Economy — released a 23 page report titled, "A Human Resource Development Plan for the Unites States." This report, which you can no longer receive from the National Center by request, listed the goals they hoped to set in stone over the next four to eight years.

In the preface of the report, Marc Tucker, the president of the center wrote,

> The advent of the Clinton administration cre-
> ates a unique opportunity for the country to
> develop a truly national system for the devel-
> opment of its human resources, second to none
> on the globe. The National Center on
> Education and the Economy and its predeces-
> sor organization, the Carnegie Forum on
> Education and the Economy, have been elabo-
> rating a national agenda in this arena over the
> last eight years.

There it is in black and white — and in their own words.

A group of social engineers exists — and they have an agenda. In fact, they have been hard at work for years. We won't call it a conspiracy, but an aggressive agenda is being promoted by some of America's most liberal social engineers to change America and its institutions.

Ten years from now, when elected officials have come and gone, agents of change such as those who sit on the board of the National Center on Education and the Economy will remain.

Who are these social engineers on the board of the National Center?   Of the 27 board members, one stands out above the rest — Hillary Rodham Clinton.

Hillary has and will for many years to come play a big role in America's educational system. Ira Magaziner, the social engineer of national health care and Hillary's personal friend, also serves on the National Center board. Other board members include David Rockefeller Jr. and Vera Katz.

At the time this report was released, Vera Katz was the Speaker of the House of Representatives in Oregon. Presently, Vera is the Mayor of Portland. Now you know why Oregon became the test state for the rest of the nation.

Vera Katz introduced and sponsored the Oregon bill titled, the Oregon Educational Act of the 21st Century, which became the model for the national version, the School-to-Work Opportunities Act of 1994.

Before we look at the Oregon bill and its federal version, let me share with you a few more of the goals included in the report put out by the National Center on Education and the Economy.

Parents — Suppliers of Raw Material

The National Center sees a "great opportunity in front of the country." What is it? "To remold the entire American system for human resources development."

Who are the human resources? America's students.

Our children today are considered by the government as human resource — or as raw material. You, the taxpaying parent, are no longer the customer, even though you pay the bill for your child's education.

Under today's liberal educational agenda big business is the customer. The child is the product, and the parent is the supplier of the raw material.

Educational researcher Carol Pomeroy has said,

> The OBE model defines parents as merely the suppliers of human capital, or human resource material. It makes one wonder if the "customers" of this model will at sometime demand licensing of the suppliers to produce a "quality" raw material.

Parents today are "the suppliers" of the raw material. To

produce a "quality" product some lawmakers have actually discussed the idea of requiring adults to attend parenting classes in order to receive a marriage license.

The National Center report goes on to mention that "it needs to be a system driven by client needs." Who is the client? Big business.

In the preface of the National Center's report, Marc Tucker writes,

> What is essential is that we create a seamless
> web of opportunities to develop one's skills
> that literally extends from cradle to grave.

For whom will the system be developed? Whose skills do they want to develop?

According to Marc Tucker, everyone will fit into the "same system" — young and old, poor and rich, worker and full-time student.

What would you call such a "system"? Socialism?

Look out adults! This program is not only for your children but for you as well.

Look out employers! The federal government wants you to help pay for this new system through a 1 1/2 percent levy — which is really a tax.

National Standards for Every Student

Marc Tucker goes on to say that they will "take advantage of legislation on which Congress has already been working to advance the elementary and secondary reform agenda."

What legislation in Tucker referring to? America 2000, or course, which became known as Goals 2000 in the Clinton administration.

When he wrote about taking advantage of legislation, Tucker and his friends knew that the reauthorization of the Elementary and Secondary Act of 1994 was just around the corner.

The National Center report states that "the vision" includes "clear national standards of performance in general education." These national standards can also be called out-comes.

The report goes on to say that "students get a certificate when they meet this standard, allowing them to go on to their next stage of education."

Students who do not meet the set outcomes will not be permitted to continue their education.

This is happening right now in Oregon. Students who do not meet the states 11 outcomes in order to receive their Certificate of Initial Mastery can be held back until they meet the politically correct standards.

What else does the National Center's report envision?

> A national system of education in which cur-riculum, pedagogy, examinations and teacher education and licensure systems are all linked to the national standards.

Who will set these national standards? The Department of Education and particularly the Department of Labor and the SCANS board are already at work on developing "standards."

What is their goal? To create "a system that rewards stu-dents who meet the national standards with further education and good jobs."

Those students who do not meet the national standards or outcomes do not receive a Certificate of Initial Mastery and cannot receive further education or get a job.

Originally, the Oregon Educational Act of the 21 Century states in section 25:1, that "by July 1, 1996, it shall be unlawful for an employer to employ any person under 18 years of age who has not obtained a Certificate of Initial Mastery."

Due to public pressure, the wording was changed, but the framework still remains.

The National Center on Education and the Economy (NCEE) report states that "a student who meets the standard at 16 would be entitled to two free years of high school and one of college."

That sounds nice — until we realize the national centers report states that "this idea redefines college."

A Nation of Students

As President, George Bush, who introduced America 2000 — which became Clinton's Goals 2000 — said the goal is for America to become "a nation of students." Keep in mind that George Bush was at one time U.S. Envoy to China.

In 1977, Assistant Secretary of Education Mary Frances Berry of the Carter administration delivered a speech at the University of Illinois in which she outlined the newest forms of education reform. And where did she get these new reforms? From the four pillars of the Chinese model of lifelong learning and community education.

What is the purpose of the Chinese program? To keep people working for the benefit of the state for their entire lives.

The four pillars of the Chinese model laid out by Ms. Berry are:

1. Eliminate tests and grades.
2. Make truth a relative concept.
3. Make education serve the masses.
4. Combine education with labor — or in other words, combine education with industrial production.

A report issued by the National Center on Education and the Economy titled, "Education and Training for Employed and Unemployed Adults," reveals America is already on the way to implementing the Chinese model. After all, Hillary calls her plan a "cradle to grave" program.

This NCEE plan includes adults as well as children and states that this "is a system for everyone, just as all the parts of the system already described are for everyone."

If you are out of a job, you can receive training "through the federal programs for that purpose and by state unemployment insurance funds. The chronically unemployed are funded by federal and state funds established for that purpose."

How would such an extensive program be funded? For those who are not unemployed, the federal government will force the employer to pay for his employees' training. The NCEE report states:

> Employed people can access the system
> through requirements that their employers
> spend an amount equal to 1 and 1\2 percent of
> their salary and wage bill on training leading
> to national skill certification.

The goal is to have every working adult who is in the work force "nationally certified."

How do employers feel about paying for education? The NCEE already knows the answer, as their own report states:

> Everything we have heard indicates virtually
> universal opposition in the employer commu-
> nity to the proposal for a 1 and 1\2 percent
> levy on employers for training to support the
> costs associated with employed workers gain-
> ing these skills, whatever the levy is called. The
> President may choose to press forward with
> the proposal nevertheless.

In other words, "We don't care what employers think! We are going ahead with our liberal, socialist agenda, no matter what the opposition says!"

No need to worry, you think, this program will never get off the ground. It will not last from one administration to another. Right?

Wrong! Currently, three bills — Goals 2000, H.R. 6, and the School-to-Work Opportunities Act of 1994 — are already feder-al law. Everything is in place for the adult training program to be massively funded and continue for at least the next four years — unless we the people get these three bills repealed.

If we fail, American students will be trained like the Japanese — under a system that educates children according to the specifications of big business. The only remaining obsta-cle is convincing America's corporations that such a program would be profitable and lucrative.

Outsmarting Big Business

Under the heading, "An Agenda for the Federal Government," the report by the NCEE says that this is not being done, "as a pilot program, not as a few demonstrations to be swept aside in another administration, but everywhere, as the new way of doing business."

Don't forget, this report was written by Hillary and her friends in 1992 when Clinton was first President elect. They have succeeded in getting three major pieces of legislation passed. As a result, long after Clinton is out of office, Hillary and her friends will still be serving on their little boards and committees, cutting deals with lawmakers and trying to further their socialist, new-world order.

Implementing the plans these social engineers have for our nation will not be easy, but they are off to a good start. Unless their plans are presented to the American people in just the right way and at just the right time, their agenda will fail.

The members of the NCEE are well aware that how they "package" their programs is pivotal to their success. In fact, the NCEE report itself states,

> Creating such a system means sweeping aside countless programs, building new ones, changing deeply embedded institutional structures. . . . Trying to ram it down everyone's throat would engender overwhelming opposition. . . . This is not the usual scale experiment nor is it a demonstration program. . . . As soon as the first set of states is engaged, another set would be invited to participate.

In the past few years, I have studied so many reports and proposals put out by the Department of Education, the Department of Labor, the National Standards Project, the National Center on Education and the Economy, and other such groups that I could write one myself.

In fact, it would easy. Why? Because, although every proposal has a new name with new wording, they all have the

same goal as every previous program that has been proposed.
Why is that?

These fascist, social engineers will continue to throw out
educational program after program until big business finally
buys one hook line and sinker. They may even take one part of
one proposal and another part of another plan and merge
them — if that is what it takes to appease American business
and get them to buy into and use the government plans.

It doesn't matter what the plan is called or which one
American business finally chooses. All plans accomplish the
same goal — governmental control of private business.

The Labor Market System

The NCEE also calls for developing a "labor market system" that is "fully computerized." This labor market system
would follow every citizen from cradle to grave.

Part of the "systemic change in public education" that the
NCEE is calling for is to "deploy advanced technologies to
support the learning of students in and out of school."

Just what kind of technologies are they interested in
deploying for out of school use?

According to Department of Labor reports, the SCANS
Board wants to develop a system called WORKLINK, which
would asses students' personal qualities that could be shared
with businesses electronically.

The National Center on Education and the Economy, the
non-profit board that Hillary Rodham Clinton sits on along
with David Rockefeller Jr. and others, has laid out their plans
for a Labor Market Systems.

The Department of Labor, and the Department of
Education has willingly worked with the NCEE as well as the
National Standards Project. All of these groups have the same
goals as well as many of the same board members.

The Labor Market System, as laid out by the NCEE, would
be "fully computerized."

> All available front-line jobs — whether public
> or private — must be listed by law. . . . It is no

longer a system just for the poor and unskilled,
but for everyone.[3]

Under what authority will they make it a requirement by
law that employers list all available front-line jobs? And what
are front-line jobs?

I consider front-line jobs to be low-skilled, low-wage jobs.

The advanced technology that these organizations desire is
now funded through H.R. 6, which calls for the development
of "educational technology." We will discuss the kind of educational technology that H.R. 6 funds in the next chapter,
"Computers, the Information Givers."

In August 1992, the National Center on Education and the
Economy reported that "a group of 17 states and six school
districts, involving over half of the nation's students, are participating in development and pilot testing."[4]

In summer of 1989, the National Center's board of trustees,
(which includes Hillary Clinton), created the Commission on
the Skills of the American Work force to study the skill needs
of our nation's front-line work force.

In June 1990, the Commission released its report,
"America's Choice: High Skills or Low Wages!" The report rec-
ommends that American employers alter dramatically the way
they organize work and that our nation change the way it educates and trains workers.

Goals 2000, H.R. 6, and the School-to-Work Opportunities
Act of 1994 strives to have America's students meet "world
class standards" (Outcome-Based Education standards). All of
this is being rammed down the throats of the American people
by the Department of Labor and the Department of Education
to serve big business.

For example, the School-to-Work Opportunities Act established inside the Department of Labor a new bureau called the
Bureau of Apprenticeship and Training. This new bureau will
administer skill certificates that are "industry recognized."

When the federal government caters to big business, look
out! Such a system is called "corporate fascism."

Why is this so dangerous?

The American Heritage Dictionary defines corporate fascism as "a philosophy or system of government that advocates or exercises dictatorship through the merging of state and business leadership."

Now, do you get the picture?

Our Way or No Way!

The School-to-Work Opportunities Act states,

> Career awareness and career exploration and counseling [will begin] (at the earliest possible age, but not later than the 7th grade) in order to help students who may be interested to identify, and select or reconsider, their interest, goals, and career majors.[5]

The federal bill goes on to say that interested students will choose a "career major not later than the beginning of the 11th grade."

Why must the student select his career major no later than the beginning of 11th grade? Because at this time he must choose from the list of available Certificate of Advanced Mastery endorsement areas.

Remember Jay Tennison? Once he received his Certificate of Initial Mastery, he had to choose from one of six career tracks as offered by the state of Oregon.

The wording of the School-to-Work Opportunities Act sounds so free and unrestricted when it says that "interested students" will choose their career major no later than the beginning of the 11th grade. But what if a student is not interested in their "plan" or not interested in choosing a "career major" until he is ready — which may not be until after high school? Will that be acceptable? No!

The way the plan has been written, and once it is fully implemented accordingly, a student cannot receive a "certificate of advanced mastery" until he chooses a career major and completes the required two to three years of training required to receive the Certificate of Advanced Mastery. In short, a student either chooses his career major at the beginning of his

11th grade year or he does not graduate on time. If he never chooses a career major, he does not graduate at all.

The School-to-Work Opportunities Act states that students will be required to meet set "requirements necessary to prepare a student for post-secondary education and the requirements necessary for a student to earn a skill certificate."

Who sets these "requirements"? The SCANS board inside the Department of Labor and individuals within the Department of Education.

As we have seen from Jay Tennison's Certificate of Initial Mastery, the requirements being set have very little to do with cognitive, academic data and everything to do with ensuring students possess a politically correct, humanistic worldview. The system is being established so that if you do not possess the correct worldview, you will not be given certain advantages or opportunities.

CAREERS — A Dangerous Alternative

In the spring of 1994, Congress introduced a new bill, H.R. 1617, whose official name is the Consolidated and Reformed Education, Employment, and Rehabilitation Systems Act (CAREERS).

Sponsored by two Republicans, Bill Goodling of Pennsylvania and Buck McKeon of California, the CAREERS bill has the support of many conservatives because it does away with the School-to-Work Opportunities Act of 1994. CAREERS supposedly also eliminates several duplicate job and educational programs.

Those who have read the bill in its entirety — something few Congressmen have the time to do — realize that H.R. 1617 contains much of the same wording as the School-to-Work Act, plus several dangerous alternatives. What are they?

CAREERS creates a centralized plan and agenda in Washington for the kind of "human resource development" that Hillary, Mark Tucker, David Rockefeller, and Ira Magaziner have been lusting after for some time.

To make matters worse, Republican Congressmen Steve Gunderson of Wisconsin and Bill Goodling of Pennsylvania have proposed a bill called, "A proposal for the Establishment of the Department of Education and Employment." This bill would simply merge the Department of Education with the Department of Labor.

That should be enough to scare any conservative capitalist!

I don't understand how these Congressmen could even suggest such a proposal. Granted, the School to Work Opportunities Act of 1994 came to us under the Democratically-controlled House and Senate. But unless we wake up our elected officials in Washington, the federal government's stealth takeover of education will be aided and abetted by the Republicans.

I am not exaggerating when I say that H.R. 1617 comes right out of the tenth plank of the Communist Manifesto by Karl Marx, which calls for, "Free education for all children in public schools. . . Combination of education with industrial production."

How can other Republicans, including Republican Whip Tom Delay, House Republican Conference Chairman John Boehner of Ohio, and House Budget Committee Chairman John Kasich of Ohio, support this obvious attempt at corporate fascism? Have they forgotten the mandate from the American people in November 1994 for smaller government and the return of local control to the states? Why would Republicans want to beef up the Department of Education that already costs the taxpayers of America $33 billion each year?

The Big Picture

Reliable sources in Washington indicate that the problem is not that conservatives are knowingly caving into the liberal, socialist agenda. They probably think they are doing what is best for America.

However, even lawmakers who are more informed on educational issues than their colleagues find it difficult to sort out this kind of complicated legislation. In addition, many of them lack qualified staffers who understand all the ramifications of CAREERS. As a result, our elected officials have no idea where this kind of legislation would take America.

With that in mind, allow me to paint the big picture for all concerned to see:

• H.R. 1617 will further the concept of Outcome-Based Education diplomas called "certificates."

• H.R. 1617 allows for the continuation of the Bureau of Apprenticeship and Training, which is housed inside the Department of Labor. The bureau will continue to administer skill certificates that are industry recognized as called for in the School-to-Work Act.

• H.R. 1617, as does the School-to-Work Act, calls for "Career exploration and guidance counseling . . . in as early a grade as possible."

• H.R. 1617 allows for "workplace mentoring." Students in their final two years of school will be spending many hours each school week outside of the classroom in a "workplace mentoring" or "job shadowing program."

• H.R. 1617 discuss in great detail the development of "one-stop career centers." Often times these centers will be connected with and inside of the local school. The "one-stop career centers" will provide job training, counseling, re-mediation where necessary, and assist in helping individuals get entitlements which H.R. 1617 allows for.

• H.R. 1617 allows the Department of Labor to divide the United States up into ten "federal regions."

• H.R. 1617 requires states who want to receive federal dollars under this bill to establish a "local workforce development board in each local workforce development area within the state."

• H.R. 1617 requires states who want to receive funds under this bill to provide the Secretary of Education information on how the state will "coordinate the Goals 2000: Educate

America Act, and Improving America's Schools Act of 1994."
Remember the Improving America's Schools Act is also known
as H.R. 6.

• H.R. 1617 will allow for major funding to be used in our
schools to train America's students for specific jobs. The
acquiring of skills will be stressed at the expense of acquiring
knowledge. In other words, children will be "trained" instead
of educated.

• H.R. 1617 will have students picking their career majors
at the earliest possible age.

• H.R. 1617 will create a labor market information system
to guarantee that students in America's schools are being
trained according to the demands of the work force.

• H.R. 1617 will allow individuals to come to the one-stop
career center in their area to apply for entitlements. People
who have been fired or laid off will be given a check every
month to support them while they go through training or retraining at the career center.

Students Who Don't Fit the Mold

What is the labor market information system? A computer
database that will contain personal and private information on
each student that has been collected throughout the child's
school years. This information will follow the child the rest of
his life, especially into the work force, and be shared between
the private and public sectors.

How is this information obtained? From tests, essays, port-
folios, and assessments that are routinely performed on
American students. Sounds like an invasion of privacy to me.
Our legislators, however, seem to be looking the other way
when it comes to allowing schools to violate students' constitutional rights.

In some cases, these tests are actually mandated by the
United States Congress such as the National Assessment of

Educational Progress, (NAEP).

How will all this personal and private information be used? To weed out students who don't fit the mold or have the mindset of either an intellectual elitist or an easily-controlled laborer.

What about students who demonstrate, during their school career, the wrong worldview or exhibit individualism, patriotism, or the belief in national sovereignty? What if they have strong religious convictions and are not afraid to voice them? The answer is simple.

Outspoken, creative, God-fearing students can forget about graduating and receiving their government recognized diploma. If, by some chance, they are permitted to graduate, the students' beliefs, convictions, and worldview could dog them the rest of their lives, keeping them from getting a good job and moving up the corporate ladder.

The tracking of students is not a new concept. The Chinese government keeps a "dangan" on its citizens. The March 16, 1992 *New York Times International* revealed that a dangan is a "file opened on each urban citizen when he or she enters elementary school, and it shadows the person throughout life, moving on to high school, college, employer. . . the dangan contains political evaluations that affect career prospects and permission to leave the country. . . the file is kept by one's employer. The dangan affects promotions and job opportunities. . . any prospective employer is supposed to examine an applicant's dangan before making hiring decisions."

Look at what the cultural elite have imported from Red China, what will they think of next?

Fools or Conspirators?

Why do we need another bill — like H.R. 1617 — that allows for the continuation of Outcome-Based Education? We don't. But our legislators have been fooled by the skillful wording of CAREERS.

H.R. 1617 calls for a student's "career pathway plan" to include "vocational education," which includes "competency-based applied learning," "higher-order reasoning," "problem-solving skills," and "work attitudes." Sounds like a cover-up to me. Instead of including the more commonly used wording of "higher-order thinking," H.R. 1617 calls it "higher-order reasoning."

Remember, it was Benjamin Bloom, the father of Outcome-Based Education, who developed this concept of "higher-order thinking skills." Also keep in mind that Benjamin Bloom, as a highly decorated humanist, actively embraced the Communist Manifesto and its tenth plank of combining education with industry.

To make matters worse, the CAREERS bill, H.R. 1617, contains some of the exact wording found in the Human Resource Development Plan written by Hillary Clinton, Ira Magaziner, David Rockefeller, and others.

Portions of Section 3 of H.R. 1617, (a)(5) clearly spell out a socialist plan for creating a worker class in America managed by an elite ruling class. (The following italics are mine for emphasis.):

> (E) . . . encouraging lifelong learning and skills upgrading through a *seamless system* connecting elementary, secondary, postsecondary, rehabilitation, adult, and work-based training and education; and (F) to establish a comprehensive, integrated *labor market information system* to ensure that workforce preparation and development programs are related to the demand for particular skill requirements in local labor markets.

Hillary's Human Resource Development plan puts it this way: "What is essential is that we create a *seamless web* of opportunities to develop one's skills that literally extends from cradle to grave."

Educrats seem to like the word "seamless."

The Human Resource Development plan also calls for a "labor market system" that is "for everyone" and it is "fully computerized." In fact the plan calls for "all available front-line jobs — whether public or private — must be listed in it by law."

Could this be the same as a "labor market information system?" Duh!

How could Republican lawmakers support H.R. 1617 when it mandates the same programs as the Democrats' School-to-Work Act and H.R. 6?

I can only come up with two reasons: Either our Republican friends are ignorant of the CAREERS bill's content — or Steve Gunderson and Bill Goodling are working with Hillary and her cronies to accomplish their liberal, socialist agenda.

I hope their excuse is ignorance.

On September 19, 1995 a few days before this book went to press, H.R. 1617 was passed by the United States House of Representatives. Due to the overwhelming support H.R. 1617 received in the House it is on a fast track for passage in the Senate. Call your elected officals for additional information on this bill.

When "the Same" is Insane

Unfortunately, we don't have to wait for either plan to be implemented. Why not? The goals of those who signed the Humanist Manifesto are being accomplished even now.

What are those goals? Dr. D. James Kennedy explains:

> The means of production belong to the state. For supporters such as Paul Kurtz, B.F. Skinner, John Dewey, Francis Crick, Isaac Asimov, and the other signers of the manifesto, communism and state socialism were the only logical solutions to mankind's problems. In the first edition of that thin volume, they wrote, "A socialized and cooperative economic order must be established to the end that the equitable distribution of the means of life be possible. . . . Humanists demand a shared life in a shared world.[6]

How are today's socialists accomplishing their goal of a "shared world"? By working within America's democratically elected government and using its *unelected* bureaucratic officials

All the topics discussed in this book — Outcome-Based Education, the Certificates of Initial and Advanced Mastery, the U.N. Convention on the Rights of the Child, the financial condition of our nation, the robbing of religious freedoms, the constant attacks on the traditional family, private schools, and homes schools, and the establishment of federally controlled schools — share a common goal: the creation of a humanistic, socialistic, communistic nation where everything is shared and everyone is the same.

What is the humanist's idea of "the same"? An uneducated, unmotivated, non-controversial, compliant, humanistic worker and citizen who marches in lock step to government orders and plans.

Who benefits from this kind of controlled society? The cultural elite, of course. People like Bill and Hillary Clinton and other social engineers who think they know what is best for you and me. Make no mistake, they want to live and rule their lives, and yours, as they see fit — and at your expense.

Believe it or not, everything is now in place to accomplish just that in America — and it will adversely affect your faith, family, and freedoms — unless we reclaim this nation at risk.

Notes

[1] *Citizens for Academic Excellence Letter,* December 1994, (P.O. Box 1777 Corvallis, Oregon 97339).

[2] Charlotte Iserbyt, "The OBE Attack," *The New American,* August 8, 1994 p.32.

[3] "A Human Resource Development Plan for the United States," National Center on Education and the Economy, p. 9.

[4] "Program Overviews," National Center on Education and the Economy, August 1992.

[5] "The School to Work Opportunities Act of 1994," *Public Law* 103-239, May 4, 1994, 20, USC 6112 Sec. 102. School-based learning component.

[6] Dr. D. James Kennedy, *Character and Destiny,* (Grand Rapids, MI: Zondervan Publishing, 1994) p. 135.

6

Computers:
The Information Givers

Have you ever wondered why the educrats today are calling for computers in every classroom for every student? To give kids access to better education. Right? But who will determine the material and methods by which the student is "educated" using the computer?

What if the actual purpose is to use computers to reinforce and correct thoughts and attitudes on a proper and timely schedule?

Dustin Heuston of Utah's World Institute for Computer-Assisted Teaching has said:

> We've been absolutely staggered by realizing that the computer has the capability to act as if it were ten of the top psychologists working with one student. . . . You've seen the tip of the iceberg. Won't it be wonderful when the child in the smallest county in the most distant area or in the most confused urban setting can have the equivalent of the finest school in the world on that terminal and no one can get between that child and that curriculum? We have great moments coming in the history of education. [1]

"No one can get between the child and that curriculum."
The question arises, then, Who will determine the content of
the curriculum?

Charlotte Iserbyt, who served as a Special Assistant in the
Office of Educational Research and Improvement in the U.S.
Department of Education in the 1980s, has said that until
recently, "parents could examine their children's textbooks;
now, thanks to technology, nothing or nobody will be able to
get between the child and his computer. Except, of course, the
agents of change."

Computer Disc DJs

Along with radical changes in the school curriculum
brought on by Outcome-Based Education, the job of the
teacher is being transformed. In fact, some believe that the role
of the teacher is disappearing from America's classroom.

Under OBE, mandated by Goals 2000 and H.R. 6, the computer will be the new "teacher." Someone has noted, "Our
teachers will be reduced to computer disc DJs."[2]

The Minnesota Department of Education in a publication
titled, "Technology and Outcome-Based Education in
Minnesota," described this changing role of teachers:

> Machines are becoming the information givers
> of our society. Since professional information
> givers of the past may quickly be replaced by
> these machines, teachers need to define them-
> selves, and act as diagnosers, prescribers, cre-
> ative climate makers, instructional designers,
> coaches, and learning facilitators. . . . Teachers
> must stop functioning as information givers,
> putting learners in rows, trying to transmit
> information through worksheets and lectures.

This idea is not new. In fact, as early as 1968, the "education reform movement" was laying the groundwork for its
future policies at a U.S.A. Goals 2000 conference. Their own
reports reveal the agenda of the educational elite:

> The teachers will have disappeared, and his
> place will be taken by a facilitator of learning,
> focusing attention on the prime period of learn-
> ing . . . from infancy to age six or eight . . . He
> [the student] will never be graduated.

This is what the social engineers call "life-long learning."

When George Bush introduced America 2000, which later
came to be called Goals 2000, the President said we would
become "a nation of students." There is nothing wrong with
that as long as the student — or his parents — can determine
what he will learn.

Forcing Students Into Line

In the future, every child will be working on his own computer, with his own projects and assignments. Why? Because
every child will have different attitudes, values, feelings, and
emotions that need re-mediating. In other words, every student will have varying shades and types of political incorrect-
ness that must be changed.

According to the educational elite, every child is sick and
in need of help.

Dr. Pierce, professor of Education and Psychology at
Harvard University, has said,

> Every child who enters school at the age of five
> is mentally ill because he enters school with an
> allegiance toward our elected officials, our
> founding fathers, our institutions, the preserva-
> tion of this form of government that we have,
> patriotism, nationalism, sovereignty. All this
> proves that the children are sick, because a
> truly well individual is one who has rejected all
> of those things, and is what I would call the
> true international child of the future.[3]

Outcome-Based Education is designed to correct the mental sickness of every child. Of course the question that arises is:

What makes every five-year old in America sick? Could it be the five years of love and attention the child has received from his parents?

Yes, that is what the "experts" think makes the child sick.

Dr. Pierce said that the child comes to school with a set worldview, a worldview with which he disagrees. Where did that worldview come from? Who instilled into the five-year old this worldview that Dr. Pierce finds so sickening? The child's parents.

What Dr. Pierce really objects to the child's parental authority, parental influence, traditional values, the traditional American family, and the Christian worldview.

Research journalist Geoffrey Botkin notes that it is at this point that the computer comes into play:

> In coming stages of OBE, the government can determine how to re-mediate, or fix, the way the child thinks with custom software for every child . . . [the software] can create custom individualized computer drills that can force every student into line.[4]

Does this seem unlikely to you or maybe even extreme? I wish that were the case. However, the facts prove this is exactly what the educrats in Washington have in mind.

Collecting Data About Your Child

The Washington Star, April 15, 1970, printed in an article titled, "Set up Data Banks, Allen Urges Schools" by John Matthews. In this article, U.S. Commissioner of Education James Allen is quoted as encouraging local school systems to have a central diagnostic center and explains its purpose:

> . . . to find out everything possible about the child and his background. . . . (The Center) would know just about everything there is to know about the child — his home and family background, his cultural and language defi-

ciencies, his health and nutrition needs and his
general potential as an individual.

Allen then implied that professionals would write a "prescription" for the child "and if necessary, for his home and
family as well."[5] How would they determine which children
need a professional "prescription"? According to Allen's Plan,
each child would "be evaluated before 6 years of age, then
again at 11 and 15."[6]

Research journalist Geoffrey Botkin, in a television documentary on America's educational system, discovered that in
1978, the Institute of Electrical and Electronic Engineers
warned about the unlawful political abuse of electronics technology.

The warning was not heeded, and in 1994 they published a
summary of the abuses, which included:

1. The collecting of psychological, medical, sociological
data on students and their families without their knowledge or
consent via the NAEP, the National Assessment of Educational
Progress.

2. The "going on line" of the education supercomputer, the
Elementary and Secondary Integrated Data System in 1989.
This system linked the U.S. Department of Education with all
50 state education departments.

3. Promoting the above under the rubric of "educational
restructuring" under names like Outcome-Based Education
while withholding from the public the nature and extent of the
data collection.

America's social engineers will stop at nothing to achieve
their goal of reprogramming our youth — even if it means
"withholding from the public" their secret methods of collecting data about our children — and us!

Programming Humans

Certainly computers are a tremendous asset to our society
and to education, but such technology has the potential to

perpetuate and facilitate the "Big Brother" thinking of bureaucrats who see education and schools as a means of controlling
society.

B.F. Skinner, an atheist, humanist psychologist who taught
at Harvard University, was one of the first to promote the use
of a machine for remediation. Its purpose was to aid in developing programmed learning or corrective thought control. As
a behavioral psychologist, B.F. Skinner believed that man is
controlled by stimuli from the environment and, therefore, can
never make a decision in which he exercises free will.

B.F. Skinner believed "the hypothesis that man is not free
is essential to the application of scientific method to the study
of human behavior."[7]

Skinner went on to write, "We must expect to discover that
what a man does is the result of specifiable conditions and that
once these conditions have been discovered, we can anticipate
and to some extent determine his actions."[8]

In other words, once an individual discovers the right
stimuli, or the right conditions, he can control anyone.
According to Skinner, there will be those who are controlled
and those who are the controllees.

In his book, *Beyond Freedom and Dignity*, Skinner wrote that
man "plays two roles: one as a controller, as the designer of a
controlling culture, and another as the controlled, as the products of a culture."[9]

B. F. Skinner and Karl Marx had the same mindset that
dominates today's social engineers. They believe that a perfect
world or utopia can be created by establishing the right conditions through proper conditioning, programmed learning, corrective thought control, coercive thought control, brainwashing, and manipulation.

Dr. Skinner was so skilled at behavioral programming that
he trained pigeons during World War II to pilot and detonate
bombs and torpedoes. In the book, *B.F. Skinner, The Man and
His Ideas*, by Richard Evans, Skinner is quoted as saying, "I
could make a pigeon a high achiever by reinforcing it on a
proper schedule."

Skinner believed, by using the teaching machines he developed to reinforce desired behavior in animals, he could program humans.

Alienating Children From Parents

Professor Kenneth Goodman, former president of the International Reading Association, wrote a letter to President Jimmy Carter denouncing programs that were based on the philosophies of B.F. Skinner and were being funded by the U.S. Department of Education. In his letter, Professor Goodman did an excellent job explaining exactly what B.F. Skinner's programmed learning was all about.

Professor Goodman wrote:

> In behavior management, outcomes are assumed or arbitrarily determined and the behavior of human learners is shaped, conditioned, reinforced, extinguished, rewarded or punished until the learners achieve the target behavior.[10]

Under Mastery Learning and Outcome-Based Education, teachers are expected to track, record, and correct the improper attitudes, values, feelings and emotions of students. That is an impossible task — unless the teacher has help. Today computers and specialized software can track and correct students who exhibit the politically incorrect responses — without the aid of a teacher.

Dean Corrigan, in a 1969 speech before the 22nd Annual Teachers Education Conference held at the University of Georgia, predicted that Skinner's "teaching machines will pace a student's progress, diagnose his weaknesses and make certain that he understands a fundamental concept before allowing him to advance to the next lesson."

Why do the agents of change want to track the beliefs of our children? For one reason: to aid them in their diabolical quest to inculcate into our children *their* beliefs and values. First, however, they must make sure that this inculcation is not hindered by the beliefs of the child's parents.

When children exhibit the wrong attitudes and beliefs, which were instilled into them by parents, then remediation, corrective thought control, and re-programming will be the order of business. The computer is the fastest and most effective manner by which to track a student's moral and character development. The computer is also the fastest, most accurate and consistent way to correct wrong developmental behavior.

Using Eskimos to Mold Beliefs

In 1963, under contract with the U.S. Office of Education of Health Education and Welfare, the National Education Association oversaw the Technological Development Project, which published a supplement stating:

> Another area of potential development in computer applications is the attitude changing machine. Dr. Bertram Raven in the Psychology Department at the University of California in Los Angeles is in the process of building a computer-based device for changing attitude. This device will work on the principle that students' attitudes can be changed effectively by using the Socratic method of asking an appropriate series of leading questions logically designed to right the balance between appropriate attitudes and those deemed less acceptable.[11]

In the 1970s, a controversial Social Studies program called, *Man: A Course of Study* was introduced into America's schools. This course can still be found in schools today.

What was the purpose of this program ? "To help children by exploring in depth the lifestyle of an obscure Eskimo tribe."[12]

Who designed the course and how was it supposed to help children?

> The course was designed by a team of experimental psychologists under Jerome S. Burner and B.F. Skinner to mold children's social attitudes and beliefs along lines that set them apart and alienate them from beliefs and moral values of their parents and local community.[13]

That assessment was made by Congressman John Conlan of Arizona on April 9, 1975 on the House floor.

John Conlan hit the nail on the head. Skinner's programmed learning focuses on setting children apart and "alienating them from the beliefs and moral values of their parents" — particularly if those parents are instilling into their children traditional values.

The Secret Test

Are computers being used to track more than students' test scores? Some people think so.

Many involved parents fear that personal and private information — which many tests and assignments draw out of their children — will be filed on a data base developed by their state or the U.S. Department of Education.

During the 1993-1994 school year, more than 7,000 schools in California had to give up the old academic achievement test and pass out a new one called the CLAS Test, (the California Learning Assessment System test). The test was so secret that the California Department of Education officials were threatening to sue those who leaked its content. Some California legislators were considering Senate Bill 1273, that would have made it a felony for a student or parent to disclose the content of the test.

The *Press-Enterprise* in Beaumont, California reported that, "Sherry Loofbourrow, a member of the Newport-Mesa Unified School District board in Orange County, has said she believes some of the questions violated state law."

A parent from Menifee, California by the name of Debra Hills said, "Look at the eighth-grade test; it is so invasive."

The *Press-Enterprise* in Riverside, California reported on April 14, 1994, that critics of the test object to it because they believe that the test, 'violates students' rights by asking about religious and family beliefs."

Gary Kreep, director of the U.S. Justice Foundation, which sued one school district in California over the CLAS test said, "Questions ask for specific experiences from students' own lives, not general experiences drawn just from the reading selections."

Susan Kettner of Beaumont, California wrote in a letter to
the editor of the *Press-Enterprise*, which was published in the
paper on April 23, 1994, that her superintendent had not even
seen the CLAS test. "John Wood is not comfortable with the
test as it is. He should not be put in a position to administer a
mandated test he is not even allowed to see."

Susan Kettner also wrote in her letter to the editor about a
school board meeting she attended. "The meeting, I found,
was very frustrating. The State Department of Education representatives from the County of Riverside, who have never
seen the test, refused to answer our questions. I left the meeting wondering, 'Who has seen this test?'"

It was reported in the *Press-Enterprise*, April 16, 1994, that
Don Lauder, a school board member in Beaumont, California,
"defended the state's refusal to let parents examine the CLAS
test because doing so would compromise it."

Concerning many of the test questions, which numerous
parents felt invaded their families privacy, the *Press-Enterprise*,
reported,

> The purpose of such questions, Lauder said, is
> to measure the students' ability to use higher-
> thinking skills. . . . "The state is trying to go
> beyond having students memorize lists of facts.
> They want students to organize facts and eval-
> uate them and produce something called
> 'authentic achievement,'" Lauder said. "That
> means students are able to adapt or use the
> basic knowledge they've learned."[14]

As a school board member, Lauder, either out of ignorance
or honesty, knowingly or unknowingly, spilled the beans when
he said the purpose of the test is to see if students have or are
"able to adapt."

Adapt to what? Change?

That is exactly the purpose of these types of tests. With
their intrusive questions, such tests are used to determine in
what areas a student needs remediation. After a battery of
drills and assignments, the student is tested once again. The

test will disclose whether or not the student has adapted to the change as requested, without protest.

In certain states such as Oregon, students who do not demonstrate that they have adapted to the desired and requested change, thus possessing the correct worldview, are not permitted to go on in their education or receive a diploma.

The $55 Million "Desired" Response

The April 16, 1994 *Press-Enterprise* issue went on to report:

> Lauder acknowledged that some of the questions could constitute invasion of privacy, but students are not graded on the "rightness or wrongness" of their answers, but on how well they state their case.

The reason students are not, as school board member Lauder said, "graded on the rightness or wrongness" of their answers is because the questions are open ended. Even the math portion of the CLAS test called for easy answers. To the casual observer there is no real right or wrong answer. As with most such tests, however, there is a "desired" answer or response.

I have read the CLAS test for all three grades, and it has absolutely nothing to do with cognitive, academic knowledge. The test is nothing less than an evaluation of the child's attitudes, values, feelings, and emotions.

Governor Pete Wilson has, for the time, repelled the law that required that every fourth, eighth, and tenth grader take the CLAS test.

The question remains, however, what was done with the information we know was collected on thousands of children?

Many newspapers in California, including the *Los Angeles Times*, reported that only about 25 percent of the fourth, eighth, and tenth graders who took the state mandated CLAS test actually had their test graded.

If the state was grading only 25 percent of the tests, what was the purpose of having students take the test?

Once the fact that only 25 percent or less of the tests were being graded, parents became even more suspicious. Because the state did not grade all the tests or have any such intentions, many believe this proves the state was never really interested in gaining statistically data on the condition of education in California but to gain personal data on their children and families.

Many parents still have a lot of unanswered questions. What was the real goal and purpose of the CLAS test? Why would the state of California plan on spending $55 million a year to administer the CLAS test only to correct 25 percent of the test?

The CLAS test in California was an attempt by the cultural elite and educrats to implement a part of their "school reform" agenda. Thanks to passionate, involved, courageous, and committed parents and citizens, the attempt was foiled.

The battle is not won,. however. In fact, it is just beginning. I have first-hand reports from one involved mother, whose husband is also a police officer, that the CLAS test, which was supposedly done away with, is back. Apparently, teachers are giving the test in small segments during regular class time so as not to arouse student or parental suspicions.

The CLAS test is just one example of how the "agents of change" hope to assimilate personal information about students for their computer database, which will later be used to channel them into the "right" career track after they have received their certificates.

The IRS: Getting to Know You

Students, however, are not the only Americans the government has targeted for data collection.

In January 1995, it was reported that the Internal Revenue Service has plans of expanding the secret computer database of information that it keeps on virtually all Americans. Developed in the 1970s, this database will be expanded to include "credit reports, news stories, tips from informants, and real estate, motor vehicle and child support records, as well as conventional government financial data."[15]

According to an IRS notice filed in December 1994, "any individual who has business and/or financial activities" can expect upgraded agency computers to put such information before IRS auditors promptly.

What if the information they collect is wrong?

"Although agency officials concede that some of the data collected will be inaccurate, taxpayers will not be allowed to review or correct it."[16]

Phyllis DePiazza, chief of the agency's Privacy and Education Branch has said, "Only when undergoing audits — which the system is designed to target and assist — will taxpayers be able to rebut the system's inaccuracies."[17] Ms. DePiazza acknowledged that even then taxpayers will not be permitted to see actual raw data about them that the IRS has collected.

Coleta Brueck, the agency's top document processing official has said:

> If I know what you've made during the year . . . if I know what your withholding is, if I know what your spending pattern is, I should be able to generate for you a return so that I only come to you and tell you, "This is what I think you should file for the next year, and if you agree to that, then don't bother sending me a piece of paper."

Does that mean the IRS is collecting enough data on you so that they could file your income tax return without your help?

Evan Hendricks, editor and publisher of *Privacy Times*, a bi-weekly Washington newsletter, has said the IRS wants to "wipe out the line between the private sector and government."

After America's radio talk show hosts got hold of this information and reported it to the American people, the IRS issued a statement saying it was going to reconsider plans to collect personal data.

Only time will tell.

Gary Bauer, former Under Secretary of Education and policy adviser in the Reagan Administration and now President of the Family Research Council, reported in his daily update, February 16, 1995:

> The IRS has quietly implemented a new program called Compliance 2000. Under the program, any information that is linked to your Social Security number will be accessible to federal tax agents. That includes, believe it or not, orders from catalogs, whether your family has cable T.V., what videos you rent, what magazines you read, etc. All of this information will be warehoused by the IRS on computers that its agents can use for investigations. What's more, the IRS is exempt from most privacy act requirements. This needs attention from the Congress right away.

For more information on the IRS, read chapter eight, "Your Family and Freedoms At Stake."

Risking Your Privacy On-Line

If you use your personal computer to log onto a computer on-line service such as Prodigy, Compuserve or American Online, you may risk being monitored without knowing it.

In a speech given June of 1995, Rich Frank, president of the Academy of Television Arts and Sciences told a group of TV and radio executives,

> You will have instant access to an enormous database, which will provide you with a consumer's age, number of children, color of hair, height, weight, credit card number, Social Security number and favorite soft drink. . . . As marketing executives, this is an incredibly exciting prospect. You will know intimate details about millions of consumers. At least

it's exciting until you realize that you're also
one of those consumers, and your intimate
details will also be accessible to others.[18]

How will marketers get this information without talking to
you? An Article by Robert S. Boyd, published in the *St. Paul
Pioneer Press*, explains how the system works:

> Every time you click the mouse, hit the "enter"
> key on your PC or press a button on your inter-
> active-television remote, the signal can be cap-
> tured by a computer, stored and analyzed. . . .
> Electronic marketers call it the "click-stream,"
> and they're using it more and more. It gives
> merchants and advertisers a new way to gather
> personal information about potential customers
> who use the Internet, the World Wide Web or
> commercial on-line services such as Prodigy
> and Compuserve. . . . Combined with informa-
> tion from other sources, the click-stream can
> reveal who you are, where you live, what inter-
> ests you, what you are willing to pay for and
> sometimes much more.

The selling of this information is becoming a big business
in itself. You can bet if marketers have this information, the
government will have access to it, too.

The next time you are browsing the Internet and are
offered a free catalog or you pick a category for a free sample of sports, books, cars, music entertainment, or whatever
else, remember it may cost you dearly. It may cost you your
privacy.

I Smell a Rat!

The potential for misuse of computer collection of personal
consumer and student information abounds.

Suppose our government puts a vaccination tracking system in place — as we discussed earlier. Not only are they

tracking vaccinations, but under OBE they are tracking attitudes, values, feelings, and emotions. Add the IRS into that component, and I smell a rat!

I would like to think that these tracking systems were established by our current government for moral and practical reasons. Their motives are probably sincere and, hopefully, in the best interests of children and adult citizens. Under a moral and honest government, we have nothing to fear from the gathering and compiling of information about us.

What happens, however, if our leaders are not moral and not honest? What if those in control of these tracking systems decide that certain individuals and groups of people hold "politically incorrect" values and beliefs and need to be "retrained"? Could such a vaccination and attitude-tracking system be used to persecute or eliminate those who do not accept the government's way of thinking?

Consider what happened in Waco, Texas to the Branch Davidian cult.

What about pro-life groups who have peacefully and prayerfully protested against abortion in America? Many pro-life Americans have been repeatedly jailed — some for long periods — because they dared to confront the establishment with the murder of innocent children.

Injustices occur everyday in America against God-fearing, freedom-loving people. You won't always read about such incidents in your newspaper or see them reported on the network news.

Conservative and Christian media — television, radio, newsletters, etc. — however, abound with reports of persecution of Christian students, IRS intimidation of churches and pastors, and aggressive attempts to silence anyone who confronts and exposes the liberals with their socialistic agenda. Just ask me and others who consistently broadcast the truth.

Computer tracking systems, in and of themselves are not evil. But I for one will not sit idly by and passively let government thugs develop a centralized bureaucracy that could some day be used against me and my family.

How about you?

Notes

1 Dustin Heuston, "Discussion-Developing the Potential of An Amazing Tool," *Schooling and Technology,* Vol 3. Southeastern Regional Council for Educational Improvement.

2 Carol Pomeroy, "Education According to Corporate Fascism," (unpublished speech delivered March 3, 1994, at Northwestern College).

3 From a keynote address to the Association for Childhood Education International, Denver, Colorado, April 1972, quoted by John Steinbacher and Dr. Dennis Cuddy.

4 "Certain Failure", a documentary on H.R. 6 by Geoffrey Botkin.

5 Dr. Dennis Cuddy, *Chronology of Education with Quotable Quotes,* (Highland City, FL: Pro Family Forum, Inc., 1993), p. 47.

6 Ibid.

7 B.F. Skinner, *Science and Human Behavior* (New York: Macmillan, 1953), p. 447.

8 Ibid, p. 6.

9 B.F. Skinner, *Beyond Freedom and Dignity,* (New York: Macmillan, 1953), p. 197.

10 Kenneth Goodman, "The President's Education Program: A Response," *Support for Learning and Teaching of English Newsletter,* March 1978, Vol. 3 No. 2.

11 March/April: A special supplement of *AV Communication Review* is published as "Monograph No. 2 of the Technological Development Project of the NEA." The project is under contract #SAE-9073 with the U.S. Office of Education of HEW, as authorized under title VII, Part B, of the National Defense Education Act of 1958. The contractor is the NEA. I was made aware of this fact by Dr. Dennis Cuddy.

12 Charlotte T. Iserbyt, "Back to Basics Reform or...OBE Skinnerian International Curriculum?" 1995, p. 6.

13 *Congressional Record,* April 9, 1975, p. H. 2585

14 *The Press Enterprise,* April 16, 1994, p. B-7.

15 "IRS Plans to Collect More Data on Individuals to Nab Tax Cheats," *St. Paul Pioneer Press,* January 20, 1995.

16 Ibid.

17 Ibid.

18 Robert S. Boyd, "Click. Be Monitored. Click. Fight Government Agents," *St. Paul Pioneer Press,* June 13, 1995.

7

When Child "Rights" Become Parental "Wrongs"

Ronald Reagan said: "Today, more than ever, it is essential that . . . each of us remember that the strength of our family is vital to the strength of our nation."[1]

No one knows this better than the agents of change. In fact, they have made it their goal to diminish the role parents play in their children's lives. Why? Because they want to control the way our children think, feel, and behave.

The U.N. Convention on the Rights of the Child

As a board member of the Children's Defense Fund, Hillary Clinton actively supports the United Nations Convention on the Rights of the Child. While the idea of "children's rights" may sound nice, this is just one more effort by the liberal agents of change to demean and negate traditional family values.

In November 1973, *The Harvard Educational Review* published Hillary Rodham's radical views of children's rights in an article entitled, "Children Under the Law." In her article, Ms. Clinton states that some children "may have interest independent of their parents or the state."[2]

Ms. Clinton disapproves of "the belief that families are private, non-political units whose interests subsume those of children."[3] In other words, she prefers to view the child as distinct from the family.

With that in mind, it is no wonder Hillary suggests that government age restrictions on children's activities must be legally justified:

> The state should no longer be allowed to
> assume the rationality of regulations based
> upon age, and should at least be required to
> justify its action on the basis of modern legisla-
> tive or administrative findings.[4]

What does that mean?

Dr. Dennis Cuddy, national syndicated columnist and former U.S. Department of Education official, explains that Ms. Clinton is really saying, "If individuals can vote at eighteen years of age, drive at sixteen, and have sex and abortions at a particular age, then the state should have to justify why they're not allowed to do those things at earlier ages."[5]

In the October 1992 issue of *Harper's* magazine, Christopher Lasch wrote an article titled, "Hillary Clinton, Child Saver: What She Values Will Not Help the Family."

Lasch defines Ms. Clinton's opinion in this way:

> The traditional family is, for the most part, an
> institution in need of therapy, an institution
> that stands in the way of children's rights — an
> obstacle to enlightened adults. . . . She con-
> demns the State's assumption of parental
> responsibilities, not because she has any faith
> in parents themselves but because she is
> opposed to the principle of parental authority
> in any form. . . Her writings leave the unmis-
> takable impression that it is the family that
> holds children back; it is the state that sets
> them free.

Why all this emphasis on the "state"? Could it be that

Hillary plans to use the federal government to set children free from parental authority? Why would she want to do that?

What is the purpose for the United Nations Convention on the Rights of the Child and who came up with this idea anyway? The text for the Convention was provided by Poland in 1979 as their contribution to the Year of the Child. Let us not forget that in 1979, Poland was controlled by a Marxist-Leninist, socialistic government.

Does that give you an idea of why this treaty is so dangerous — and why Hillary is no friend of the family?

The All-Powerful Social Worker

What are some of the legal "rights" that would be guaranteed by the U.N. Convention on the Rights of the Child? Consider this sweeping statement proposed by the treaty:

> The right of every child to a standard of living adequate for the child's physical, mental, spiritual, moral, and social development.

Who will determine the adequacy of these kinds of intangible factors? On what basis will judges and social workers determine what is "adequate"?

An Alabama social worker testified under oath that even if she received *anonymous* complaints against the Governor himself, she would need to inspect his home, no matter what evidence was offered to rebut the allegations.[6]

What if your sixteen-year-old son demands his own car upon receiving his drivers license and you won't provide him with a car? Your child could claim that he is not living in an environment that is adequate for his physical, mental, or social development.

What if your family only has one car, and your son is unable to go out with his friends on a Friday night because you are using the car? Will you have hindered his "social development"? Not to mention that you may have also deprived him of his "right to freedom of association and peaceful assembly," according to Article 15 of the U.N.

Convention on the Child.

Does this analogy sound far-fetched? Not if you are aware of what is taking place in courts across America today.

Recently, the Supreme Court of Washington state ruled that it was not a violation of parents' rights to remove a child from her family because she objected to — what was termed — their "reasonable rules which were reasonably enforced." The parents had grounded their eighth-grade daughter because she wanted to smoke marijuana and sleep with her boyfriend. She objected, and the court removed her from the home.[7]

Unexplored "Frontiers"

Article 13 of the Convention lists the right of every child (individual under 18), to be:

> The right of freedom of expression; this right
> shall include freedom to seek, receive and
> impart information and ideas of all kinds,
> regardless of frontiers, either orally, in writing
> or in print, in the form of art, or through any
> other media of the child's choice.

This article would give the child the right to view pornography whether in print or through the computer, which is accessible today over the Internet. Who knows what other unexplored "frontiers" our socialist friends have in mind for our children.

According to the U.N. Convention, every child has the right of "access to information and material from a diversity of national and international sources," and the state must "encourage the mass media to disseminate information and material of social and cultural benefit to the child" as well as "encourage the production and dissemination of children's books" (Art. 17).

Who will decide the content of these "children's books" to be produced and disseminated by the state? Can we trust the same government who funds blasphemous and homo-erotic art through the National Endowment for the Arts to decide what is of "social and cultural benefit"?

What about parents who don't want their children reading books the state has deemed as "information"?

The battle lines are drawn. It is only a matter of time before there is all-out war — unless, of course, no parents show up to fight.

When Rights Become Wrongs

Other "rights" provided for under the U.N. Convention on the Rights of the Child are:

• the right of "freedom of thought, conscience, and religion" (Art. 14);
• the right of the child to "education" (Art. 28);
• the "right . . . to benefit from child-care services" (Art. 18);
• the "right of the disabled child to special care" (Art. 23).

I have no problem with the right of every child to receive an education, or for the disabled to receive necessary care. Potential problems arise, however, from the vague wording of many of these rights.

Hillary Clinton believes that some families can go "to the point of depriving [children] of an advanced worldly education."[8] Most of the Christians I know are doing everything they can to keep their kids from having a "worldly" education!

The question then becomes: How do Hillary and other "agents of change" define education?

If you home school your child or send him to a private school that does not fit the government definition of an "education," will you then be guilty of depriving your child of an education?

Could it happen in America? It already has.

The Ohio Supreme Court took children out of the custody of a "fit and good mother with normal, delightful children" solely because she had chosen to conduct a legal home-school program.[9]

What about Article 23 that provides for the rights of the
disabled child? Who will define and determine which children
are disabled. After all, every time we turn around, liberal educators are handing out a new disability.

What if your child is determined to have dyslexia or to
have A.D.D. (attention deficit disorder) — or any other myriad
of so-called disorders? What if you don't want your child put
on Ridalin or some other mind-altering drug to control his
hyperactivity?

Suppose you refuse to allow your child to take part in special classes, programs, or courses — many of which are filled
with psycho-babble, new age thinking, and humanistic
garbage. Will you then be depriving your "disabled" child
from special services?

Consider this real-life example.

A school guidance counselor who examined a first grader
diagnosed the child as hyperactive and recommended psy-
chotherapy. The mother dutifully took the little girl to four sessions but stopped after concluding that her daughter's problems were due to the classroom environment at school and not
the result of any personal or emotional causes. It was also
apparent that the therapy was not helping her daughter.

When the mother refused to take the daughter back to
therapy, social workers removed the child from the home. The
court, claiming the right to intervene whenever "medical intervention will have a beneficial effect," ruled the mother guilty
of child neglect.[10]

The Family Substitute

We cannot deny that there are children in this country and
around the world who do not receive the kind of love and nur-
turing that every child craves and needs. Sure, there are parents who do not take the responsibility of parenting seriously
and some who should have their children removed from their
custody because of physical and sexual abuse.

Nonetheless, this does not mean that the problem in our
nation is so great that *every* parent should have the right and
the responsibility of parenting taken from them. Why strip the

constitutional freedoms of the majority in order to serve an irresponsible minority? There is no cause nor justification for such action.

Will all child abuse and neglect cease just because the U.S. has ratified this invasive U.N. treaty?

Has the government ever been qualified to replace or substitute for the family? The United Nations Convention on the Rights of the Child is not the answer to the needs of children.

The answer is found in local communities where civic, community, and church groups work together to meet the needs of those who are less fortunate. Signing a treaty such as this one will not begin to solve the problems.

The intent of the U.N. Convention on the Child is not to help under-privileged children, but to undermine parental authority and to break down the very foundation of our society — the family. Day after day, America's liberal court system proves that this is their agenda.

When Maryland required every elementary school to provide comprehensive sex education for all students, parents went to federal court demanding an "opt-out" provision. The judge dismissed all their claims outright.[11]

Are you getting the picture? Your rights as a parent are in serious jeopardy.

Taking Parents Out of the Picture

Article 37 of the U.N. Convention of the Rights of the Child provides every child "deprived of his or her liberty" with the right of free legal counsel and access to the courts to let his case be heard.

Will your child be encouraged by his or her public school teacher, guidance counselor, school nurse, school physiologist, or friends to sue you the next time you deprive him of his liberty?

Under the right of freedom of religion, you could be sued by your child for forcing him to go to church with you.

Under the right of freedom of expression, you could be sued by your child if you refuse to let him pierce his nose with an ear-ring or deny him the "right" to wear a t-shirt with profanity written on it.

Dr. Lucier, a former congressional staffer, in a report for the Family Research Council, explains how these "rights" of the child could be used against parents:

> The child is guaranteed these rights, no matter what the parents' religion, political, or other opinion. If the parents, on the basis of their religion or political views, or even ethical views, object to the so-called "rights" guaranteed in the Constitution, the state must step in and uphold those rights "irrespective" of the parents' opinion. The state, or an agency acting on behalf of the child, can sue in court against the parents so that the child can think what it pleases, and associate with whomever it pleases. . . .
>
> If parents refuse to grant these rights, even on the basis of conscientiously held religious or other opinions, the child may be removed from the parents "when competent authorities subject to judicial review determine, in accordance with applicable law and procedures, that such separation is necessary for the best interests of the child."

Common sense tells us that any treaty developed from the then-communist regime of Poland cannot be good for America, Americans, or U.S. Constitutional freedoms.

Why do the liberal, socialistic, agents of change want such a treaty? What is there goal?

The answer is clear: To undermine parental authority and to take all power, control, and influence away from moms and dads.

Author and syndicated columnist, Thomas Sowell, provides this warning:

> Parents are the greatest obstacle to any brainwashing of children . . . if parents cannot be

gotten out of the picture or at least moved to the periphery, the whole brainwashing operation is jeopardized.[12]

Such brainwashing is not new. In the 1940s, Nazi Germany tried to do away with parental influence. In her book, *The Story of the Trapp Family Singers,* Maria Trapp recalls her childhood experience with the Nazis:

> This morning we were told [by the Nazis] at the [school] assembly that our parents are nice, old-fashioned people who don't understand the new Party. We should leave them alone and not bother. We are the hope of the nation, the hope of the world. We should never mention at home what we learn at school now.[13]

Think about it. Do you really know what is going on in your child's classroom? If you ask him, will he tell you? If you visit the school and request permission to sit in on one of your child's classes, will you be allowed? I suggest you try, and then write and tell me what kind of response you received.

Just a Phone Call Away

The United Nations Convention on the Rights of the Child gives children the right to do almost anything. Why do I say *almost* anything? Because there is one very important right that this treaty does not grant every child.

It does not give a child the right to say, "I was wrong."

When, in a moment of anger and rebellion, a child picks up the phone and files a complaint against his parents for supposedly violating one of his liberties, this treaty does not give the child the right to say later, "I was wrong." The treaty does not allow the child to change his mind and have the complaint withdrawn.

Your child is sure to receive at school or through radio or television the proper number to call when he feels his liberties have been violated.

How many parents will find themselves embroiled in a court case or being subjected to the regular visits of a social worker simply because their child got angry and made a call, which the child later regrets but cannot reverse?

Who will provide the official interpretation of this treaty? A group of parents? No. Interpretation will be up to the U.N. Committee on Children.

In Great Britain and some European countries, the committee has already determined that it is in the best interests of the child to outlaw corporal punishment and conduct public educational campaigns to cause society to accept the prohibition of corporal punishment. That means it is illegal for parents to spank their children.

The Associated Press reported in August 1995 that a Norwegian father who smacked his four-year-old daughter on the bottom was fined $470 for violating Norway's strict child protection law. The law bars corporal punishment — even in the privacy of a family's home.

But the U.N. has not stopped there. The committee wants to limit the rights of parents to withdraw their children from sex education classes and change laws to increase the ability of children to participate in their parents' decisions concerning them.[14]

The socialist, liberal agenda, with their one-worldviewpoint, seeks to take away America's pride, prestige, and prosperity. They know the best way to do that is to remove any influence that traditional family values may have on children. When all else fails, they must resort to removing children from homes that are not politically and socially correct.

In order to do that, they need laws on the books that will give social workers, teachers, judges, and psychologists the authority to determine whether you are a fit parent and if your child's constitutional "rights" are being denied.

The Law of the Land

What is the present status of the U.N. Convention on the Rights of the Child? It was "approved by the U.N. General Assembly on November 20, 1989, and entered into force on

September 2, 1990, after the 20th nation ratified."[15]

What about the United States? So far, the liberals and social engineers of our country have done a fine job of sugar coating and packaging this bitter pill that they hope Americans will swallow.

During the first years of the Clinton administration, over 47 U.S. Senators in the 103rd Congress co-sponsored this U.S proposal in the Senate and called for the President to sign the treaty and send it up to the Senate to be ratified.

These co-sponsors of Senate Resolution 70, the United Nations Convention on the Rights of the Child, included:

Alaska (HI), Biden(DE), Bingaman (NM), Boren (OK), Boxer (CA), Bradley (NJ), Bumpers (AR), Campbell (CO), Chafee (RI), Daschel SD), DeConcini (AZ), Dodd (CT), Dorgan (ND), Durenberger (MN), Feingold (CA), Feinstein (CA), Ford (KY), Glen (OH), Graham (FL), Harkin (IA), Hatfield (OR), Inouye (HI), Jeffords (VT), Kennedy (MA), Kerrey (NE), Kohl (WI), Lautenberg (NJ), Leahy (VT), Levin (MI), Lieberman (CT), Lugar (IN), Matthews (TN), McCain (AZ), Metzenbaum (OH), Mikulski (MD), Mitchell (ME), Moseley-Braun (IL), Murray (WA), Packwood (OR), Reid (NV), Riegle (MI), Rockefeller (WV), Sarbanes (MD), Simon (IL), Spector (PA), Wellstone (MN), Wofford (PA).

If the United Nations Convention on the Rights of the Child is ever ratified by a two-thirds majority vote by the U.S. Senate, it would become the law of the land — as the U.S. Constitution Article 6, paragraph 2 states:

> This Constitution and the laws of the United
> States which shall be made in 'Pursuance there-
> of; and all treaties made, or which shall be
> made, under the authority of the United States,
> shall be the supreme law of the land; and the
> judges in every state shall be bound thereby,
> any Thing in the Constitution or Laws of any
> State to the contrary notwithstanding.

If this treaty is passed, parents will find themselves on the wrong side of the "law of the land."

Fortunately, some Senators have had the courage to stand up to Hillary Clinton and the political pressure put on them to cave in on this issue of parents' rights. One of the most vocal critics of the U.N. Convention on the Rights of the Child has been Senator Jesse Helms of North Carolina.

Safeguarding the Family

At the time of this book's publication, Senator Helms is still the Chairman of the Senate Foreign Relations Committee, which must approve the U.N.'s proposal before it can be sent to the Senate floor. Since Senator Helms refuses to allow the treaty to move through his committee, it has become a dead issue.

Recently, however, several legislative experts have indicated that the treaty could possibly be pulled from the Senate Foreign Relations Committee by a high-ranking Democrat and given to another committee where it would have a better chance of moving through and making it to the Senate floor.

In an effort to bolster support for opposing the U.N. Convention on the Rights of the Child, Senator Jesse Helms offered Senate Resolution 133 on June 14, 1995. A resolution is different from a bill in that it is non-binding. By having a vote on Resolution 133, voters would have a record of how many Senators are for the U.N. treaty and how many are opposed.

The first paragraph of Mr. Helms' resolution states:

> Expressing the sense of the Senate that the primary safeguard for the well-being and protection of children is the family, and that, because the United Nations Convention on the Rights of the Child could undermine the rights of the family, the President should not sign and transmit it to the Senate.

As of the publication date of this book, the resolution has yet to go to the Senate floor. You can call Senator Helms' office for an update on this crucial issue. In order for the treaty to be ratified by the U.S. Senate, it needs the approval of 67

Senators. Currently, there are not enough senators in favor of the treaty to pass it.

Even though the votes are currently lacking for the treaty to pass that does not mean we can relax. Senators will often cut deals with each other, voting for bills they oppose in return for their colleagues' votes in passing pet bills of their own. Should the treaty ever get out of a committee, it would go to the Senate floor.

We must continue to stay on top of this important issue. Keep writing your two U.S. Senators expressing your dislike for the U.N. Convention on the Rights of the Child. If they know how strongly the voters feel, they might be less likely to swap your parental authority in a back-room bargaining session.

The Parental Rights Act of 1995

To counteract the U.N. Convention on the Rights of the Child, Democratic U. S. Congressman Mike Parker of Mississippi and Representative Steve Largent of Oklahoma introduced, in June 1995, a federal bill to reassert and protect parental authority. Senator Charles Grassley of Iowa sponsored the bill in the Senate.

The Parental Rights and Responsibilities Act of 1995 lists the following Congressional findings.

1. The Supreme Court of the United States has properly recognized that the right of parents to direct the upbringing of their children is a fundamental right implicit in the concept of ordered liberty within the Ninth and Fourteenth Amendments.

2. The role of parents in the raising and rearing of their children is of inestimable value and deserving of both praise and protection by all levels of government.

3. Governments should not interfere in the decisions and actions of parents without compelling justification.

The purpose of the Parental Rights Act is:

1. To protect the right of parents to direct the upbringing of

their children as a fundamental right.

2. To protect children from abuse and neglect as those terms have been traditionally defined and applied in the common law of this nation.

3. While protecting the rights of parents, to acknowledge that those rights carry with them responsibility; specifically parents have the responsibility to see to it that their children are educated, for the purpose of literacy and self-sufficiency, as defined by the Supreme Court in *Wisconsin V. Yoder*, 406 U.S. (1972). [See Chapter 12 for a list of Landmark Court Cases pertaining to parental rights.]

The Act would uphold the parents' right to provide discipline for one's children, including reasonable corporal discipline, and the right to direct or provide the religious training of one's children.

It is a sad commentary on our nation when we need a Parental Rights Act to provide protection from the very state that is supposed to protect us. That, however, is exactly what parents and children need in order to guard against the intrusion of government nannies who are trying to steal our children.

To check on the current status of the Parental Rights Act, you may call Congressman Mike Parker's office at (202) 225-5865. When calling, remember to thank Mr. Parker for his leadership in this area.

Deadly Vaccines

In 1993, Ted Kennedy proposed legislation known as the Comprehensive Child Immunization Act to "help the government ensure that all two-year-olds get immunized by the year 2000."[16]

Doug Phillips of the National Center for Home Education, which is a division of the Home School Legal Defense Fund, has said, it is "a violation of parental rights for the state to assume the role of deciding what is in the best interest of the health of the child."[17]

Most parents have their children immunized against

potential diseases. However, as Christy Hamrick of the Family
Research Council noted,

> There's a big difference between a tried and
> true vaccine . . . and another vaccine that has
> resulted in the deaths of some children. We
> have always left that decision up to parents.[18]

The *World Magazine* reported in October 1993 that "in a 24
month period ending in July 1992, 2,525 serious injuries were
reported to the federal government following vaccinations,
and 360 persons died."

Some parents object to certain vaccines, but under such
federal legislation as the Comprehensive Child Immunization
Act, parents who do not have their child immunized could be
found guilty of child abuse.

The *Wallstreet Journal* reported in 1993 that one father who
failed to have his daughter Christine vaccinated for measles
was convicted of breaking state child neglect laws.

> Because of his conviction, the Court had the
> right to place Christine under social service
> agency supervision, or even take her away
> from her father and put her in a foster home. In
> this case the judge did neither of those things,
> since the measles epidemic was long over.[19]

The judge did not require Christine's father to get her vaccinated against measles.

Gary Bauer of the Family Research Council was quoted in
the *Washington Times* as saying "that the next parent accused of
child abuse for refusal to immunize, 'may not be so lucky.'"[20]

One vaccination that many parents object to is the hepatitis
B vaccine that is given to all twelve-hour-old infants. This vaccine was originally developed for people in high-risk jobs or
who engage in high-risk activity such as doctors, nurses, other
health care workers, drug users, and prostitutes.

Doug Phillips of the National Center for Home Education
has said that for the state and government to run around push-

ing the hepatitis B vaccine is proof that they are operating
under the pre-tense "that all kids are going to grow up with
the possibility of being a homosexual, prostitute, or intra-
venous drug user."[21]

A National Tracking System?

Senator Kennedy's Comprehensive Child Immunization
Act may sound like a positive endeavor, but apparently the
Senator has something more in mind — the registration and
tracking of America's children through a government database
of medical and personal information.

Christy Hamrick of the Family Research Council puts it
this way: "Today we're going to all track the measles vaccine,
but tomorrow maybe we're going to track the measles vaccine
and the religion of children."[22]

Add Outcome-Based Education into the mix, which is all
about teaching and then testing children's attitudes, values,
feelings and emotions, and Senator Kennedy's intentions
become suspect.

Did you realize that the attempt is being made by our government to establish some sort of national data base to track
just about "everything there is to know" about your child? You
weren't aware that such a system was in the works? Why not?
Because the social engineers attempt to hide such tracking systems behind what appears to be beneficial programs.

U.S. Commissioner of Education James Allen discussed in
the *Washington Star* the purpose for setting up a central diagnostic center:

> To find out everything possible about the child
> and his background. . . . [The Center] would
> know just about everything there is to know
> about the child — his home and family back-
> ground, his cultural and language deficiencies,
> his health and nutrition needs and his general
> potential as an individual.[23]

Remember, these are Mr. Allen's own words.

Because public schools already require proof that your child has been vaccinated before he can go to school, a vaccination tracking system would be seen by most Americans as not only helpful but nothing less than normal. Once there is some sort of tracking program established, regardless of its initial proposed purpose, the program can be tailored by those in charge for the purpose of good or evil.

Senator Kennedy's Comprehensive Immunization Act is just one more attempt by the social engineers of our nation to gain more and more control over the American family through requirements and mandates, thus minimizing the parents' role as the primary teacher, protector, provider, and care-giver.

It is at this point that the child's "rights" become parental "wrongs."

Notes

1 Brannon Howse, *Cradle To College*. (Green Forest AR: New Leaf Press, 1993), p.13.

2 Dr. Dennis Cuddy, *President Clinton Will Continue the New World Order*. (Oklahoma City, OK: The Southwest Radio Church, 1993) p. 26.

3 Ibid.

4 Ibid.

5 Ibid.

6 Transcript from trial court in *H.R. V. Alabama Dept. of Human Resources*. 609 So. 2d 477 (Ct. Civ. App Ala. 1992).

7 *In re Sumey*, 94 Wash. 2d 757, 621 P.2d 108 (1980).

8 Cuddy, p. 26.

9 *Gardini v. Moyer*, 575 N.E. 2d 423 (Ohio 1991).

10 *Matter v. Ray*, 408 N.Y.S. 2d 737 (1978).

11 *Cornwell v. State Board of Education*, 314 F. Supp. 340 (D. Md. 1969), aff'd. 428 F. 2d 471 (4th Cir. 1970), cert. den. 400 U.S. 942 (1970).

12 Thomas Sowell, from one of his syndicated columns.

13 Cuddy, p. 44.

14 "Concluding Observations of the Committee on the Rights of the Child," United Kingdom, CRC/15/add. 34 (Jan. 1995).

15 Dr. James P. Lucier, *Family Policy*, "Unconventional Rights," Family Research Council.

16 Mark Horne, "Big Mother is Watching You," *World Magazine*, October 2, 1993 p. 10.

17 Ibid.

18 Ibid.

19 Ibid.

20 Ibid.

21 Ibid.

22 Ibid.

23 Dr. Dennis Cuddy, *Chronology of Education with Quotable Quotes*, (Highland City, FL: Pro Family Forum, Inc. 1993), p. 47.

8

Your Family and Freedoms at Stake

On April 26, 1995, *USA Today* and CNN, working with the Gallop organization, released an interesting poll.

A nationwide sample of adults were asked, "Is the federal government so large and powerful that it poses an immediate threat to the rights and freedoms of ordinary citizens?"

Forty percent of those polled said, "Yes."

A month later, the May 16, 1995 *USA Today* reported that 39 percent of Americans believe that government has grown so big it represents an "immediate threat" to basic freedoms. Remove the word "immediate," and 52 percent of Americans believe the government represents a threat to basic freedoms.

After you read this chapter, you will understand why so many Americans feel that their freedoms are in jeopardy.

Serfs or Slaves?

Many Americans are finding it increasingly hard to make ends meet. Most earn more than enough money to survive, but they are simply not permitted to keep it. Between state, federal, city, and county taxes, Americans work until May 6 before they get to keep what they earn. In some states, it takes even longer:

New York extends to May 24, some 144 days
into the year. Connecticut pays until May 22,
followed not far behind by Minnesota, New
Jersey, and California.[1]

When we total up all the taxes we pay, such as FICA tax
(Social Security and Medicare); regular IRS Income tax; property tax, local sales tax, state sales tax, capitol gains tax, small
business tax, license tax, telephone tax, hotel and airline tax,
gasoline tax, car taxes, and on and on, the average American
pays 40-50 percent of his income in taxes.

When we read accounts of the Saxon lords taxing the serfs
30 percent of their income, history refers to them as slaves.
What does that make us? Government hostages?

The problem, however goes beyond money. American people are in a battle for their freedom.

Why do we pay so many and so much money in taxes?
The answer becomes clear when you realize that, as of July
1995, there were an estimated 85,006 governments in America.
How is this number obtained? From adding together the federal government along with all the state, city, and county governments.

The high tax rate in our nation has had a devastating
impact on our culture, quality of life, productivity, and expan-
sion. It is difficult for a businessman to expand his business
and hire more employees when he is hardly making a profit
due to the incredible tax burden placed on him.

The self-employed American gets hit twice as hard as the
employed American when it comes to FICA (Social Security,
Medicare) tax. Employed Americans have 7.65 percent of their
income taken out of their pay check, and the employer pays an
equal amount to total 15.3 percent. The self-employed
American has to pay the entire tax himself, meaning he pays
almost double in FICA tax as the employed American.

Without a doubt, the current tax system discourages individuals from pursuing the American dream of owning your
own business and being your own boss.

An ideal solution would be to allow all Americans to opt
themselves out of Social Security and invest in their own
retirement accounts.

I know that the chances of my ever seeing a dime of the thousands of dollars I have paid in FICA tax is very slim. As far as I'm concerned, the federal government is involved in extortion. Why? Because not only will that money not be there when I retire, but it's not there now.

The Social Security Administration takes my money each year and uses it to pay current retired American citizens. In addition, the Treasury Department takes billions each year from the Social Security Administration and uses our money to keep the government running.

If your employer took money from your company's retirement account to use as he sees fit, he would be charged with extortion. Yet our government gets by with it every year. Why? Because you and I, Mr. and Mrs. America, have let them.

It is high time we pull together and take back our government, money and lives.

Taxing Families

How does our nation's heavy tax burden affect today's average American family? There are many ways, but I will discuss only three.

1. Mom is forced into the workplace.

Because the government takes so much from dad's paycheck, mom is forced into the work force in order for the family to keep the bills paid. Many American mothers work because they want to, but I also know that numerous mothers would love to stay at home and raise their children.

I could cite many studies that show the difference between children whose mothers stayed at home and raised them versus those children raised in a daycare center. Common sense, not an expensive study, tells you children are much better off if raised at home by mom versus being dropped off at a center to be cared for by strangers.

Countless mothers' hearts are breaking because they have no choice but to work outside of the home — all to pay the incredible tax burden placed on their families. On the other hand, some couples have chosen for mom to work when, in fact, mom could stay at home if they were willing to make a few sacrifices.

Nevertheless, we as a people must tell our elected officials that it is time they quit talking the talk and start walking the walk. Flowery speeches on the how important the American family is to the survival of our nation is nice at election time, but I am much more interested in results versus a lot of hot air.

It is way past time for implementing a reasonable flat tax or national sales tax.

2. Our government encourages couples to live together instead of getting married.

One of the fastest ways to increase your tax burden is get married. Couples who live together and even have children without being married are financially rewarded by our government.

Couples who choose to enter into holy matrimony, however, are severely penalized by the IRS. Two income couples have to pay more in taxes, making the penalty for getting married incredible. When the salary of both husband and wife are combined, most couples fall into a higher tax bracket.

Being married and filing separately, however, does not solve the problem either. Our government punishes those who choose to get married, thereby encouraging couples to live together versus making a life-long commitment as a family.

3. The large tax burden on today's average American family makes it difficult for them to afford private education for their children.

Over the past few years, our nation has seen a large increase in the enrollment of students in private schools. This increase in attendance at private schools is due to the poor state of America's public schools.

In Milwaukee's public schools, only 48 percent of students graduate, while inner city private schools report an average 88 percent graduation rate. According to columnist George Will, "in 11 public high schools, the average grade is 1.5 on a scale of 4.0, and the failure rate in core academic subjects range from 26 percent to 43 percent."[2]

Unfortunately, few parents — especially those living in the inner cities — can afford to send their children to private schools, leaving these kids trapped in gun-invested, academically deprived institutions where little learning is taking place.

C.S. Lewis in the preface of his book, *The Screwtape Letters*, predicts that the government's increasing tax burden on families will be part of a plan to keep them from being able to afford the tuition at a local private school. C.S. Lewis wrote,

> Penal taxes, designed for that purpose, are liquidating the Middle Class, the class who were prepared to save and spend and make sacrifices in order to have their children privately educated.

The last thing the social engineers want is educated young American men and women. Why? Such educated young people are a threat to their elitist agenda because of their knowledge and commitment to truth, history, leadership, and individuality — not to mention their commitment to faith, family, and freedoms.

I myself am a product of my parents and a private education. There are countless numbers of authors, radio hosts, columnists, teachers, pastors, attorneys, doctors, accountants, and mothers and fathers who are products of a quality private school education. Many of these private schools also offer religious training. Therefore, graduates of private Christian schools graduate possessing the Christian worldview.

This Christian worldview is a threat and in direct contrast to the secular humanist worldview of the social engineers and agents of change. Therefore, I believe the social engineers will do their best, through the tax burden, to make it increasingly difficult for the average American to have their child educated in a private religious school.

Between the tax burden and intrusive legislation, private schools that want to maintain independence from state and federal control are facing some of their most challenging days.

Guilty Until Proven Innocent

The Fourth Amendment of the Bill of Rights grants every American citizen, "the right of the people to be secure in their persons, houses, papers, and effects, against unreasonable searches and seizures, shall not be violated, and no warrants shall issue, but upon probable cause, supported by Oath of affirmation, and particularly describing the place to be searched, and the persons or things to be seized."

The Fifth Amendment says, ". . . nor shall any person be . . . deprived of life, liberty, or property, without due process of law."

Not only is the tax load on Americans too great, the agency currently responsible for collecting those taxes burdens every Americans with paperwork, rules, regulations, audits, and the fear of the IRS' wrath. Most of the conduct the IRS engages in, is in complete and total violation of the Constitution and Bill of Rights.

Martin Gross, a *New York Times* bestselling author of many books, including *The Tax Racket,* has written:

> When they conduct an audit, they search your papers without a warrant, claiming that it is "voluntary" on the taxpayer's part.
>
> When they place penalties on your taxes due, they do it without a court order.
>
> When they levy your bank account and take out your money without your permission, they are making a seizure without a legal judgment against you.
>
> When they seize your home because they say you owe money, they are depriving you of property without due process of the law.
> You've lost your constitutional right to defend yourself in court.
>
> When you contest the IRS in Tax Court, you are guilty until you can prove yourself innocent, the opposite of our whole system of jurisprudence.[3]

Sound unbelievable? The following story from *The Tax Racket* proves how unjust and illegal IRS practices are:

> A house painter in Texas quickly learned that the other side holds all the cards in an audit. It seems the computer had spewed out a conflict, and the painter was called in to explain it. His Form 1040 showed he had received some $14,000 from a general contractor for painting a house. But the contractor's Form 1099 showed that he had paid the painter $35,000.
>
> The contractor could only document the $14,000 payment, claiming he paid the painter most of the $35,000 in cash. The painter denied it, swearing that the $14,000 was all he had received. Who was telling the truth?
>
> As is IRS custom, the local office decided the painter was guilty until he could prove himself innocent. He had to show that he didn't get the cash. Not only was that impossible, but it was a backward version of our usual justice system. Having failed to prove he didn't do something, the painter was billed $17,000 by the IRS, including penalties and interest.
>
> An immigrant from Mexico with five children, he was frustrated. How could he oppose the powerful IRS? He'd have to sell his pickup truck and his small house to satisfy the debt.
>
> Luckily, he had previously painted the house of a local tax attorney, who listened, then took the case without a fee. When the attorney read the IRS file, he was outraged. The IRS admitted that they didn't believe the contractor's story that he had paid the painter in cash. But since the IRS had the painter in their collection clutches, they pressed their case.
>
> The attorney filed suit in the U.S. Tax Court where, topsy-turvy, the painter was

guilty unless he could prove himself innocent.
The IRS won the case, and the painter had to
pay up.

The distraught painter borrowed $17,000
from his relatives and paid off the IRS.
Meanwhile, his attorney was furious at the
injustice. He personally borrowed $75,000 to
continue the case in the U.S. Court of Appeals.
This time, the verdict was different. The higher
court overturned the Tax Court, stating that the
IRS had acted in a "clearly arbitrary and erro-
neous" manner.[4]

If the painter had not been fortunate enough to know the
tax attorney, who in turn was compassionate and angry
enough to donate his time and use his own money to fight this
injustice, the outcome would have been much different.

This could just as easily happen to you or me. Such injustice, however, is expressly prohibited by the Constitution and
Bill of Rights.

Stopping the Tax Racket

Don't wait until you or your friends or family are dealt
such injustice, join the battle being waged by Martin Gross
and United States Congressman Bill Archer of Texas to abolish
the IRS.

Martin Gross in his book, *The Tax Racket*, sheds light on
why some kind of tax reform is so important. Gross reveals
that Americans now face 200 kinds of levies. The federal government alone imposes excise taxes on 66 different items,
many of which we don't even notice.

For example, we pay $3.50 per month to the Federal
Communications Commission for each phone in use. The Feds
also add 10 percent to every airline ticket and 15 percent of
gasoline prices account for taxes.

United States Democratic Congressman James Traficant of
Ohio had a run-in with the IRS himself and won. He is now
committed to undoing injustice.

In a letter to his colleagues to gain support for a bill he introduced, H.R. 390, Congressman Traficant wrote,

> The IRS is an agency out of control . . . All too
> often the IRS terrorize and threatens taxpayers.
> Too many lives have been ruined unjustly, and
> it is time to rein in the IRS and insure that it
> respects the rights of every taxpayer.[5]

The bill that Congressman Traficant introduced on January 4, 1995 said, "A bill to amend the Internal Revenue Code of 1986 to provide that the burden of proof shall be on the Secretary of the Treasury in all tax cases, and for other purposes."

H.R. 390 now has 305 co-sponsors and is expected to be added to a Taxpayers Bill of Rights now being worked on by the House Ways and Means Committee.

Americans need to put pressure on our elected officials to end the injustice. If we don't, the IRS will continue to take advantage of taxpayers, as this incident indicates:

> In San Francisco, a retired postal worker
> sent his $1,300 mortgage payment to his bank.
> By mistake it was delivered to the IRS office in
> Fresno.
>
> Did they return the check which was made
> out to the bank?
>
> No. The IRS merely altered the name of
> payee and deposited it, claiming he owed $300
> in back taxes. They had never sent him a defi-
> ciency notice, and gave him no warning the
> check would be altered — which is illegal — or
> that his money would be seized.[6]

The next mistake could be yours.

Write your United States Congressman and your two United States Senators telling them that you want them to sup-port any bill put up by Congressman Archer of Texas dealing with the abolishment of the IRS. Also tell them you are in favor of ending all federal income tax and support the idea of a national sales tax.

In April 1995, Newt Gingrich and Bob Dole appointed Jack Kemp to head a new commission on economic growth and tax policy. The commission may study such issues as a flat tax and replacing the income tax with a national consumption tax.

Getting Out While the Getting's Good

Larry Burkett, the author of the book, *The Coming Economic Earthquake*, also authored, *Whatever Happened to the American Dream?* In this book, he shares a sad but all-to-common and true story that symbolizes the battle faced by many hard-working and honest Americans — a battle that gets harder with almost every bill passed by Congress.

> He owned a company in the western United States and a sizable portion of his business was providing parts for catalytic converters on automobiles. A part of the manufacturing process involved the use of potent acid catalyst, which was recaptured, cleaned, and reused.
>
> Three years earlier he was required by the Environmental Protection Agency (EPA) to install some very expensive equipment to monitor the plant's environment to ensure that no workers were exposed to the caustic fumes. He did this willingly, believing it was in the best interest of his employees.
>
> Recently he received a bill from the EPA for his "share" of an environmental cleanup. It seems the company he bought the monitoring equipment from also used toxic chemicals in their testing facility. The facility failed to meet EPA standards and was required to decontaminate their entire complex, which meant chipping out several hundred yards of concrete and storing it in sealed containers for the next 150

years or so. Rather than absorb these costs, the company, a subsidiary of a foreign firm, declared bankruptcy and closed its doors.

The EPA then sent a portion of the cleanup estimate to all the companies that had ever done business with the firm, including this businessman. The thing about it that bothered him the most was the only slightly veiled threat he received. The attorneys for the EPA warned him that if he refused to pay his "share," amounting to tens of thousands of dollars, he could be held liable for the entire cleanup, amounting to several million dollars. The timing was significant since he had just returned from an industry meeting where other owners shared horror stories of similar conflicts with various government agencies. Many of them had their assets attached when they refused to comply.

"Enough is enough," he told me. "Government officials from another country want me to relocate my business there, and they've offered me tax breaks, low-interest loans, and governmental guarantees of no interference. I can see the handwriting on the wall here. So I'm going."

He offered his employees a chance to relocate also. As expected, no one took the offer, so 1300 employees were out of a job, and another industry left the U.S.

I'm sure some newspaper or television station in his area will eventually do a report on the callous businessman who dumped his employees for a few dollars. But that was not the case at all. He grieved over his decision, and then he provided liberal benefits to those who were dismissed.

"My great concern," he said, "is that one day the rules will get so oppressive that I

won't be able to operate profitably and laws
will be passed to keep me from relocating. So
I'm getting out while I still can." He saw the
EPA in the same role as the KGB in Russia.
They have become a paramilitary enforcement
group running amok throughout the free
enterprise system.

This oppressiveness of the government not only effects
American business but ordinary American families living quiet
lives in their suburban homes.

Homeowners, Beware!

In Bakersville, California a controversy arose over the
opening of a "group home" for the "developmentally disabled" in a residential subdivision. It is not uncommon for
controversy to surround such group homes when located in
residential areas. Many homeowners feel that the placement of
a group home in their neighbor home will adversely affect the
value of their homes and lots. Often times, such group homes
are only permitted in areas specially zoned for such services.

In early 1995, five homeowners who chose to exercise their
legal rights went to court to get a temporary restraining order
to prevent the opening of the home until the controversy could
be resolved.

The actions of the homeowners, however, did not set well
with the United States Justice Department, who filed suit,
charging the homeowners with discriminatory practices in violation of the Fair Housing Act. In simple terms, our government is claiming that filing a case in court is a civil rights violation that could result in heavy fines.

The five homeowners, fearful of losing thousands of dollars through a battle with the Unites States Justice
Department, offered to end their legal challenge. Federal officials, however, would not agree to drop their lawsuit against
the homeowners.[7]

Choosing to exercise your right to petition a governmental
body for redress of grievances could cost you dearly in this

age of political correctness. Remember, political correctness is really a masking term for socialism.

Sobering Statistics

One dragon that must be slain in this battle for freedom is the United States Department of Education. Why? Because the Department of Education violates the Tenth Amendment.

The Tenth Amendment of the U.S. Constitution makes it very clear that the powers the federal government has are very limited and very specific. Unless the Constitution specifically grants the power to the federal government, the unlisted power belongs to the states and the respective people thereof.

The framers of the United States Constitution purposed for education to be controlled by parents and taxpayers in the state where they live and not by the federal government.

The Department of Education's abuse of power and tax-payer's money can be documented by their duplication of services and far-reaching programs.

Jim Jacobson, vice-president of the National Right to Read, conducted a study entitled, "The Federal Role in Education, a Program Review and Analysis." In his research, Jacobson discovered that, "the U.S. Department of education budget counts for only $33 billion of the $70 billion spent on education."

That means that approximately $37 billion spent on education at the federal level comes from agencies other than the Department of Education. In other words, more federal dollars are spent on education by agencies outside of the D.O.E. than the D.O.E. itself spends each year.

Jim Jacobson also discovered that the D.O.E. administers 244 education programs while other agencies administer another 308. More education programs exist outside of the Department of Education than inside it.

Jim Jacobson also discovered that there are 86 federal programs in nine federal departments that offer teacher training. The money from these programs are used for organizing and planning teachers' conferences. Why? So the federal government can continue to promote and sabotage America's educational system by indoctrinating teachers into implementing

Goals 2000 and other federally mandated programs.

Jim also uncovered 90 pre-school and child-care programs in 11 federal agencies. If that were not bad enough, the 90 programs are very similar in the services they offer, but very different in costs.

The abuses by the Department of Education are only one indication of how big our federal government has become and how large a role it plays in our children's education. I believe this data gives us a sobering account of the work that must be done to eliminate the federal government's role in education.

The Same Old Tune

Many of the freshman in the 104th congress were elected with the mandate to downsize the federal government. Republican freshman Congressman Joseph Scarlabourgh has wasted no time in working to fulfill the wishes of his constituents by introducing H.R. 1883, which calls for the elimination of the U.S. Department of Education over a four to five year period.

I applaud Congressman Scarlabourgh's leadership, but his bill contains a few key flaws.

First of all, we cannot wait four to five years for the elimination of the D.O.E.

Secondly, H.R. 1883 also allows the most dangerous D.O.E. programs to survive by finding shelter at another agency.

If we do not abolish the D.O.E. and every program in it, the programs will be scattered throughout the government, making my job of tracking them even harder than it is now.

What is the solution?

Legislative analyst, Mike Hammond, has written a bill that would return all of the power that now belongs to the D.O.E. back to the states. Mike's bill, which still needs a sponsor in Congress, would abolish the D.O.E. in one year along with every program inside the D.O.E.

Abolishing the United States Department of Education and the federal role of education is not going to be as easy as we thought. After the elections of 1994, enthusiasm and determination ran high to slay the education dragon — until July 1995.

In early July, U.S. Congressman John Kasich of Ohio, who serves as the budget chairman, made a very discouraging remark. Mr. Kasich proclaimed that he believed we would be able to keep the U.S. Department of Education and the Department of Labor if we would do away with the Department of Commerce. Many anti-D.O.E. conservatives do not believe Congressman Kasich was speaking for himself but for a more powerful politician.

Some of the most powerful people and organizations in our nation do not want the federal role of education decreased. In fact, they want it increased. Many who sing the conservative song at election time only hum that tune once elected.

I fear that the fate of the D.O.E. is being hammered out in back rooms where so-called conservatives are backing off the idea of abolishing the D.O.E. in exchange for protection or passage of their pet projects and programs.

I suggest you take note of those individuals who sang the loudest at election time only to hum the quietest after being elected. In 1996, tell political soloists to put a sock in it — and vote against those who talk the talk but are afraid to carry a big stick.

You — a Lobbyist?

Many Americans got involved in a strategic battle in the fall of 1994 and helped through their faxes, phone calls, and letters to defeat a bill that would have created one more money-wasting, freedom-robbing agency.

Many legal experts believed that the Lobbying Disclosure Act would have required conservative and family organizations like the American Family Association, the Heritage Foundation, and others to turn over supporters' names and addresses to a government official appointed by the President.

With its vague wording, this bill would have put numerous restraints and loads of paperwork on the average conservative think tank. Many experts who reviewed the legislation feared that it could have required politically involved citizens to register themselves with the Office of Lobbying Registration that would have been established in the executive branch.

The Family Research Council, based in Washington D.C., noted in its research on the Lobbying Disclosure Act that fines could have been imposed on activist citizens and/or grassroots organizations of $200,000 if the bill's proposed regulations were violated.

The Lobbying Disclosure Act would have also required organizations attempting to influence federal decisions with the help of a grassroots operations to reveal the specific names, addresses, and principle places of business involved in conducting grassroots lobbying.

This means that if my organization, the American Family Policy Institute, was attempting, and we are, to enlist your support in abolishing the Department of Education, you and I would both be a target. Under this Act, if we were asking you to order a video to show in your community about the importance of abolishing the Department of Education, and you responded to our call for action by ordering the video, we would be required by law to list your name and address in our reports to the Office of Lobbying Registration.

Thanks to you and your tens of thousands of phone calls, faxes, and letters this bill never won congressional approval.

A Part-Time Congress?

Aside from abolishing many of the unneeded, freedom-robbing federal agencies, we need to encourage our elected officials in Washington, as well as in our own states, to take an oath before the voters that they will not vote in favor of any bill unless they have personally read every page.

If that were the case, many detrimental bills would never have become law. If our senators and congressmen knew that the voters were going to ask them questions about the bill in order to verify their having read it, our elected officials would not be so quick to create a piece of legislation that contains a thousand pages. The bigger the bill, the easier it is for pork and freedom-robbing amendments and sections to get lost in the shuffle.

Another way to save time and money — and get more qualified elected officials — would be to make the holding of a congressional and senatorial position a part-time job. Our founding fathers did not intend for U.S. Congressmen and Senators to be employed full-time by the federal government. Instead, the intent was for elected officials to be ordinary citizens who own their own businesses or work for someone else.

Many states do not employ their elected legislators full-time. Instead, state representative are full-time doctors, teachers, plumbers, accountants, carpenters who serve their state on a part-time basis. Such a system allows elected officials to stay in touch with the real world as well as requires them to live and work under the laws they pass.

If both houses of Congress were operated on a part-time basis, think of the money America could save on paper and postage alone — not to mention phone bills and air travel. In addition, congressmen and senators would have less time to meddle in our affairs. The results could only be positive, as this report proves:

> A report in the *New York Times* in 1992 suggested that the nation and the economy suffer in proportion to the meddling of government in our private lives. Their study compared the performance of the Dow-Jones stock averages when Congress was in session and when it was in recess. The statistics showed that in the 45 years from the end of World War II to 1991, the level of the Dow was 17 times higher when both houses of Congress were out of town.[8]

This data alone is proof enough we do not need a full-time Congress.

Judge Breyers' Snow Job

Every school year, many Americans silently — and with their pocketbooks — protest big government's intrusion into their lives by opting out of public schools. Parents do this in spite of the fact they must pay tuition and/or pay for textbooks in addition to rendering taxes to support the local school district.

For now, it is legal for parents to home-school or send their children to private and Christian schools. But that is not a guarantee.

Most home-school and private school parents believe they are protected from government control and intrusion by the "Home-School, Private-School Freedom Amendment" passed into H.R. 6 by U.S. Congressman Dick Armey. While this is a needed amendment, and we are thankful for Dick Armey and his leadership, it is just a band-aid.

Several loop holes in H.R. 6 and the vague wording of both this bill and Goals 2000 create horrendous problems. As a result, the ultimate interpretation of these bills will more than likely be made in the federal courts — and perhaps ultimately by the U.S. Supreme Court.

Why would such a legal battle ensue? Because Bill Clinton has stuffed America's federal benches with his liberal cronies. These agents of change, of course, will remain long after the helicopter lifts off the grounds of the U.S. Capitol, taking Bill Clinton back to Arkansas.

In early 1994, Bill Clinton appointed Judge Stephen Breyers to the United States Supreme Court. This Judge — who received high praise during his confirmation hearings from liberals, moderates, and conservatives alike — pulled off a snow job only surpassed by that of his appointer — Bill Clinton. The test of time will prove Stephen Breyers true ideology when the mask is unveiled to reveal a soul-mate of the Clintons.

How do we know? Judge Breyers' record proves the point.

In 1987, New Life Baptist Academy in Massachusetts found itself fighting off a hostile takeover from the East Longmeadow School District.

In writing his opinion on *New Life Baptist Academy v. East Longmeadow School District,* Judge Stephen Breyers — who was then on the First Circuit U.S. Court of Appeals — revealed that he believed it is constitutional for states to effectively ban home education.

When justifying his decision to subject New Life Baptist Academy to massive control and intrusion by the East Longmeadow School District, he cited three previous cases —

one from North Carolina, one from Arkansas, and one from California — involving both private school and home school freedom. In his opinion, he wrote that these cases "uphold effective and total ban on home schooling."

Without a doubt, Breyers believes it is legal and constitutional to have this kind of control and intrusion into a local church's educational ministry.

As private school associations and home school organizations fight for freedom and independence, my fear is that such cases could ultimately land at the feet of the U.S. Supreme Court. If our presidents continue to appoint liberal judges and Congress continues to approve them, this could put our constitutional freedoms in jeopardy.

Any judge who seeks to limit the power and control that parents have over their child's private, Christian school education and/or their home school education poses a danger to God-fearing, freedom-loving Americans.

It is very clear from reading Judge Breyers' opinion in *New Life Baptist Academy v. East Longmeadow School District* that he will, in cases such as this, have the tendency to ignore the U.S. Constitution and Bill of Rights and side with America's social engineers who want total and unquestioning control of you and your children — from womb to tomb.

Unnecessarily Burdensome

Let's look at the issues that were raised in the New Life Baptist Academy case.

In Massachusetts, a child cannot satisfy the Massachusetts' compulsory school attendance laws unless the local school committee "approves" the education the private school provides. New Life Baptist Academy viewed the district's proposed approval procedures as vague and unnecessarily burdensome upon the right of the free exercise of religion.

As a result, the academy countered with the proposal that they would voluntarily take a standardized test to prove to the district that the school was effectively educating their students. The district refused this proposal, so New Life Baptist Academy filed a law suit in order to stop the district from carrying out it proposed vague approval process.

The district court conducted a hearing and determined that the school committee's proposed procedures were unnecessarily burdensome upon religion, compared to the less burdensome possibility of standardized testing. The district court also ruled that the school district's proposed evaluation methods were unconstitutional, violating "free exercise" and "establishment" clauses of the first Amendment.

The public school committee, joined by the Commonwealth of Massachusetts, appealed this ruling to the United States Appeals Court, first circuit, upon which Judge Stephen Breyers sat — and won.

New Life Baptist Academy was more than willing — as most private schools and home schools are — to take some sort of standardized test as long as it was not mandatory. The real problem arises when a state or the federal government wants to make such tests mandatory.

If a certain test is made mandatory and that test is testing a child's attitudes, values, feelings, and emotions — as many tests do today — the correct answers on this test could be in violation of the religious rights of parents or of a certain religious school. Such a test would force the child's parents or school into teaching the politically correct views with which they disagree in order to ensure that the student or students pass the test and thus allow the private school or home school to continue operating.

Why are most private schools and home schoolers not opposed to administering some sort of standardized test? Because private school and home school students across our nation continue year after year to score well above public school students. It seems to me that our public officials should be more concerned with the quality of the public schools than worrying about the private and home schools!

The point of disagreement between New Life Baptist Academy and East Longmeadow School District was the fact that the district insisted on approving or disapproving the education being offered by New Life Academy based on very vague and intrusive methods. The district refused to articulate any concrete, measurable standards for approval, giving them complete control over New Life Baptist Academy by making up the rules as they went along.

The Amendment Shell Game

Without a doubt the battle over H.R. 6 was a hotly contested one.

On Thursday, March 24, 1994, Congressman Mel Hancock of Missouri offered an amendment to Title XI of H.R. 6. The amendment would keep federal tax dollars from being used to pay for curriculum that promoted or encouraged the homosexual or lesbian lifestyle.

The Congressman's amendment read as follows:

> No local educational agency that receives funds under this Act shall implement or carry out a program or activity that has either the purpose or effect of encouraging or supporting homosexuality as a positive lifestyle alternative.

Unfortunately, Democratic Congresswomen Jolene Unsoeld of Washington state offered an amendment to Congressman Hancock's amendment, watering it down and rendering it virtually ineffective

While the Hancock Amendment prohibits schools who choose to accept federal funds under H.R. 6 from using any public resources — local, state, and federal — to promote the homosexual lifestyle, the Unsoeld Amendment would limit this restriction only to federal dollars.

The Unsoeld Amendment explicitly affirmed the right of schools to spend state and local resources to promote homosexuality as a positive alternative lifestyle — allowing schools to play a shell game, much like NEA grantees, regarding the use of federal dollars.

The Unsoeld Amendment also limited the Hancock Amendment's restrictions to those programs or activities with the "purpose" of promoting the homosexual lifestyle. The original Hancock Amendment targeted programs with the "purpose or effect" of promoting the homosexual lifestyle.

The deletion of the word "effect" left the bill to mean that you could buy curriculum for sex education or AIDS awareness just as long as you did not use it for the "purpose" of promoting the homosexual lifestyle even if that were its effect. The Hancock Amendment targeted programs with the "purpose or effect" of promoting the homosexual lifestyle.

Gutting the School Prayer Amendment

America's social engineers are forcing change on Americans despite their protest.

On February 3, 1994, the U.S. Senate voted 75-22 in favor of the Helms-Lott School Prayer Language as an amendment to H.R. 1804, the Goals 2000 bill. The amendment read as follows:

> No funds made available through the Department of Education under this Act, or any other Act shall be available to any state or local educational agency which has a policy of denying, or which effectively prevents participation in, constitutionally protected prayer in public schools by individuals on a voluntary basis. Neither the United States nor any state nor any local educational agency shall require any person to participate in prayer or influence the form or content of any constitutionally protected prayer in such public schools.

On that same day, February 23, 1994, the U.S. House voted 367-55 to instruct the house conferees on the "Goals 2000" bill to accept the Helms-Lott school prayer amendment from the Senate.

Despite these overwhelming legislative victories for freedom, less than a month later, on March 18, 1994, the House and Senate "Goals 2000" conferees dropped the Helms-Lott Amendment and substituted "do-nothing" language authored by Rep. Pat Williams:

> No funds authorized to be appropriated under
> this Act may be used by any state or local edu-
> cational agency to adopt policies that prevent
> voluntary prayer and meditation in public
> schools.

Why is Rep. Williams' amendment being called a "do-
nothing" amendment? Because it merely prevents schools
from using federal funds in the Goals 2000 bill "to adopt policies" preventing school prayer. Schools never use federal
funds of any kind "to adopt" school policies — local money
pays the school board and school administration salaries and
expenses in this regard.

The "Goals 2000" conferees substituted the Helms-Lott
Amendment with Rep. Williams amendment during the last 60
second of the conference without a vote on the issue.

Despite the overwhelming votes in favor of the Helms-
Lott Amendment in both the House and Senate and the
numerous phones calls made by the American people in support of the amendment, Senator Kennedy (then chairman of
the Senate labor and Human Resources Committee) and Rep.
William Ford (then Chairman of the House Education and
Labor Committee) agreed to gut the Helms school prayer
amendment by substituting the Rep. Williams "do nothing"
amendment.

Are we still living in a democracy? Or are we living in a
dictatorship? This is one loophole that must be closed in order
to ensure that the American people have representation in
Washington.

On Wednesday March 23, 1994, the U.S. House passed the
"Goals 2000" conferees' report and sent it on to the U.S.
Senate.

On Wednesday night, Senator Jesse Helms called for the
reading of the entire bill. This took over four hours, which
gave Senator Helms a chance to run around and try to get at
least 60 Senators to agree not to go to cloture — which means
there can be no more amendments added to the bill. At the
same time, if Democrats were able to get cloture, they could
keep Senator Helms from having his school prayer amend-

ment added back onto Goals 2000.

Early on Thursday morning, after the reading of the bill, the Senate agreed to move on to other business. Once a motion has been made for cloture, unless there is 100 percent consent by all Senators, the Senate must wait two days before actually voting on cloture.

The Senate debated Goals 2000 all Friday afternoon and late into the night on March 25th. At 11:00 p.m., the U.S. Senate took a one-hour recess and reconvened at 12:01 a.m., Saturday March 26th, ending the two-day waiting period. After a roll call to bring absent Senators to the floor, the vote on cloture, the obtaining of cloture, and the roll call vote on the passage of Goals 2000 occurred at approximately 1:15 a.m.

Goals 2000 passed the U.S. Senate to become law.

Getting Around Goals 2000

Is there a way around the massive government intrusion that Goals 2000 will bring? Yes.

The states must reject the federal funds allowed for by ESEA, which they are accustomed to receiving, and the new funds, however small, available under Goals 2000. States who wish not to comply will have no option but to withhold federal taxes from the federal government and fund their schools themselves — until the government complies with the tenth amendment.

I said earlier in this chapter that we need protection from legislation like Goals 2000 and H.R. 6, but I was wrong. We already have protection from such freedom-robbing legislation through the U.S. Constitution. The problem is that many of our federal judges and legislators are not following or complying with the principles our founding fathers wrote.

Even if we had an education bill of rights written and put into law, the chances are slim that it would be honored. Why? Because the U.S. Constitution itself is being ignored in spite of the fact that every judge and state and federal lawmaker swears to protect and uphold the U.S. Constitution.

When a U.S. Congressman or U.S. Senator takes the oath of office, he or she is swearing before God and this country to first and foremost defend the U.S. Constitution. Congressmen enter into a contract for two and senators for six years.

If and when an elected official does not support, or goes against, the U.S. Constitution, it is a clear and definite breach of contract — and the voters should organize a re-call or simply vote the traitor out of office next go round. It is high time the American people defend their rights and freedoms guaranteed by the Constitution by voting out those elected officials who so arrogantly and deliberately break their oath of office.

A lot is at stake in the 1996 elections. We must let our voices be heard at the polling booth — for the sake of our family and freedoms.

What's At Stake?

If this on-going battle for our freedoms is to be won, we must start disassembling the bureaucracy that hinders Americans from being the enterprising, productive, creative, capitalists that made this nation strong.

Whether it is the unconstitutional tax burdens and procedures placed upon Americans, the money-wasting, bureaucratic, socialistic, mandates of the Department of Education or the Environmental Protection agency, we must return America to Americans.

If we let them have their way, they will destroy everything that made our nation great — like freedom of religion, free enterprise, industry — and people. How do I know? Because that is what they say, as these quotes illustrates:

> The Humanist view is that marriage is a human institution. . . . in no sense sacred and immutable. Some opponents of Humanism have accused us of wishing to overthrow the traditional Christian family. They are right. That is exactly what we intend to do — *the British Humanists Association.*

> Christianity is our foe. If animal right is to succeed, we must destroy the Judeo Christian reli-

gious tradition — *Australian philosopher, Peter Singer, the "Father of Animal Rights."*

Free enterprise really means rich people get richer. They have the freedom to exploit and psychologically rape their fellow human beings in the process . . . Capitalism is destroying the earth — *Helen Caldicott of the Union of Concerned Scientists.*

Isn't the only hope for the planet that the industrialized civilizations collapse? Isn't it our responsibility to bring that about?— *Maurice Strong, Head of the 1992 Earth Summit in Rio.*

In order to stabilize world population, we must eliminate 350,000 people per day — *Dr. Jacques Cousteau.*

This will give you an idea of the radical thinking of the environmental movement and other groups who have the ear of the White House through Vice President Al Gore, who wrote the book, *Earth in the Balance.*

Since the 1994 elections, Vice President Gore seems to have gone underground, but you can bet he is tunneling behind the scenes to accomplish his environmental goals through government channels.

Just how big have our governments become? Currently in our nation, "20 percent of all Americans work directly for federal, state, and local governments, and such create no new goods and services."[9]

Our over-sized government creates out-of-control rules and regulations that serve no real purpose other than to give some bureaucrat something to monitor and enforce so he can collect a paycheck. That paycheck, however, comes from our hard-earned tax dollars — which are getting harder to earn because of all the rules, regulations, and permits that cost Americans and American business millions of dollars. That money could have been spent by businesses to expand their companies, creating jobs and growing the economy.

Today many of our hard-earned dollars are going to feed unnecessary state and federal agencies that spring up like powerful weeds and crowd, cramp, and steal the precious resources that weaken and stifle the beautiful life-giving flower of freedom.

Capitalism and ultimately the American dream — the American way of life — is at stake in this battle for freedom.

Notes

[1] Martin L. Gross, *The Tax Racket* (New York, NY: Ballantine Books, 1995) p.2.

[2] George F. Will, "Poor Students Blocked From Escaping," *Greensburg Tribune Review,* Sept. 10, 1995.

[3] Ibid. p. 27.

[4] Ibid., p. 40-41.

[5] Ibid., p. 240-241.

[6] Ibid., p. 242.

[7] Gary Bauer, "End of the Day Briefing Memo," Family Research Council, May 31, 1995.

[8] Dr. D. James Kennedy, *Character and Destiny,* (Grand Rapids, MI: Zondervan Publishing House, 1994) p. 32.

[9] Larry Burkett, *The Coming Economic Earthquake,* (Chicago, IL: Moody Press, 1991, 1994) p. 95.

9

Financial Nightmare or American Dream?

W hen I think about America's financial future, I am reminded of a story a friend once told me.

A young man wanted to be a truck driver. The thought of being out on the open road, driving one of those big eighteen wheelers from town to town all across the county really appealed to him.

One day the young man thought it was time to quit talking about it and make his dream come true.

After weeks of studying and training at truck driving school, the young man passed his written and driving test with flying colors. There was only one requirement left, the oral exam. If the young man passed this test, he would receive his truck drivers license.

When the day of the oral exam finally arrived, the young man walked into the exam room. There sat three men — old, retired, truck drivers who now spent their days conducting the oral exam.

The young man took his seat in front of the three old truckers, and they began asking him questions. With great skill and articulation, the young man answered question after question.

Finally the oldest of the three truckers said, "Son, if you

193

can answer this final question correctly, you will walk out of this room today with your truck drivers license.

"Here is the question. You are driving your eighteen wheeler, and you are coming down on the other side of the Blue Ridge Mountains. It is a cold day, and the road is slick because it has been sleeting. You wind around and come upon the last and final incline. It is a very long and steep incline. On your left is a school bus filled with school children, on the other side of the school bus is a mountain wall. On your right, there is a 300 foot drop off into the valley. Suddenly directly in front of you, at about 150 yards, in your lane, is a jack-knifed semi. What do you do?"

The young man began to think out loud.

"Well," he said, "I can't go to my left because there is a school bus filled with kids. If I try moving over toward them, I could cause them to crash into the side of the mountain. On my right is a 300 foot drop off. The roads are very slick and due to the steep incline. . . . Suddenly, the young man stopped speaking.

The room was filled with silence.

Finally after what seem like forever, he spoke.

"I know what I would do," he said, "I would wake up Harold."

The three old truck drivers looked at each other in shock.

The oldest of the three men asked the question that was on all their minds, "Who is Harold? And seconds before you crash, why would you bother to wake him up?"

In a very serious tone, the young man responded, "Well, you see, Harold is my partner who is asleep in the back of the cab. He is from a small town in Texas, and he has never seen a wreck like this one is going to be."

I believe that just like the young man and his partner Harold, we are headed for a crash like we have never seen. Maybe it will not be today, tomorrow, next month, or even next year. Unless, however, we wake up the Harolds of our nation and begin to make the extreme and necessary sacrifices required, a crash is inevitable.

On and Off the Record

Before we look at how America's social engineers have led us down the present financial road to disaster, let us examine our nation's present fiscal nightmare.

Currently, America is approximately $4 trillion in debt on record. I say "on record" because when our leaders talk about our nation's current debt, they seldom mention our off-record debt.

Off record, our nation is nearly $12 trillion in debt. A portion of the debt that is classified as off record is the amount of money our government borrows each year from the Social Security Administration. Each year for the past several years our federal government has borrowed $30 to $50 billion from the Social Security Administration in order to help pay our nation's bills and keep the country running. In return, the Social Security Administration receives an I.O.U.

Eventually, the Social Security Administration will need to cash in its stack of I.O.U.'s in order to meet its financial requirements and commitments to millions of Americans.

In reality, the money that the federal government borrows from the Social Security Administration is a loan, which must be repaid; thus the money the federal government owes to the Social Security Administration is part of our national debt.

The ever-increasing dollar amount owed to the Social Security Administration, however, is not included in the national deficit figure we so frequently hear reported. This figure is only part of what we call our off-record national debt.

What would happen if the company you work for borrowed from its employees' retirement fund and, instead of paying it back, simply said, "Oh well, we will repay it when we can. Here is an I.O.U."? The company's officials would be sent to prison.

If it is unlawful and determined to be fraud when American citizens conduct their business in such a fashion, what is it called when the federal government does exactly the same thing? The federal government "at work."

How Much is a Trillion Dollars?

Let's think about the $4 trillion debt our nation has on record.

How much is a trillion dollars? The typical answer is, "A lot."

The head of a conservative organization in Washington D.C. that monitors government spending has given a brilliant scenario to describe just how much a trillion dollars really is. Let me summarize it.

If you were to open a business during the time of Christ and you kept your business open 365 days a year, and you lost a million dollars every day from the time of Christ to present, you would have to leave your business open another 700 years, 365 days each year, loosing a million dollars each day, to equal one trillion dollars.

Here is another way to look at it. If you were to tightly bind $1,000 bills until you had one trillion dollars, you would have a stack of $1,000 bills that would reach 63 miles into the sky.

Remember, our national debt is approximately $4 trillion on record and over $12 trillion including the off-record debt.

Currently, federal figures report that 40 percent of the federal taxes collected today goes to cover just the *interest* on the national debt. That means everyone west of the Mississippi is paying their federal taxes not to build roads or to pay for education but to cover the interest on the national debt.

According to federal figures, the debt is compounding so fast that by 1996, every dollar collected in federal taxes will go just to cover the interest on the national debt. That means that by 1997, this nation will not even be able to cover the *interest* being accrued on the national debt, much less pay anything on the principal.

Congressman Phil Crane, (R-IL) has said, "I believe we will just ride this thing out until the economy crashes and burns; then we'll see what we can salvage from the ashes."[1]

On March 24, 1992, then U.S. Senator Warren B. Rudman said, "This recession will be a picnic compared to where this country will be in the year 1997."[2]

Senator Rudman knows that very few politicians are truly interested in making the serious sacrifices required to get our yearly federal deficit — and ultimately our national debt — under control.

What's the Difference?

America's financial situation baffles many Americans. Begin talking about the national debt or the federal deficit, and eyes will glaze over.

As a result, most Americans have no idea how serious the problem has become in terms of America's current financial condition and the economic nightmare that will haunt most Americans when this house of cards comes crashing down.

What is the difference between the national debt and the federal deficit?

The *federal deficit* is our nation's yearly financial debt and is derived from the difference between what we as a nation bring in each year — through taxes and the selling of treasury bonds, etc. — and the amount we spend.

Larry Burkett wrote in his 1994 book that "the government has an income of approximately $1.2 trillion a year, yet it is spending approximately $1.5 trillion a year."

The difference between those two figures is what makes up the federal deficit.

For instance, if you made $50,000 one year, yet you spent $110,000, you would have a deficit that year of $60,000.

When our nation spends more each year than it makes, it must borrow the difference in order to meet its financial obligations and pay its bills. The amount our government borrows each year is referred to as the federal deficit.

What, then, does the term *national debt* mean? It is the combined total of our yearly federal deficits.

For example, if you make $50,000 a year, yet it costs you $110,000 a year to meet your financial commitments and maintain the standard of living you desire, you would have to come up with an additional $60,000 each year. Where would you get the extra $60,000? More than likely you would go to your local bank and take out a loan to cover your commitments and maintain your desired standard of living.

That is exactly what our federal government does.

If each year, for five years, you borrowed $60,000 from your local bank to cover your yearly deficit spending, your total deficit after five years would be $300,000 ($60,000 x 5 = $300,000).

Actually, you would owe more than $300,000 to your local bank. Why? Because your bank makes its money by charging interest on the money you borrow.

Our nation is so far in debt that the interest we are paying each year on our national debt is eating us alive. "In 1995 interest will take $244 billion (15.5 percent) of all government spending."[3]

Our *federal deficit* is the amount our government over-spends each year, above and beyond what it brings in through taxes and other means.

The *national debt* is the combined total of all our years of deficit spending with interest added and accruing daily.

Not Will, But When

What would you do if you realized your family was spending more than twice your income? More than likely, you would quickly learn to live within your means, even if that meant doing without some things you want but don't need.

This seldom practiced discipline, called "making sacri-fices," is foreign to many Americans — and even more alien to those running our federal government. Most Americans, how-ever, are pragmatic enough to realize that our nation needs to cut back on spending in order to balance the budget.

Solving your personal as well as our government's finan-cial problems could be very simple. Unless the problem goes uncorrected for so long that you find yourself in such great debt that you cannot get out because you don't — or can't — bring in enough revenue to cover the initial amount you bor-rowed — much less the amount being added daily due to interest. Eventually you would have no choice but to file bank-ruptcy.

That is where America finds itself today. Our nation is now

on the verge of bankruptcy.

The problem is so great that Harry E. Figgie Jr., CEO of Figgie International, Inc., the company that owns Rawlings Sports among other businesses, wrote a book in 1992 titled, *Bankruptcy 1995*.

Mr. Figgie reports that the government spends $1.68 for every $1.00 it takes in through taxes and other means.

No one can predict whether or not America will go bankrupt and have an economic collapse in 1995. The question is no longer, *Will* America suffer an economic collapse? But, *When* will America an economic collapse occur?

Four Reasons Why I Am Not Hopeful

Larry Burkett, author of the book, *The Coming Economic Earthquake* wrote, "If the elections of '94 confirm Clinton's policies, I would change my previous estimate of an economic collapse from near the turn of the century (around the year 2000) to '96-'98."[4]

Fortunately, the American people did not confirm Clinton's policies in the November 1994 elections. However, despite Republican control of both the House and the Senate, and their Contract with America, I am not hopeful about the future for several reasons:

1. It is too little too late.

The Republicans are claiming to end our nation's yearly deficit spending, which means no more federal deficits, sometime around the year 2003. I do not think we have until the year 2003 to get our yearly deficit spending under control.

2. Our politicians lack backbone.

Once our nation achieves the enormous task of no more deficit spending, we must create a yearly surplus. It will be a major victory for Congress and the White House to bring our government to the point of spending no more than it brings in each year through taxes and other means.

Not only will zero deficit spending have to continue each year, but the government will need to bring in more than it spends, leaving the government with a surplus. This surplus could then be used to begin paying off our national debt. It will never happen. Our government will never have enough years of zero deficit spending, plus a surplus, to even put a dent in the national debt.

I seriously doubt whether we will ever see our government operate for one year without a deficit. Why? Because we do not have enough elected officials who are truly serious about getting our financial problem under control. We have *some* but not enough fiscal conservatives who understand the seriousness of the situation. Nor do I believe that enough of our elected officials are willing to make the greatly needed massive sacrifices necessary to get our deficit spending and national debt under control.

Author and historian, David Barton, has said,

> Unfortunately our political leaders are no longer required to face or to accept personal responsibility for the long-term consequences of their actions. Contemporary politicians often look no further than 2, 4, or 6 years into the future, depending on the term of their office. Consequently, their own short-term decisions, often taken to help ensure re-election, frequently jeopardize the people's long-term security and prosperity.[5]

It is difficult for politicians to get elected or re-elected when they go around talking about cutting Social Security and other entitlement programs like welfare, food stamps, school lunches, pensions for federal employees, etc. Yet, unless we get the entitlement programs under control, we will never get our yearly federal deficit or national debt down to manageable levels. The long term results of such irresponsibility will inevitably be devastating.

How much is our nation spending on entitlement programs?

"In 1962 all entitlements took $32 billion (28 percent of all government spending). In 1995 they will consume $795 billion

(50.4 percent of all government spending)."[6]

Recently, there has been a lot of talk about getting the problem under control, but for the most part, you are hearing nothing but political posturing. The politicians are telling you what they think you want to hear.

The entitlement spending has gotten so crazy that families are now receiving just that, "crazy checks." Several investigations have shown parents are having their children do poorly in school, misbehave and even fake being crazy in order to get an extra check from the government that has been nicknamed, "the crazy check."

Under the federal governments SSI program, individuals who have a so called disorder can receive a very healthy check for their supposed disorder.

NBC news reported on September 15, 1995 that the federal governent is giving families extra money in the form of "the crazy check" for such off the wall disorders as a child who has been diagnosed with "oppositional defiant disorder." Now I have heard it all.

3. Bill Clinton's presidential policies.

Despite the Republican takeover of the House and Senate in 1994 and their Contract With America, Bill Clinton has been in office for nearly three years and is still President.

Clinton has financed our debt through short-term bonds. As the interest rate was raised several times in 1994 alone, so moved up the interest on the short term bonds that Clinton used to finance our debt. Therefore, due to the increasing interest rate, our national debt began — and continues — to grow at an even faster rate.

Despite Clinton's claims to have cut the national debt, he has not! The only thing Clinton has cut is "projected spending." For example, instead of borrowing $100 million for some pet program, Clinton proposes only borrowing $50 million — and then says he saved American taxpayers $50 million.

4. New legislation continues to drain our economic resources.

Finally, I am not hopeful because our leaders continue to pass legislation that only makes the problem worse — such as

GATT, the General Agreement on Tariffs and Trade.

Phyllis Schlafly has said, "GATT. . . is a budget breaker. It will add at least $31 billion to the federal debt as a result of lost revenues from tariff cuts."[7]

Larry Burkett, writes, "This country is so far down the road to disaster now that, in my opinion, there is very little that can be done to avert it."[8]

Soaring Prices

When, and not if, the economic disaster that so many authors, economists, and national leaders are predicting occurs, what effect if any, will it have on you and your family?

Unless you and your family are out of debt and well-diversified, you could be facing some very difficult times ahead. Under an economic collapse, the dollars you now hold will be worth very little if anything. Prior to an economic collapse, we could experience a recession, depression, inflation, and possibly hyperinflation.

Many economists are predicting a deflationary period that will cause the government to resort to more credit to make up for a rise in the federal deficit. Such a move could put inflation on a fast track.

If we see the return of inflation — prior to and after an economic collapse — it could lead to hyperinflation. Through hyperinflation your paper money would have less buying power to the point of becoming virtually worthless.

In countries that have experienced hyperinflation, such as Argentina and Germany, the price of goods sky rocketed while the value of their currency dropped like a stone. In Germany in 1918, "retirees who held government or bank bonds saw their assets devalued by 2000 percent in one day."[9]

Due to hyperinflation the price of goods was increasing continually. Prices changed so fast due to the rate of inflation that stores found it futile to put prices on their goods. Instead, the prices were computed at the counter at the time of purchase.

The German mark became so worthless as a monetary symbol that the paper it was printed on was actually worth more than what the mark represented.

In some countries, inflation, which led to hyperinflation, was so bad that the factories would pay their employees every hour. The men would then take their wages and pass it through the factory fences to their wives. The wives would run and buy the needed groceries and items as fast as possible because every minute wasted meant that their money had less buying power.

Men who worked in factories that paid them every hour counted themselves fortunate. Some greedy businessmen would pay their workers at the end of the week, saving money for themselves.

Suppose, due to hyperinflation, you work for $500 a week. On Monday, that $500 may have the buying power of only $300. By Friday, suppose the decline in value of the dollar due to hyperinflation means that $500 only has the buying power of $200. Would you prefer to be paid each hour, the end of the day, or at the end of the week?

The problem with hyperinflation is that wages never stay consistent with the cost of living. Prices are soaring while wages remain the same, or move up very slowly.

Inflation — Less Buying Power

This might be a good place to stop and define some terms. What is inflation?

Webster's dictionary defines inflation as: "An increase in the volume of money and credit relative to available goods resulting in a substantial and continuing rise in the general price level."

In other words, inflation occurs when people have access to money or to more credit to buy products and goods. The increase of availability in credit or money being pumped into the economy creates a demand for certain products. The demand for products creates an increase in the price because of the law of supply and demand.

Inflation makes your money less valuable. Due to the demand for products, there is a rise in the cost of those prod-ucts. The rise in the cost of living means your money will buy you less than it did a year ago. Inflation makes your money worth less or causes it to have less buying power.

The difference in the price of goods from one year to the next is the rate of inflation. In order to achieve the most accurate figure concerning the rate of inflation, the government compares the prices of certain goods each year.

In 1994, the Federal Reserve raised interest rates seven times. The reasons for this rise in interest rates is debatable. The Federal Reserve claimed it was raising interest rates in order to stop the rise of inflation. Because banks were loaning money and credit cards where extending credit, people were given the means by which to buy products.

The increase in available cash or credit created a demand for certain products. In turn the demand created an increase in prices. The increase in the price of goods and services due to demand gives your money less buying power, which means inflation.

In order to slow down the rate of inflation or to hold back inflation, the Federal Reserve said it was necessary to raise interest rates. The hike in interest rates meant that it cost American's more to buy products and goods on credit because of the increase in the interest rate at which they are borrowing.

This increase in the cost of borrowing money from your bank or credit card company usually discourages many people from buying that new car or sofa until they have all or most of the cash.

Slowing down the rate of spending and the demand for products — and ultimately the increase in the price of certain goods and services — means slowing down or stopping the increase of inflation.

The rise in interest rates means among other things that you are paying more when you carry a balance on your credit cards. Therefore the rise in interest rates will cause your debt to grow when you carry a balance on your credit cards.

Big Banks and Bad Government

What is hyperinflation?
Hyperinflation is "a condition of inflation that is so severe

— ranging from 1,000 percent to even 1 billion percent — that people try to get rid of their currency before prices render the money worthless. Technically, it is defined as a monthly inflation rate exceeding 50 percent."[10]

America could experience a period of hyperinflation because we are the biggest debtor nation in the world with a declining credit rating. Approximately 18 to 20 percent of the money our government borrows to keep operating each year comes from overseas.

When — due to our economic situation — it appears to our creditors (the nations who loan us money) that we will be unable to repay the massive amount of money we already owe them, much less the interest, they will cease lending us money.

What can we do to prevent that from happening? Pass a constitutional amendment requiring our lawmakers to balance the budget.

In early 1995, the Balanced Budget Amendment passed the House but failed to pass the Senate by one vote. The failure of the BBA Amendment sends the message to current and potential investors around the world that the United States is not interested in getting its financial house in order. Who can blame foreign investors for choosing to invest in the more stable Japanese yen or German mark instead of in a nation that acts financially irresponsible?

The other 78 to 80 percent of money our government borrows each year to make up for our yearly federal deficits comes from big U.S. banks like the Chase Manhattan Bank and individuals like you and me who buy U.S. Savings Bonds and other Treasury notes.

When you buy a T-bill, the federal government pays you interest on the money they have borrowed from you. Eventually millions of Americans will have good reason to believe that the federal government cannot repay what it has borrowed, plus interest. At that point many Americans will no longer purchase such T-bills, thus adding to the shrinking credit line of the federal government.

Around this same time, the big U.S. banks who have been loaning the federal government millions and millions of dollars each year, will deny the government's request for another loan. As a result, these big banks will not be willing to risk loosing money on a government that is on the verge of going bankrupt.

You need to know that these big U.S. banks have, over the past many years, made billions and billions of dollars in interest alone by loaning the federal government money each year.

I am a true capitalist and believe in the free market. There is nothing wrong with a U.S. bank loaning our federal government money and making large profits on the interest it charges. The problem and conflict of interest arises when those who own the big U.S. banks are involved in setting the interest rates via the Federal Reserve — thus causing the government to have to borrow more and more each year from their banks.

Today the Federal Reserve, a non-government institution, and the Federal Reserve banking system have tremendous control over our economy and, therefore, our nation.

President Andrew Jackson at one point abolished the Bank of the United States because he recognized the power and control such a centralized banking system could have over the country. President Jackson warned us not to ever accept such a system, saying, "the bold effort the present bank had made to control the government, the distress it had wantonly produced . . . are but premonitions of the fate that awaits the American people should they be deluded into a perpetuation of this institution or the establishment of another like it."

Funny Money

What will happen when other countries, the American people, and the big U.S. banks are no longer willing to loan money to the U.S. Government?

The federal government needs billions of dollars each year to make up for its short fall. Why? Because the federal government spends more than it makes. The difference must be obtained somehow, or the federal government will not be able to continue operating.

The government will have three options when it no longer has credit from the current three existing sources.

1. Default on all its loans.

2. Cut spending by 40 percent across the board. That means cutting Social Security, welfare, government employees, and every expenditure by 40 percent. In addition, the federal government will have to tax 50 percent of every American's income. That is just federal income tax, you will still have to pay your state income tax.

3. The federal government can simply tell the Treasury Department to print more money.

In order to get the money the government needs to continue operating, it will print more money. This is called "monetizing the debt."

Printing more paper money beyond what the economy can support will create inflation which can lead to hyperinflation. The paper money you now hold will become worth much less because there will be more of it in circulation.

Years ago, our paper money was backed up by gold and silver. Instead of carrying around gold and silver, the Treasury Department printed paper money called gold or silver certificates that represented the gold and silver that the federal government had in its vaults. If you desired, you could walk into your bank, hand them a ten dollar bill, and ask for $10 worth of gold. Try that today, and you will get a blank look from your teller.

Under his "New Deal," President Roosevelt took us off the gold standard making it easier for the social engineers to control and manipulate the economy. The gold and silver certificates were replaced with Federal Reserve notes, which is the paper money you now hold.

Larry Burkett gives this example:

> Think of the dollars you hold like stock in a company. Suppose a company with a total worth of $100,000 is authorized to issue 100 shares of stock. So you buy one share with assurance that it's worth $100 shares of stock. So you buy one share with assurance that it's worth $1,000 based on current value of the company. Later the com-

pany needs more capital, so the directors issue
100 more shares and sell them to the public for
$1,000 a share.

At first glance, you might think, well, it does-
n't hurt me. I still have my share worth of $1,000.

But is it really worth $1,000? If the company
is still valued at $100,000 and there are 200 shares
outstanding, your share is only worth $500.
However, it is possible that no one else know
that another 100 shares have been issued. The
"logical" thing to do in that case is to dump your
shares before the others discover the company
has diluted your stock by 50 percent.[11]

Due to the fact that our government can simply print
money at will, you are at great risk of having your money
drop in value. When the government prints paper money with
nothing of value backing it up, your money really becomes
funny money. In reality, the government is printing counterfeit
money.

You Ain't Seen Nothing Yet!

Millions of Americans who now live paycheck to paycheck
will — under such poor economic times — find themselves
unable to meet their daily needs for existence.

If you think we have a problem with crime today, you ain't
seen nothin yet! Just wait, and the growing numbers of have-
nots will be violently taking from those who have.

Crime in the big cities will be like scenes out of a fiction
movie. There is something to be said for living out in the
sticks on your own land where you can live and survive on
your hard work. Having a house and some land that is paid
for, along with a few good shot guns, might be the way to go.

Many of the middle class who lived in the city during the
great depression found themselves out of a job and standing in
soup lines. Those who lived on farms, which they owned,
were much more self-sufficient. Aside from buying sugar,
flour, and other such basics, there was very little they could

not raise on their own.

A big garden, a few chickens, a couple hens, a milk cow, a husband who is handy with tools, a wife who knows how to can food and sew — and you could survive. You would not be living the life of luxury, but you would survive. Compared to the situation many would find themselves in, you would be doing very well.

Unless the government decides to confiscate your farm and land because you violated one of the Environmental Protection Agencies petty regulations. But that's another book!

Give Us a Break!

In 1960, the average taxpayer worked 36 days to pay all of his or her taxes. In 1993, it took 123 days.

The American taxpayer now works four months to pay federal taxes and a fifth month to pay state and local taxes.

In 1994, The average taxpayer's "contribution" to the federal budget, based on an annual income of $38,000, operates our government for approximately one seventh of one second.

Florida and Texas, two states that have no state income tax and generally low property taxes, have led the way. According to a University of Florida study, these two states topped the nation in 1993-1994 in job growth.

Other positive approaches gaining in popularity are a national sales tax and a flat tax instead of the present income tax system. Income tax taxes hard work while a sales tax taxes consumption.

Why should you pay more taxes simply because you work hard, save, and create jobs? The guy who works as little as possible, sits around drinking beer and smoking, makes no real contribution to society or to the well being of our economy. Yet, he pays less in taxes under our current flat tax system than the individual who is hard working, frugal, and contributes to the economy by creating jobs or products.

Part of the problem with our current tax system — which uses a flat tax — is that it creates class envy. The "rich" are tired of the poor living off them, and the poor think the "rich" should pay more in taxes to guarantee them a better standard of living. The current system is one based on socialism — the re-distribution of wealth.

A national sales tax or consumption tax makes everyone equal. You are only taxed on what you consume. The more you consume, the more you pay in taxes; the less you consume, the less you pay in taxes. You decide when and how much you pay in taxes based on what and when you purchase that boat, car, stereo, or case of beer or carton of cigarettes.

Through this system the lazy, beer drinking, cigarette smoking, MTV types don't continue to get a free ride. At the same time, hard-working Americans are not punished for making a living and saving money.

Some people argue that a national sales tax would help only the rich. Not true. The poor would not be hurt by a national sales tax because housing, food, and medical care would be tax free.

Why a National Sales Tax?

What are the benefits of a national sales tax? A national sales tax will enable Americans to:

1. *Have access to more of their pay check* — instead of having big chunks taken out before they ever see what was earned.
2. *Decide when they will pay taxes* — based on what and when each individual or family wants to purchase an item.
3. *Save more money.* Presently, frugal savers are penalized because they are taxed on the interest they receive. A national sales tax would encourage people to invest their money.
4. *Create lower interest rates.* Increased saving would cause banks to lower interest rates in order to be competitive.
5. *Save millions of lost productive work hours* — hours that are now spent filling out complicated forms. It has been estimated that our national economy loses $200 billion dollars each year in lost productivity due to bureaucratic red tape.
6. *Abolish the IRS* — and put the $10 billion dollars allotted for their yearly budget to better use. In its place, the government would create a National Sales Tax Office.
7. *Put an end to the "underground economy,"* operated by

those who do all their business in cash to avoid paying taxes — like drug dealers. They would have to pay taxes like the rest of us when they purchase a new Mercedes or speed boat.

8. *Do away with the inheritance tax.* Many families end up loosing the farm or business their fathers or grandfathers worked for years to leave behind. Why? Because they are required to sell all or half of the farm or business to satisfy the inheritance tax — which can be as high as 50% of the property's value.

9. *Stimulate the economy.* With more money in their pockets, Americans will be more likely to purchase the things they need.

10. *Lessen impulse buying.* The idea of having to pay tax on everything we buy, however, should make us think twice before purchasing things we don't need.

These are only a few of the positive results that a national sales tax could have on American families — and on our economy in general. I suggest you write your congressman and senators and get their opinion on this important issue.

The Quest for the American Dream

Every young couple who falls in love and gets married desires to achieve the "American Dream." While the definition of the American dream differs, for most couples it means owning your own house, two cars, a dog, raising two children, and living at a standard that is equal or exceeds that of their parents.

Obtaining the American dream is harder today than ever. Why is that? In my estimation, there are two main reasons

First, I believe that many young couples start their lives together having never been taught how to properly manage their money. For this reason they wake up one day to realize the American dream they were pursuing has turned into a financial nightmare.

Whether you have been around the block a few times or find yourself well down the road of life, the principles I am about to discuss may be familiar to you.

I am continually shocked, however, when I meet people

who know these basic financial principles yet do not practice them. In that case, I hope this information will cause you to sit down and re-evaluate your finances and how you can become debt free and prosperous.

The second reason I believe the American dream is harder to achieve today than ever before is due to the ever-growing power and intrusion of both state and federal government.

While in San Antonio, Texas this year, my friend Steve Troxel, who is the senior pastor of large church there, shared this amusing story with me. It highlights the point I am trying to make.

> A church had a stewardship drive, and one of the members sent the pastor the following letter: "Dear pastor, in reply to your request to send a check, I wish to inform you that the present condition of my bank account makes it almost impossible. My shattered financial condition is due to federal laws, state laws, county laws, corporation laws, mother-in-laws, brother-in-laws, and outlaws.
>
> Through these laws, I am compelled to pay a business tax, amusement tax, head tax, school tax, gas tax, light tax, water tax, sales tax, even my brains are taxed. I am required to contribute to every organization or society that the genius of man is capable of bringing to life. Women's relief, unemployment relief, every hospital and charitable institution in the city — including the Red Cross, the purple cross, and the double cross.
>
> For my own safety I am required to carry life insurance, earthquake insurance, property insurance, liability insurance, accident insurance, burglar insurance, business insurance, tornado insurance, unemployment insurance, fire insurance. I am inspected, expected, respected, dejected, examined, reexamined, informed, reformed, summoned, fined, com-

> manded, and compelled until I supply an inex-
> haustible supply of money for every known
> need, desire, or hope of the human race.
>
> Simply because I refuse to donate some-
> thing or other, I'm boycotted, talked about, lied
> about, held up, held down, robbed until I am
> ruined! I can tell you honestly, had not the
> unexpected happened I could not enclose this
> check. The wolf that comes to so many doors
> now-a-days just had pups in the kitchen, I sold
> them, and here's the money.

Many entrepreneurs are finding it increasingly difficult to
start and maintain a business because of all the red tape. You
can hardly sneeze today unless you have a permit.

To make matters worse, the legal system is out of control.
Every American has a good chance of being sued at least once
in their lifetime. Owning a business today, however, puts you
at even greater risk of finding yourself involved in a meritless
law suit.

The law suits being filed against big and small business
today is not simply the work of individuals but of state governments, the federal government, and extreme activist
groups. Many ridiculous laws keep small, medium, and big
businesses — and many families — from reaching their full
productivity and potential.

I Want It Now!

On the road to achieving their dreams, most couples make
the mistake of thinking that in order to achieve the American
dream they must go into debt. This ultimately has led to many
shattered dreams and worst of all many broken homes and
marriages.

Americans are unaware that interest is eating them alive.
Not only is the interest on our national debt threatening
America's future for generations to come, debt and compounding interest in personal finances has eliminated hope for
many of ever having a secure future.

Most Americans will never enjoy true prosperity and financial security because they are in debt. Much of this debt is due to paying interest on the money they have borrowed to finance their desired standard of living.

Notice that I said "desired" standard of living and not "necessary" standard of living. Americans have a "I want it now" way of thinking and managing their finances that causes them to pay for an item two or three times over the real cost just so they can have it today.

John Cummuta in his book, *Debt Free and Prosperous Living*, gives this example of how buying an item on credit instead of waiting until you can pay cash for it can costs you dearly:

> Suppose you bought $2,000 worth of furniture on a typical credit card, (a credit card that charges you 19.8% interest plus a $40 annual fee), and paid only the minimum monthly payments requested by the credit card company, it would take you 31 years and 2 months to pay it off. Plus — in addition to the original $2,000 cost for the furniture — you would have paid $8,202 in interest! Long after you had thrown the furniture out, you would be draining your wealth away paying for it. In this example, using a credit card would cause you to pay five times the furniture's value!

Simply being willing to *wait* until you had the $2,000 would have saved you over $8,000. Most people can certainly live with their old furniture until they can save $2,000 even if that means waiting six months or even a year.

The more than $8,000 dollars you would have paid in interest could have been put toward paying off your house. By paying off your house earlier, through wise management of your resources, you can save literally thousands and thousands of dollars.

Because of mismanagement and the "I want it now" way of living, most Americans are paying thousands of dollars toward interest simply because they do not have enough self control to wait until they can pay cash.

Paying Three Times for a House

If Americans managed their resources correctly and waited until they were financially ready, most could either pay for their house with cash or put down a large sum of cash as a down payment. That would enable them to pay for their home in a few years as opposed to waiting 30 years.

You may be thinking, How much does he think I make a year? The problem is not with how much you make, but with how much you spend. Most people maintain a standard of living that is beyond what they can afford. In other words, most Americans spend what they make and more.

Maybe you could not buy a home that cost $185,000 and pay cash or even pay for half of it with cash. If you are in such a situation — and you were honest with yourself — you are probably wanting or living in a home that is beyond your means — at least beyond *sound* financial means.

Getting a 30-year mortgage and taking the entire 30 years to pay off your home is not the smart thing to do. If it will take you 30 years to pay for your home, you need to do a reality check. Should you really have bought and continue to live in a home that will take you 30 years to pay for?

Remember, the banks and credit card companies do not want you to face reality. Why? Because they make their money by selling you their money and the lie, "You can afford it."

Author John Cummuta writes, "If you buy a home with a 30-year conventional or adjustable rate mortgage, you will pay for that loan about three times."

That means that two-thirds of that total is interest. That's 200 percent interest!

If you buy a $250,000 home, with a $200,000 mortgage, you will end up paying about $600,000 over 30 years. This means you will pay nearly a half million dollars in interest!"

In this very realistic example, you would have been working for many, many years in order to pay your bank $400,000 for loaning you $200,000. Instead of getting rich and becoming debt free, you would have been working to make your bank rich.

A Good Investment?

I am often intrigued when I hear someone say, "You should buy a house, It is such a good investment." At one time, that was true. Today, it takes real planning for the average American to make money on the purchase of a house.

Most people think if they buy a house for a set price and sell it for a few thousand dollars more, they have turned a profit. Most forget that they had to pay interest on the money they borrowed. Add in the interest, and most people quickly find that they did not turn a profit on the purchase and selling of their home.

Don't get me wrong, I am not trying to discourage anyone from buying a house. If you have done your homework and are buying within your means, and you are buying for the right reasons, then you will be happy in your new home. If, however, you are buying for an investment — unless you know exactly what you are doing and are very disciplined — you may be disappointed in the return on your investment.

In today's economy, the value of homes in most cities is not increasing enough to counterbalance the investment with the cost of interest paid. In many cities, the housing market is not increasing at all but is, in fact, declining.

For many years, anyone hoping to buy a home in the Los Angeles area had to have a small fortune. Those who paid a high price for their house are now gritting their teeth as they see the value of their home decline. Those who bought homes before or during the time when the value of homes was rising and sold at the right time, walked away with a tidy profit.

In the 1990s, turning a profit on a home is not impossible, but to do so requires serious planning.

Many couples purchase a home and are not quick to pay off their mortgage because of the belief that it is a great tax shelter.

John Cummuta, however, explains away this myth:

> If you have an accountant who tells you that
> you should never pay off your mortgage,
> "Because it is the last tax shelter for the aver-

age consumer," get a new accountant. Think about what they're saying. Let me translate it for you. They're really saying, "Keep on paying a dollar of interest to get back 28 cents in tax deductions."[12]

The $500,000 House

Money is most certainly just a medium of exchange. A house that you can eventually call your own can bring great satisfaction. Money is simply the means by which you acquire that desired house. By applying sound financial principles based on common sense, you can own that home and not pay two to three times the asking price.

Do you know anyone who wants to pay $300,000 for a $100,000 home because of interest? If you can have the $100,000 home and only pay $150,000 for it, with interest, then why not do so? If you plan ahead, it is actually possible to pay no interest or very little.

Remember, the bank or mortgage company wants you to take years to pay off your house because they make their money by charging you interest.

John Cummuta puts it all in perspective with this example. If you borrow $100,000 from your local bank to purchase that house, over the course of 30 years you will pay your bank around $200,000 in interest plus the initial $100,000 you borrowed. Just how long would it take you to earn $300,000?

If you make $25,000 a year, it would take you 12 years to make $300,000 right? Wrong. Remember you have to pay taxes on that $25,000 dollars. That $25,000 is your gross salary before taxes.

In order to pay your bank $300,000, you would have to make around $500,000 before taxes. If you make $25,000 a year, it would take you 20 years to make $500,000 before taxes. From that $500,000 you will have to pay taxes. After taxes you would have just enough left over to pay your bank the $200,000 in interest you owe, plus the initial $100,000 you borrowed.

If you fall into a low tax bracket, you may have to earn just

$400,000 to pay $200,000 in interest and to pay back the initial $100,000 you borrowed. Either way, you are going to have to make around half a million dollars before taxes in order to pay your bank $300,000.

How to Pay Off Your Debts

The social engineers in our country have done so much damage that I believe, as do many, that a severe economic downturn or collapse is inevitable.

By practicing sound financial concepts, you can find yourself out of debt and with a cost of living that is next to nothing. Remember, in a free society no one can take away from you what you own. If an economic downturn means you loose your job, it does not mean you have to loose your home and car.

Most people spend their entire lives in debt because they simple do not know how to manage money. The next time you go to purchase an item, ask yourself, "Do I need this or do I just want it?"

Unless you are buying a house or a car, a good rule to follow is: If you cannot pay cash for it, then you don't need it.

You and I both know people who will get a pre-approved credit card in the mail and go right out and charge up the full limit. If a large part of your budget every month goes to paying off debts and credit cards, the majority of your monthly budget is going to pay for interest you are being charged on the money you borrowed.

Let's say you have two credit cards. One is a department store credit card and one is a national credit card. You owe $1,000 dollars on your department store card and $2,500 on your national credit card. For sometime now, you have simply been paying the minimum required on both cards.

I challenge you to look at your budget and find $200 you can cut from your budget. That may mean you don't go golfing for awhile or to the movies and out to eat. Make some sacrifices and cut $200 from your monthly budget. Maybe you will need to put in a little overtime at work or develop a little business on the side. Even that is probably not necessary if you are willing to make the needed sacrifices.

Take your smallest debt — or the one that has the lowest interest rate — which in this example is your department store credit card. Let's say the minimum monthly payment is $75. Take the $200 you cut from your monthly budget and begin paying $275 each month on your department store credit card until you have the entire balance paid off.

What about your national credit card? Let's assume your minimum monthly payment on that credit card has been $100. Take the $275 you were spending each month to pay off your department store credit card and combine that with the minimum payment of $100 that you have been paying on your national credit card and begin paying $375 each month on the balance you owe on your national credit card until the balance is paid in full.

Now take the $375 you were spending to pay off your national credit card and add that to your monthly car payment of $250. You are now paying back $625 each month instead of $250. Before long you will have your car paid for, and save hundreds of dollars on interest for the money you were borrowing from your bank, local department store, and national credit card company.

Once your car is paid off, take that $625 a month and add that to your monthly mortgage, which is let's say, $600. You are now paying $1,225 each month on your mortgage.

In not too many years, you will be debt free. Over the course of a few years, you will have easily saved yourself thousands of dollars. I am talking about real dollars that you would have been sending to your credit card companies and bank, most of which were simply interest payments.

Once all these debts are paid off, you can take that $1,225 each month and put it in sound investments. In just two years, you will have put away in an interest bearing account $29,400. Remember this does not include the interest that has been accruing on your account over the past 24 months.

The next time you need to purchase a car, you can simply pay cash. But, be sure you use good sense and buy a vehicle that suits your needs and at the best price possible. Do not take your $29,400 and spend it all on a new car if you can pick up a nice used car a year or two old for $10,000.

Protect Yourself

We have just barely scratched the surface in how to best manage your finances. I would highly suggest you order the entire cassette tape, video, and manual series by John Cummuta titled, *The Debt-Free and Prosperous Living Basic Course.* (See the list of recommended resources in Chapter 12, "The Revolutionary's Survival Guide.")

You can have the American dream without obtaining it through the most common American way — debt. Don't let those who make their money by taking yours convince you there is no other way. There is another way. It is the common sense way that is so uncommon in today's "I want it now" society.

By planning ahead and using wisdom, you can protect your family's future and well-being no matter what America's social engineers do to our economy. Yes, it will affect you, but you do not have to be ruined and find yourself and your family on the street standing in a soup line.

Wake up and take action now before you discover your American dream has turned into a financial nightmare.

Notes

[1] Larry Burkett, *The Coming Economic Earthquake*, (Chicago, Il: Moody Press, 1991, 1994), p. 11.

[2] Harry E. Figgie, Jr., *Bankruptcy 1995, The Coming Collapse of America and How to Stop It*, (Boston, MA: Little Brown and Company, 1992), front page.

[3] Ibid;, p. 22.

[4] Larry Burkett, *The Coming Economic Earthquake*, (Chicago, Il: Moody Press, 1991, 1994), p. 149.

[5] David Barton, *The Myth of Separation*, (Aledo, TX: Wallbuider Press, 1992).

[6] Ibid;, p. 22.

[7] "The Phyllis Schlafly Report," October 1004, Vol 28, No. 3

[8] IBid;, p. 9.

[9] Ibid;, p. 84.

[10] Harry Figgie Jr., *Bankruptcy 1995*, (Little Brown and Company, Boston, Mass., 1992), p. 189.

[11] Larry Burkett, *The Coming Ecomomic Earthquake* (Chicago: Moody Press, 1991, 1994), p. 159.

[12] John Cummuta, *Debt Free and Prosperous Living*, (Marketline Press, Algonquin, IL., 1991-1994), p. 3.

10

What Makes America, American

An important battle now being fought will affect the future heart and soul of our nation. At stake is America's religious freedoms, moral foundation, and worldview.

In the July 28, 1994 *Los Angeles Times*, Ronald Brownstein wrote in an article titled, "Dissatisfied Public May Spell Democrat Losses," that 53 percent of Americans believe the moral problems facing our country are more important than the economic problems.

One survey indicates that 80 percent of Americans believe there is a problem of declining morality within our nation.[1]

America is at a crossroads, and the path that is chosen will have a lasting impact on the future of this nation. We will continue to see a downward trend in our nation's morality as long as our nation continues to permit the only accepted form of bigotry permitted today to continue — religious bigotry.

Americans need to stand up for and reaffirm the faith of our fathers. Today, a civil war rages in Congress, in the courts, and in our schools.

Why do I believe that this battle for religious freedom will so greatly affect the future of this nation? Because as a nation we can only embrace and govern on the basis of one of two worldviews. We as a people will either embrace the Christian worldview or the secular humanist worldview. There is no middle ground.

This is not a new battle. In fact, it has been on-going since the Garden of Eden. This conflict of the ages has always been between what is right and what is wrong, what is just and what is unjust, what is good and what is evil, what makes men free and what makes them slaves.

The Christian worldview was the basis and foundation on which the founding fathers built the United States of America. Lenin, however, used the secular humanist worldview to base his ideology.

A Religious People

Fyodor Dostoyevsky in his book, *Crime and Punishment*, wrote, "If God is dead, then everything is permitted."

If there is no God, then humanism, which is based on the belief that man is god, is the moral standard. In other words, man can decide for himself what is right and what is wrong through a relativistic, humanistic worldview.

If, however, there is a Creator, as America's founding fathers believed and wrote in Declaration of Independence, then man is not god and is subject to set standards as prescribed by the Creator. Man is also obligated not only to live but to govern in a manner consistent with God's laws and standards.

The standards prescribed by the Creator are spelled out in the most important book of our western culture, the *Holy Bible*. Those who believe in God the Creator and His moral standards of right and wrong, i.e. the Ten commandments, are embracing the Christian worldview either knowingly or unknowingly.

Those of us who believe in God and seek to follow and live out the Judeo-Christian faith realize that we are not the minority that the media and cultural elite would have us to believe. Gallop surveys over the past two decades reveal that fully 85 percent of Americans consider themselves to be following the Christian faith. On an average Sunday in America, 106 million Americans attend church.

Americans need not apologize to the cultural elite for their religious convictions, no matter how strong. Indeed, it was a group of gun-toting church-going Christians who gave us the greatest nation on the face of the earth.

If you doubt me when I say that this nation was founded on the Christian worldview by people who considered themselves to be following the "Christian faith," then you do not know the facts.

Dr. D. James Kennedy in his book, *Character and Destiny,* provides interesting data about the people who founded our nation:

> As late as 1776, fully 98 percent of the people in this country professed to be Protestant Christians; 1.8 percent said they were Roman Catholics; and .2 percent said they were Jewish. Now, if you add those numbers up you will find that 99.8 percent of the people in this nation declared themselves to be Christians.
>
> As an indication of the beliefs of all thirteen colonies at that time, the Constitution of the State of Delaware required that all office holders swear in public, "I do profess faith in God the Father, and in the Lord Jesus Christ His only Son, and in the Holy Ghost . . . and I do acknowledge the Holy Scriptures of the Old and New Testaments to be given by divine inspiration."

In 1892, the Supreme Court ruled in the case, *Church of the Holy Trinity v. United States,* that:

> Our laws and our institutions must necessarily be based upon and embody the teachings of The Redeemer of mankind. It is impossible that it should be otherwise; and in this sense and to this extent our civilization and our institutions are emphatically Christian. . . . This is a religious people. This is historically true. From the discovery of this continent to the present

hour, there is a single voice making this affirmation . . . we find everywhere a clear recognition of the same truth . . . these, and many
other matters which might be noticed, add a
volume of unofficial declarations to the mass
of organic utterances that this is a Christian
nation.

Again, in 1931, the United States Supreme Court declared,
in the case of *United States v. Macintosh,* that "we are a
Christian people." And in 1952, even the liberal justice,
William O. Douglas, declared from the bench that "we are a
religious people and our institutions presuppose a Supreme
Being."[2]

Who Gave Us Liberty?

In 1774, while serving in the Virginia Assembly, Thomas
Jefferson personally introduced a resolution calling for a day
of fasting and prayer. Later, while serving as the Governor of
Virginia (1779-1781), Jefferson decreed a day of: "Public and
solemn thanksgiving and prayer to the Almighty God."[3]

Engraved on the Jefferson Memorial in Washington D.C.
are these famous words by Thomas Jefferson, the author of the
Declaration of Independence and our third President:

God who gave us life gave us liberty. And can
the liberties of a nation be thought secure when
we have removed their only firm basis, a conviction in the minds of the people that these
liberties are of the gift of God? That they are
not to be violated but with His wrath? Indeed, I
tremble for my country when I reflect that God
is just; that His justice cannot sleep forever.

We must recommit ourselves as a nation and a people to
the convictions of our Christian worldview.

John Adams, who served as our nation's first Vice

President under George Washington for eight years and then as the second President of the United States, so believed in the relevancy of the Bible that he wrote the following in his diary on February 22, 1756:

> Suppose a nation in some distant region should take the Bible for their only law book, and every member should regulate his conduct by the precepts there exhibited! Every member would be obliged in conscience to temperance, frugality, and industry; to justice, kindness, and charity towards his fellow man; and to piety, love, and reverence toward Almighty God. . . . What a Utopia, what a Paradise would this region be.

John Adams also said, "We have no government capable of dealing with an irreligious people." In other words, those who disregard religion are disregarding what makes America, America.

I could fill hundreds of pages with quotes from our founding fathers proving that they both publicly and privately believed in and possessed the Christian worldview. Many of our founding fathers were convinced that as long as we as a nation held onto and protected our Christian heritage, we would flourish. Likewise, they also believed that if we denied and rejected our Christian heritage, it would be the death of this nation they so loved.

George Washington Wrote:

> We ought to be no less persuaded that the propitious smiles of Heaven can never be expected on a nation that disregards the eternal rules of order and right which Heaven itself has ordained.[4]

George Washington also wrote: "It is impossible to rightly govern the world without God and the Bible."[5]

Benjamin Franklin wrote: "Whoever shall introduce into

public affairs the principles of primitive Christianity will change the face of the world."[6]

On June 20, 1785, James Madison wrote, "Religion [is] the basis and foundation of Government."[7] Several years later, on March 4, 1809, President James Madison said in his Inaugural address, "We have all been encouraged to feel in the guardianship and guidance of that Almighty Being, whose power regulates the destiny of nations."[8]

It is overwhelmingly clear from these few examples that our founding fathers knew just how important it was to the preservation of our nation that our Christian heritage and foundations not be eroded.

Even though our founders knew how important our Christian heritage was — and with a 99.8 percent Christian majority — still a state religion was not mandated. Our founders wanted freedom *of* religion, not as the liberals claim, freedom *from* religion. The founders did not want our nation to deny its heritage, but they wanted everyone to be free to practice and express their religious convictions and beliefs.

The "Separation" Myth

The "wall of separation" between church and state is a myth. In recent years, this myth has gone from protecting us from a state-mandated religion to denying people their constitutional right to practice their religion publicly. The ultimate result of the myth of separation has been the creating of a state-mandated religion, best known as humanism.

In two different cases, the United States Supreme court has written in footnotes to decisions handed down that humanism has a religious tone. Today, this religion is not excluded but promoted aggressively in our nation's government schools at your expense.

My friend and mentor, Dr. D. James Kennedy, put it best when he said,

> The idea of separation of church and state has been abused by judges and juries for the past 50 years, but one thing is undeniably clear: If

> teachers in public schools can't teach Johnny
> about Christianity and if they can't say that
> Jesus Christ is alive today or that faith in God
> is a good idea, then they certainly cannot teach
> their students the exact opposite, either.[9]

Yet, our schools continue to promote and teach the humanist religion that denies God as the Creator and sets man up as his own god.

Despite what the liberal ACLU says, the religious foundation of our nation gave *more* liberty to everyone not *less* as they would have us believe. Our founding fathers did so for good reason. They knew the lessons of history, as Dr. D. James Kennedy writes:

> History teaches that great nations are seldom if
> ever destroyed by invaders or other outside
> forces. Wars and invasions may be involved in
> their final collapse, but nations fall because of
> compromise of their own foundational beliefs,
> loss of faith in the values that made them great,
> and the lawlessness and disorder that arise as a
> result.[10]

Public schools are now government schools that forbid the posting of the Ten Commandments. Bible reading, even from a historical standpoint, is prohibited, and prayer is banned along with any Judeo Christian symbols.

We have compromised our foundational beliefs as a nation and a people, creating a society on the verge of moral collapse — one where crime is rampant in our streets, babies are legally murdered in their mothers' wombs, and divorce is as common and easy as ordering a pizza.

Safety Net or Hammock?

Part of our Christian heritage has always been personal responsibility and morality. With these two characteristics missing, America has become a welfare program out of control. Unwed mothers are financially rewarded for having more and more children out of wedlock. Couples who get married and have children are assessed a heavy tax for simply choosing to do the respectable and responsible thing.

Untold numbers of welfare and entitlement recipients are having their immoral and irresponsible lifestyles funded by a government that has chosen not to hold individuals to a high standard of personal responsibility and decency.

Psychologists and other misguided "professionals" only worsen the problem by "discovering" a new disorder or disability for every negative human failing. Sure, there are those who have problems and disabilities, but such real problems end up being ignored or not taken seriously by the general public because of the over-use of psycho-babble terms and victimization grouping and labeling.

This nation is being destroyed from the inside. How much longer can our nation continue down this road before we realize that the damage we are doing is increasingly irreversible?

America needs to recommit itself to the heritage that made it great — a heritage that was clearly based on a Christian worldview, a strong faith in God, and in His moral principles and standards of hard work, personal responsibility, right and wrong, good and evil, just and unjust.

Certainly we need to have compassion, but today's welfare programs are based not on compassion but on socialism. At times there are those who need a little help to get back on their feet, but as one talk show host has said, "The safety net has turned into a hammock."

There is a clear difference between compassion and encouraging and rewarding irresponsibility, immorality and laziness.

Rights Without Responsibilities

The same individuals who scream that you and I are not compassionate enough are the same group of liberals who have been behind cases where compassion, understanding, and the protection of Constitutional rights have been extremely absent.

The rights of many Americans — which are so basic that the framers of the Constitution called them self-evident — have been denied. Yet, if you and I are in favor of welfare reform, we are accused of depriving certain individuals of their so-called "rights" even though these "rights" are not granted nor protected by the Constitution.

As Dr. D. James Kennedy has written, today's young people "have been taught that their heritage of freedom gives them plenty of 'rights' but very few responsibilities."[11]

Liberals who steal our Constitutional rights are hailed by the liberal press as being advocates for equality. Yet, when a conservative tries to defend the Constitution and limit special privileges and treatment for a few, which is often times not in the best interest of the majority, we are called mean-spirited hate-mongers.

In some cases, states and/or the federal government has aggressively attached and harassed conservative groups or individuals with audits, law suits, and threats. Often such harassment is leveled at those who have — with great strength and courage — dared to stand up and defend the Christian worldview on which this nation was built.

Why should America be forced to become a secular nation when the majority of Americans are not secular in their religious beliefs. In addition, there is nothing beneficial about being a secular nation. In fact, history proves that it is detrimental to the future of a nation to reject certain principals and standards just because they can be traced back to a religious foundation.

Time magazine published a cover story on December 9, 1991, titled, "One Nation, Under God," in which they asked the question: "Has the separation of church and state gone too far?" The writer for *Time* obviously felt it had when he wrote:

> For God to be kept out of the classroom or out of America's public debate by nervous school administrators or overcautious politicians serves no one's interests. That restriction prevents people from drawing on this country's rich and diverse religious heritage for

guidance, and it degrades the nation's moral discourse by placing a whole realm of theological reasoning out of bounds. The price of that sort of quarantine, at a time of moral dislocation, is — and has been — far too high. The courts need to find a better balance between separation and accommodation — and Americans need to respect the new religious freedom they would gain as a result.

Religion plays an important part in every nation's history and destiny, as Dr. D. James Kennedy explains in his book, *Character and Destiny:*

> Every nation that has ever existed has been built upon some sort of religious foundation. Whether it is the Hinduism of India, the Islam of Saudi Arabia, the Confucianism of China, the Shintoism of Japan, the Judaism of Israel . . . every nation had some form of religious commitment that contributed to its greatness. But while the government, the courts, the ACLU, the liberal American Bar Association, and the Trial Lawyers of America are doing everything in their power to strip away our moral values and religious rights, the government is stripping Americans of their property, their incomes, their rights of self-determination, and ultimately their hopes for the future.

This is exactly where we find ourselves today.

The Galveston Gestapo

What would you think if I told you a judge in Galveston, Texas ruled that any student mentioning the name of Jesus in a graduation prayer would be sentenced to a six-month jail term?

You would say, "That's unconstitutional!"

That is exactly what parents and community leaders said when Judge Samuel B. Kent of the U.S. District Court for the Southern District of Texas ruled concerning the Santa Fe Independent School District. These are the judge's own words taken directly from court papers on May 5, 1995:

> The court will allow that prayer to be a typical nondenominational prayer, which can refer to God or the Almighty or that sort of thing. The prayer may not refer to a specific deity by name, whether it be Jesus, Buddha, Mohammed, the great god Sheba, or anyone else.
>
> And make no mistake, the court is going to have a United States marshal in attendance at the graduation. If any student offends this court, that student will be summarily arrested and will face up to six months incarceration in the Galveston County Jail for contempt of Court. Anyone who thinks I'm kidding about this order . . . [or] expressing any weakness or lack of resolve in that spirit of compromise would better think again. Anyone who violates these orders, no kidding, is going to wish that he or she had died as a child when this Court gets through with it.

I wonder if the judge would have been so outraged if a student had gone to the podium and used the name of Jesus as a swear word?

The judge, obviously suffering from delusions of grandeur, did not stop with oppressing students' rights to free speech. He went on to limit the rights of school teachers and administrators to attend, organize, or promote a private baccalaureate service:

> Now the Court is going to further order that a baccalaureate service on or about May 21, 1995 . . . not occur during school hours or as

> part of normal school functions. Since it's on a
> Sunday, that's frankly academic.
>   This Court is further going to order that
> school administration, personnel or the like
> will not sanction nor . . . have any role in
> announcing it, promulgating it, in planning it,
> in participating in it. Teachers, administrators
> and the like can certainly attend as passive
> spectators, but they will sit in the spectators'
> gallery and . . . cannot sit in any designated
> place of honor or in the first row or on any
> table specifically designated. . . .

This judge apparently believes that employees of the public schools are wards of the state who must completely separate themselves from all religious expression.

Five days after this ruling, Judge Kent — seeking to save face in the light of great public outrage and fearing that a higher court would overturn his Gestapo tactics — ruled that graduates could use the name of Jesus but not in a proselytizing manner.

What if no one had objected to Judge Kent's blatant unconstitutional order? Fortunately, there are still students, teachers, and community leaders who have the courage to stand up against high-minded government officials who seek to rob us our constitutional rights. America needs more citizens who will demand the removal of judges who seek to limit or destroy our religious freedoms.

Attacks of the Thought Police

George Orwell in his book, *1984*, called those who censored our thoughts and beliefs, "thought police." The thought police, which are really the cultural elite, are constantly on patrol looking for another opportunity to let loose the ACLU lawyers — who are eager to go to court in hopes of convincing many of our liberal judges to hand down one more freedom robbing court decision.

During the Summer of 1994, the Equal Employment

Opportunity Commission proposed regulations that would have restricted religious liberty in the work place. It was predicted by some legal experts that wearing a cross at work or leaving a Bible on your desk would have been prohibited under the EEOC guidelines.

Thankfully, due to hundreds of letters and phone calls, the EEOC voted on September 19, 1993, with a vote of 3 to 0 to withdraw the proposed regulations. That's one victory for Americans in our battle for faith and freedoms.

Other skirmishes take place every day.

On December 5, 1994, a special briefing memo from Gary Bauer, President of the Family Research Council, reported that the postal service had ordered its employees not to say "Merry Christmas" to their customers.

In a city park in San Jose, California, a $500,000 statute of Quetzalcoatl, an Aztec god was erected, but in early December 1994, a Nativity scene had to be removed from the same park.

> In Selkirk, New York, a third-grade teacher
> stopped a child from reading the Bible in her
> free reading time. The child was threatened
> and, in tears, she was told never to bring the
> forbidden book to school again.[12]

In Nevada, an elementary school student chosen to sing a solo in the school's Christmas pageant was forbidden from singing "The First Noel" because of its religious overtones.[13]

> In the case of *Reed V. Van Hoven*, in 1965, the
> court ruled that if a student in a public school
> prays over his lunch, it is unconstitutional for
> him to pray aloud.[14]

Many court decisions have the potential to effect great change nationally. For instance, the November 1980 Kentucky Court decision led to the 1985 U.S. Supreme Court ruling that the Ten Commandments could not be posted in the public school room.

The ACLU Agenda

Where there is the attack on religious liberty, you can bet the ACLU is involved either directly or indirectly. This is part of the agenda the ACLU hopes to legitimize in America:

- Legalization of child pornography
- Abortion on demand
- Tax exemptions for satanists
- Totally legalized drug use
- Mandatory sex education for all grades
- Legalized prostitution
- Legalized gambling
- Giving gays and lesbians all the legal benefits that married people have.
- Letting homosexuals become adoptive and foster parents
- Unconditional legal protection for flag-burners
- Greater benefits for illegal aliens and homosexuals who want to enter the U.S.

What is the ACLU against? Everything you and I support:

- Prayer in public school classrooms, as well as in locker rooms, sports arenas, graduation exercises, courtrooms, and legislative assemblies
- Nativity scenes, crosses, and other Christian symbols on public property
- Voluntary Bible reading in public schools, even during free time and after classes
- Imprinting "in God we trust" on our coins
- Access for Christian school children to any publicly funded services
- Accreditation for science departments at Bible-believing Christian universities
- The posting of the Ten Commandments in classrooms or courtrooms

- The words "under God" in the Pledge of Allegiance
- School officials searching students' lockers for drugs or guns
- People on welfare being required to work in exchange for their government aid
- Tax exemptions for Christian churches, ministries, and other charities
- Rating movies to alert parents about sex or violence
- Christians home-schooling their children
- Medical safety regulations and reporting of AIDS cases
- Public pro-life demonstrations
- Laws banning polygamy[15]

Bureaucrats, however, don't even need the help of the ACLU. Sometimes, they just write the laws themselves.

Dr. D. James Kennedy in his book, *Character and Destiny,* writes about an attempt in 1992 by some of our nation's agents of change to implement one more unconstitutional, freedom-robbing, power grab.

> In 1992, a friend sent me an article clipped from the newspaper in Richmond, Virginia, which described the effort of a group in the United States Treasury Department to slip a clause into the federal budget that would give the IRS authority to examine church records and even to confiscate them, to get the names and addresses of every person claiming a contribution of more than $500 a year to the church. This was not a legislative procedure, nor was it a matter brought before Congress. It was a subtle attempt to slip this into the budget unseen and, thus, to create a bureaucratic principle with the weight of law.
>
> When I read the article, I immediately called Vice President Dan Quayle about the

matter. He said he had just learned of the documents and was already taking steps to halt passage of this element of the budget. He had spoken to the President about it, and neither of
them was aware that such a statement had
been included in that thousand-plus-page document. They discovered that the offending
paragraph had been drafted by someone in the
Treasury Department, and they were outraged.
It was simply an attempt by unscrupulous
bureaucrats to pass into law a measure that
was clearly and historically unconstitutional.[16]

No "Friends" at West High

In early June 1995, the 10th U.S. Circuit Court of Appeals
issued a restraining order against West High School students
in Salt Lake City, Utah. The restraining order came after a
Jewish student at the school, sixteen-year-old Rachel
Bauchman, and her parents sued to prohibit the school's choir
from singing two traditional songs that contained the words,
"Lord" and "God."

Rachel and her parents felt that the two songs referred to
the Christian God and, therefore, the songs were equal to a
prayer and thus a violation of the First Amendment.

The school complied to the restraining order, and the choir
did not sing the two prohibited songs at the school's graduation ceremony.

A graduating student by the name of William Badger,
however, thought the court ruling was bogus and refused to
comply. William got up on the stage and invited the choir and
the audience to sing one of the forbidden songs titled
"Friends." Written by Michael W. Smith, the song contains the
following words in its chorus, "Friends are friends forever if
the Lord's the Lord of them."

The other forbidden song was "The Lord Bless You and
Keep You."

Syndicated columnist Cal Thomas, in writing about this
incident, noted: "It is hard to believe that a court would con-

sider a reference to 'God' and 'Lord' a Christian reference when the Jewish prophets, including Moses, repeatedly referred to God by these names."

The removal of young William Badger from the stage by a school official was captured on video and re-played on the national network news. Because of William's courageous action, however, he was not permitted to receive his diploma during the ceremony.

> Outraged parents castigated the school from the audience and in the newspapers. Sally Brinton, the mother of a 16-year-old student, said her family had just returned from Beijing and she was stunned to learn this was happening in the United States.[17]

The action taken by the 10th U.S. Circuit Court of Appeals was wrong, and the footage of a young American being physically removed from his own graduation ceremony for being bold in the face of adversity is discouraging, but the greatest outrage of all was what followed.

An article published in the *Washington Times* reported that "the administration is going to study videotape of the ceremony to determine which of the students sang the forbidden words. They can't do anything about graduating seniors, but underclassmen will be interrogated and could be subjected to punishment, including forced community service."

Freedom "from religion" and "diversity" is tearing America apart.

The June 11, 1995 *Desert News* from Salt Lake Utah reveals that William Badger was not the only courageous student that day:

> Just after student William Badger rushed the podium and encouraged students and the audience to sing "Friends," 17-year-old Jenny Naylor began playing the piano, leading the group in the song that had been barred by the 10th Circuit Court of Appeals.

Soon after she began playing, West High
School counselor Lorraine Hargraves tried to
stop Jenny Naylor from playing and eventually
accompanied her off the stage and into a back
room in Abravanel Hall.

When asked about the incident Jenny responded, "She
came over and tried to yank my wrists off the piano . . . I tried
to keep playing and so she grabbed my wrists . . it hurt. She
shoved me off the piano."[18]

Four weeks after the graduation incident, Jenny Naylor
went on to play with the Utah Symphony as a guest pianist in
Abravanel Hall. She was quoted in the *Desert News*, prior to
her appearance with the Utah Symphony, as saying, "It's just
ironic that I'll be playing in the same concert hall I was just
thrown out of."

All of us here at the American Family Policy Institute
salute William Badger and Jenny Naylor as two individuals
who have shown that they are serious about defending their
faith, family, and freedoms.

Getting the Point Across

Cal Thomas writing about this incident in his syndicated
column concludes his article by saying, "George Orwell's
thought police haven't been defeated. They've migrated from
the Soviet Union to America."

Mr. Thomas goes on to say with tongue in check, "Perhaps
next year's graduating class at West High should sing George
Harrison's song in which he refers to his drug of choice as 'my
sweet Lord.' Wouldn't that throw the courts into a tizzy?"

A constitutional amendment to protect the religious liberties of Americans in public places really should not be necessary. The U.S. Constitution and Bill of Rights clearly covers
religious freedom and free speech. However, with the major
mis-interpretation and myth of the separation of church and
state by our courts, such an amendment is now necessary.

The Contract with the American Family, which was put
together by the Christian Coalition and unveiled in late May

1995, does call for a constitutional amendment to protect religious liberties. Although the Contract with the American Family has wide support from congressional leaders in both parties, no time table was set for passing it as was done with the Republicans "Contract with America."

Your phone calls and letters to your Congressman and two U.S. Senators, asking for support of this idea would be helpful. For further information on this amendment and its current status you can call the Christian Coalition headquarters at (804) 424-2630.

What else can you do? Follow the example of young William Badger, the student from Salt Lake City, Utah. Be bold in standing up for your faith, family, and freedoms — even when it is not popular or politically correct.

Surely William never expected his story to be seen on television by millions of Americans, talked about by numerous radio talk show hosts, or written about by authors and syndicated columnists.

Notes

[1] Nationwide survey by Luntz Research and Strategic Services, conducted February 11-12, 1995. Sample Size: 1000. Theoretical margin of sampling error: + or - 3.1%.

[2] Dr. D. James Kennedy, *Character and Destiny*, (Grand Rapids, MI: Zondervan Publishing House, 1994), p. 34.

[3] Charles E. Rice, *The Supreme Court and Public Prayer: The Need for Restraint* (New York:Fordham University PRess, 1964), p. 63. Gary DeMar, *The Untold Story* (Atlanta, GA: American Vision, Inc., 1993), p. 116.

[4] George Washington's Inaugural Address, April 30, 1789.

[5] Henry Halley, *Halley's Bible Handbook* (Grand Rapids, MI: Zondervan, 1927, 1965), p. 18. David Barton, *The Myth of Separation* (Aledo, TX: WallBuilder Press, 1991), p. 150.

[6] Benjamin Franklin's letter to the French ministry, March 1778.

[7] Robert Rutland, ed., *The Papers of James Madison* (Chicago: University of Chicago Press, 1973), Vol VIII, pp.299, 304.

[8] William J. Federer, *America's God and Country Encyclopedia of Quotations* (Coppell, Texas: Fame Publishing, 1994), p.412.

[9] Kennedy, *Character and Destiny*, p. 45.

[10] Ibid., p. 47.

[11] Ibid., p. 26.

[12] Ibid., p. 113.

[13] Keith A. Fournier, *Religious Cleansing in the American Republic*, 1993, p. 17. The decision was later reversed after counsel intervened.

[14] Ibid., p. 112.

[15] The D. James Kennedy Center for Christian Statesmanship, summer 1995.

[16] Kennedy, *Character and Destiny*, p. 124.

[17] Cal Thomas, "Graduating Without a Prayer," *The Washington Times*, June 14, 1995.

[18] *Salt Lake City Desert News* June 11, 1995.

11

The Time Is Now

Someone has said, "The time has come for all good men to come to the aid of their country."

That time is now.

This point in our nation's history is crucial to its survival. The 1994 November elections were a good start, but much more needs to be done.

If America is to survive and once again be the nation that many desire, the American people must take back their government from the agents of change. Conservative and moderate Americans are by far the majority. If we do not begin to call for a return to the U.S. Constitution and Bill of Rights, state rights, parental rights and authority, and fiscal conservatism, in a few years, there may be little left of the America we know and love to salvage.

A Few Good Men

Winston Churchill once said,

> If you will not fight for right when you can easily win without blood shed; if you will not fight when your victory is sure and not too costly; you may come to the moment when you

will have to fight with all the odds against you
and only a precarious chance of survival. There
may even be a worse case. You may have to
fight when there is no hope of victory, because
it is better to perish than to live as slaves.

In 1776, a group of good men decided to fight because they
believed in excellence, liberty, individualism, prosperity based
on hard work and honesty, the right to keep and own what
you work for, freedom of religion, freedom of speech, freedom
from socialism and a totalitarian repressive government.

On a warm July 4th, 1776, in the city of Philadelphia, 56
brave men signed their names to the Declaration of
Independence, stating, "With a firm reliance on the protection
of Divine Providence, we mutually pledge to each other our
lives, our fortunes, and our sacred honor."

Many of these 56 were men of means. They owned land,
livestock, homes, businesses, and they risked it all for the one
thing they could not buy — liberty. Liberty and freedom had
to be earned. Even though it could not be bought with money,
liberty for America and these men came at a high price.

Of the fifty-six, few were long to survive. Five
were captured by the British and tortured
before they died. Twelve had their homes, from
Rhode Island to Charleston, sacked, looted,
occupied by the enemy, or burned. Two lost
their sons in the army. One had two sons captured. Nine of the fifty-six died in the war,
from its hardships or from its bullets.

Indeed, those brave and noble 56 men pledged and lost
either their lives or the lives they had known. Their fortunes
may have been destroyed, but their honor has remained intact
to this very day.

Taking Responsibility for America

Freedom is never obtained or maintained without a price.

The freedoms we enjoy in America today are not as abundant as they once were. They can, however, be plentiful once again if all good men would come to the aid of their dying nation. America does not have to remain in a state of intensive care, struggling for life. With your help America's condition can be upgraded. But time is running out.

The choice is ours. Will we continue the long hard fight those 56 men began on our behalf in 1776? Or, will we wait until there is no chance of victory yet fight because it is better to perish than to live as slaves.

It has been said, "To be born free is a privilege. To die free is an awesome responsibility."

Will you take responsibility for America? Will you take seriously the duty to defend faith, family, and freedoms? If you and I don't, then who will?

In Washington D.C. in front of the U.S. Supreme Court, these words are carved in stone, "The price of freedom is eternal vigilance."

One line in the "Battle Hymn of the Republic" reads, "As He died to make man holy let us live to make man free."

Many in our nation's history have paid the highest price you can pay for freedom, and for this we should be eternally grateful. Through their dying we became free, in our living, we should maintain that freedom.

You — A Watchman

On November 22, 1963, President John F. Kennedy was assassinated in Dallas, Texas as he was en route to deliver a speech. The speech he never gave concluded with these words.

> We in this country, in this generation, are — by destiny rather than choice — the watchman on the wall of world freedom. We ask, therefore, that we may be worthy of our power and responsibility, that we may exercise our strength with wisdom and restraint, and that we may achieve in our time and for all time the ancient vision of peace on earth, good will

toward men. That must always be our goal. . . .
For as was written long ago, "Except the Lord
keep the city, the watchman waketh but in
vain."[1]

Through the message of this book, I hope to be not only a
watchman but a recruiter as well. If you are not already, I want
you to become a watchman. Together we must be alert and
vigilant looking for anything that threatens our faith, family
and freedoms.

What does it mean to be a watchman?

Being a watchman is dangerous, requiring that one put
himself or herself in a vulnerable position upon the tower.
The watchman searches the horizon for any sign of a threat to
the safety of those inside the fortress. Upon the sight of danger, the watchman then sounds his trumpet alerting the occupants of the fortress that danger has been sighted and is
approaching.

A watchman's job is one of great importance, for it is the
first line of defense for those inside. Should the watchman not
take his job seriously and become apathetic in his duty, those
within the fortress could be placed in great danger. A watchman can never have the attitude of "it won't ever happen
here." He is alert and vigilant at all times and in all conditions.

When a watchman sounds his trumpet, it is crucial he do
so based on the real threat of danger. If a watchman regularly
sounds false alarms, much like crying wolf, the warning of real
danger falls on deaf ears. Under such circumstances the watchman would have lost his credibility, and those whom he was
charged with protecting would no longer trust his judgment
for recognizing potential and real dangers. The watchman who
deliberately sounds false alarms for mere attention is just as
dangerous as the watchman who sounds the alarm too late.

The watchman must immediately sound his trumpet upon
sighting danger or the threat of danger. Failure to sound his
trumpet and waiting for absolute assurance and confirmation
that what he has sighted is indeed danger could be fatal.

Waiting to acquire the needed data could mean sacrificing
precious time. The site of the enemy placing ladders against

the walls of the fortress is proof of a real threat. The watchman would be derelict in his duty, however, if he had not sounded the alarm upon citing the enemy approaching in the distance.

Friend or Foe?

The purpose of the watchman is not only to warn those inside the fortress of danger but to warn them in time to prepare for the threat of danger — whether potential or real.

The job of the watchman can be very difficult because the goal of the enemy is to go undetected as long as possible, thus allowing him to have the advantage of surprise. In order to go undetected as long as possible, the enemy will do his very best to eliminate the watchman. Therefore, being a watchman means you are a likely target for attack. In fact, the watchman is often the first target of the enemy since he is the first line of defense for those inside the fortress. With the watchman out of the way, a surprise attack is almost guaranteed.

In order to go undetected, the enemy may disguise himself as a friend. In fact, he may be so well disguised that he is able to gain entrance to the fortress to live among his foes.

Upon attack, the enemy strikes not from the outside only, but from the inside as well. Those inside the fortress find themselves in such a state of confusion that they do not know who is friend and who is foe.

In order to minimize the threat of the enemy, everyone must do his part. The watchman can do his job perfectly, but if no one responds to the sound of his warning, his effort is futile.

If those inside the fortress have not trained, planned ,and prepared in advance for an attack, simply having the desire to defend themselves will do very little to actually protect them at the time of an attack.

Those inside the fortress must keep the key objectives at the forefront at all times. The occupants of the fortress certainly do not agree on everything, but they have some very like-minded goals and values that cause them to work together for the safety and preservation of their families.

Allowing petty arguments and misunderstandings to

divide the occupants of the fortress can cause attention to be diverted from the all-important common goals and desires. When this happens, the powerful force that once existed becomes weak and venerable.

You and I will not agree on everything, some reading this book are conservative in their ideology, others are very conservative, and some are moderate. However, I believe you are reading this book because you believe the way most American's believe — in parental authority, smaller government, and the U.S. Constitution and Bill of Rights.

We can disagree on a host of issues but don't let the disagreements keep all of us from working together in the quest to defend and preserve those principles most important to us — faith, family, and freedoms.

The Power of the Silent Majority

The elections of November 1994 proved that the silent majority is alive and well and can accomplish great things when we get involved.

Who are the silent majority? Hundreds of thousands of conservative and moderate Americans who do not like to be lied to, manipulated, or looked down on by the "we know better than you" politicians and social engineers.

As the most powerful voting block in our nation, when we have had enough, the politicians better look out. The silent majority are law-abiding citizens who, for the most part, do not participate in marches, sit-ins, and protests. When the silent majority does come together, however, you will hear about it.

In 1980 and 1984, the silent majority came together and sent Ronald Reagan to the White House. Ronald Reagan won his first term with an overwhelming majority. And the second term? President Reagan won by a landslide!

In May 1993, a bake sale in Fort Collins, Colorado brought out over 50,000 of the silent majority who were also fans of Rush Limbaugh. That sunny day in Colorado was filled with fun and fellowship but no arrests and no trash.

Every January 22 for over 18 years, pro-life Americans participate in the annual March for Life in Washington, D.C., with crowd estimates consistently at over 100,000 people.

Several times in our nation's history the silent majority has became the unsilent majority shutting down the U.S. Capitol switchboard and jamming every fax machine on Capitol Hill. Since 1992, this has happened over such issues as the education bill H.R. 6, Clinton's economic plan, gays in the military, and Hillary's national health care bill.

The silent majority has some serious muscle and in November 1994, we flexed. The end result was historic.

Many lawmakers heard but did not heed, the calls, letters, and faxes of the silent majority regarding H.R. 6, and Clinton's economic agenda. In November 1994, however, the silent majority sent a message to many of their representatives which they heard loud and clear, "You are fired!"

One politician by the name of Bill Clinton, got the message and went to work trying to make true the lies that got him elected.

Candidate Clinton who promised a middle-class tax cut broke this pledge as President Clinton. Instead, America received the biggest tax increase in history. The "incredible shrinking President," as *Time* magazine called him, came out in December 1994 with his better-late-than-never, I-need-to-save-my-job, middle-class tax cut.

You just watch, in November 1996, Clinton will get the same message his liberal friends got in November 1994 from the silent majority, "You are fired!"

Virtue Alone

The silent majority has more than political power; we also have a lot of buying power.

Who do you think made Rush Limbaugh one of the most successful authors of all times by buying a combined total of over five million copies of his two books? The silent majority.

Even to the surprise of many in the media, Dan Quayle's book, *Standing Firm*, made the *New York Times* bestseller list.

The silent majority also bought well over one million copies of former U.S. Secretary of Education Bill Bennett's book, *The Book of Virtues.*

Why the book of virtues? Because even though the silent majority disagrees with each other on many issues, they agree on certain virtues. These virtues bring the silent majority together, making them the most powerful group of voters and consumers in the nation.

What are some of these virtues? Honesty, integrity, character, hard work, kindness, self-control, modesty, compassion, humility, resolve, courage, and much more.

The silent majority is not asking for a leader who is perfect — they know that no such human being exists. But the politician, author, pastor, teacher, actor, citizen, and leader who embraces these virtues will find an eager group of followers. Just look at Ronald Reagan, Rush Limbaugh, Billy Graham, Paul Harvey, Helen Keller, Margaret Thatcher, Bob Hope, Jimmy Stewart, Abraham Lincoln, and George Washington — just to name a few.

Benjamin Franklin once said, "Virtue alone is sufficient to make a man great, glorious, and happy."

We certainly cannot forget the One who did live the perfect life and died for all mankind. The One that millions around the world worship because of His virtues and characteristics. Regardless of whether they are Catholic, Lutheran, Methodist, Presbyterian, or Baptist, millions around the world and in the United States of America still believe in and follow the teachings of Jesus Christ.

It does not matter whether you are a butcher, baker, or candlestick maker, you can become a watchman and leader today. Keep reading, and I will give you a detailed list of things you can do to make a difference in our nation.

Standing for Nothing?

It is easy to blame all our nation's problems on America's social engineers. Yes, they have done the majority of the damage, but conservative Americans and parents must take responsibility for letting the agents of change have so much power and control.

Granted, most of the power grab took place behind our

backs and in slimy, deceitful ways. Many Americans, however, then as now, refuse to believe that such an evil group of people with such un-American intentions even exist.

Why have many Americans denied the existence and rise in power of these agents of change? Because to do otherwise would require action. Taking action may require risking your job, your reputation, getting out of your comfort zone and getting involved in uncomfortable discussions and situations.

Edmund Burke has said, "All it takes for evil to triumph is for good men to do nothing."

There are many good, God-fearing, freedom-loving Americans. Unfortunately, there are also many who take their freedoms for granted and, therefore, do not take seriously their responsibility to get off their duffs and stand up for what is good, right, moral, decent, truthful, and noble.

The temptation to compromise has been great. What one generation allows, the next allows even more. The result has been a sliding of our moral and civic responsibilities as a people and a nation. We have permitted the loss of more and more of our individual and corporate responsibilities because of the increasing desire of each generation to take no responsibility at all for anything — much less take responsibility for our own actions.

Many, having neglected to take personal responsibility for their actions, have no thought of taking responsibility for defending faith, family, and freedoms. Is there nothing that we hold dear?

As one of my friends likes to say, "If you don't stand for something, you will fall for anything."

America has fallen. She has fallen from the place of nobility and honor that our founding fathers intended. Nobility and honor not based on pride and arrogance but on moral principles and humility. A humility that dared to recognize our moral responsibility to God and to each other, to preserve those values and truths, which were at one time self-evident.

Yes, America is not what it once was, or what it should be. Yet, to simply blame the social engineers and agents of change for all our problems and not to examine our own lives, desires, passions, commitments, and motives is simply shrugging the personal responsibility that is so needed at this time.

Uncommon, Common Sense

Will we continue to permit the decline of America? Will we take back our individual and corporate responsibilities and rebuild the America that so many died to create and preserve? Time will only tell. America's agents of change are counting on apathy to be one of their greatest assets.

To the thousands of parents who will read this book, I say to you, never let the liberal, educational elite trap you into defending your involvement in America's educational process. This is nothing less than a cheap shot that reveals their true blue — or should I say true red — elitist colors. Stand up and challenge them on the facts. When you do — and I know from experience — they will prove to be nothing less than watermelons, green on the outside and red on the inside.

When the elite social engineers challenge parental involvement due to the absence of a parent's degree in education, remember the words of one wise man: "You do not have to be in Who's Who to know what's what."

Lest we forget, some of America's greatest leaders did not have fancy degrees. President Truman did not have a college education.

One of America's greatest thinkers today, and the most successful radio talk show host of all time, Rush Limbaugh, also does not possess a Ph.D. or even a college education. Yet, to millions he is described as the Dr. of Democracy. Why? Because of his uncommon, common sense.

And before my liberal friends get too proud, let me remind them that one of their favorite spokesmen, the perfect Peter Jennings of ABC "World News Tonight," only possesses an eighth grade education.

You and the Tenth Amendment

The time is now for the federal government to back off and recognize the Tenth Amendment of the United States Constitution.

The Republican "Contract with America" promises to return local control and shrink big government. I am all for that, and so are the majority of Americans. At the same time, you and I should be busy in our states pushing for a Tenth Amendment resolution.

If the size of government does not shrink and the government's strong-arm tactics do not cease — and if voters do not elect a conservative Congress and President in 1996, we are in deep trouble. If the power of the federal government continues to escalate, the states of this nation and its citizens will need protection. Protection from whom? From a totalitarian government.

A Tenth Amendment resolution in each and every state is the best way to maintain the enforcement of the Tenth Amendment of the U.S. Constitution, which says:

> The powers not delegated to the United States by the Constitution, nor prohibited by it to the States, are reserved to the States respectively, or to the people.

Let me give you an example of how a Tenth Amendment resolution would help states defend the rights of their citizens.

Despite the overwhelming fact that Outcome-Based Education does not work and produces a fiscal and educational nightmare for the districts and states that have tried and are trying OBE, our government continues to mandate the principles of OBE through Goals 2000 and H.R. 6.

Despite the fact that Virginia and other states have dumped OBE, legislators are held at gun point by Washington educrats who threaten, "If you want a piece of the $12.5 billion allowed for by H.R. 6 and S. 1513, (in the first year alone), you must comply with this federal legislation and implement OBE."

Why would America's social engineers implement a program that has a proven track record of failure? Because education today is planned failure to produce intellectual slavery. If you are not educated, you are easily controlled.

How then can a state get around this federal mandate?

The federal government requires that states comply with their mandates in order to receive federal funding for education.

Where does the money come from that the federal government gives the states when they comply? From your tax dollars. States are being bribed into compliance with their own money.

As one man has said," Money that goes from the states to the federal government does two things. On the way to the federal government it picks up glue, on the way back to the states, it picks up strings."

What is the answer? States who do not wish to implement OBE or any other program should withhold their federal tax dollars on the basis of violation of the Tenth Amendment.

States withholding taxes could place the funds in an account and distribute the money as the state sees fit. Once, and as long as the Federal Government is in compliance with the Tenth Amendment, then the state could again begin sending the government a check.

We must remember that the federal government did not create the states, but the states created the federal government — and the Tenth Amendment reaffirms this fact.

When Trust is Gone

Carol Innerst of the *Washington Times,* wrote in an article titled, "Parents Rebel as Outcomes Replace Three R's," that, "just a few years ago . . . parents were comfortable with their children in public schools and trusted educators to deliver a solid academic program. Now the trust is gone as a new school year gets under way."[2]

How can we see that our government restores that trust? By passing and instituting an Education Bill of Rights.

Just as many Americans embraced and supported the idea of the Republican's "Contract with America," I believe a majority of the American people would support an Education Bill of Rights.

In the February 17, 1994 issue of the *Raleigh News and Observer,* Stephen Arons wrote a well thought-out article on

how Clinton and his social engineers are taking away some of
our basic rights, which are guaranteed by the constitution,
through such legislation as H.R. 6 and Goals 2000.

> The change will begin with the nationaliza-
> tion of important areas of education policy and
> will eventually result in the creation of a
> national public secondary school curriculum
> enforced by a system of performance tests for
> all students. The last time the country experi-
> enced such a basic shift in the relationship of
> individuals to their government — the adop-
> tion of the U.S. Constitution — the protection
> of individual liberty was secured by the adop-
> tion of the Bill of Rights.
>
> Two hundred years ago, the national
> debate over the new Constitution and the pro-
> posed amendments was long, thoughtful and
> difficult. The proposed reallocation of federal
> power over schooling — and its effect on the
> freedoms of intellect and belief — has been
> accompanied by no such debate. . . . The
> Constitution created substantial new federal
> powers, raising the fear that individual liberties
> might be at risk. As a result, Congress adopted
> and the states ratified amendments called the
> Bill of Rights. It was a means of ensuring that
> the good intentions of the founders could not
> turn into the repressive manipulations of suc-
> ceeding generations of public officials.
>
> The good intentions of today's educators
> and government policy-planners are manifest.
> But the magnitude of the change in federal
> power that they are proposing in Goals 2000 is
> so great, and the importance of individual free-
> dom to the success of schooling so fundamen-
> tal, that an Education Bill of Rights is essential.

An Educational Bill of Rights

Mr. Arons goes on to suggest the following Educational Rights:

1. Secure the right of families to choose other than a government-run school, and of sub-cultures to provide schooling consistent with deeply held beliefs.
2. Secure the right of non-government schools to be free of content regulation and to adopt goals and standards of their own choosing.
3. Protect public school students and teachers from having to confess a belief in any ideo-logical point of view and from, in any other way, having imposed on them an orthodoxy of beliefs that contradicts their conscience, cultural heritage, or spiritual values.
4. Secure the status of teachers as professionals by enhancing academic freedom and due process protections against job loss, discrim-ination, textbook and library censorship or other penalties arising from political pres-sures or content-based government require-ments.
5. Protect the rights of expression, inquiry, press, and privacy of public school students.

What we really need is for our lawmakers to follow the Constitution we already have. In addition, they need to comply with U.S. Supreme Court rulings such as the 1966 decision *Grinswold V. Connecticut*, which states that "the state cannot interfere with the right of parents to control their children's education."[3]

What Can You Do?

Here are a few suggestions that you can take to regain control not only of your children's education but also of their future.

1. Run for school board.

Due to the federal control of our public schools, local school boards often find themselves fighting an uphill battle.

If there are enough reform- minded conservatives on your local school board, they can vote not to comply with Goals 2000, H.R. 6, or the "state improvement plan" developed by your state and approved by the U.S. Department of Education. By not complying with the state plan, which is really the implementation of Outcome-Based Education, the board can create a court test case.

The federal government in H.R. 6 encourages states who have districts and school boards that are not complying with the U.S. Department of Education's approved state plan to fire the school board and, if necessary, the district superintendent. If the state does not ensure that every district is in compliance with the state's "OBE plan," the state can lose its federal funding.

Talk about heavy-handed intervention by the state and federal government! Can you imagine firing a dully elected school board because they are carrying out the wishes of the parents and taxpayers versus the wishes of the liberals in Washington? Such a scenario is no joke. In fact, it is on the verge of becoming a reality.

The question is: Is there a local school board courageous enough to take a stand, take the heat, and be a test case for the courts?

Maybe. I have been consulting with school board members in Illinois who have the votes and are on the verge of voting out OBE and anything to do with Goals 2000. Others, like Hartford, Connecticut and Baltimore, are hiring alternative education companies to come in and manage their schools. Unfortunately, these companies — which operate the schools more economically — are also forced to follow state mandates in implementing the OBE standards.

Imagine what would happen if school board members all across the country were to take a stand and help us reclaim America by reclaiming their local control! If that seems possible in your district, get informed, get busy, gain support, and get elected to your local school board.

Under Goals 2000 and H.R. 6, however, your local school board has very little power, unless — and until — your state passes a Tenth Amendment resolution and regains control from the federal government. If this situation occurred, your local school board would once again have substantial power. In that case, running and getting elected to your local school board means you are in position to bring about change should H.R. 6 and Goals 2000 be overturned or should your state pass a Tenth Amendment resolution.

2. Distribute information.

Informing people is one of the most effective things we can do.

I have come across many people who were in favor of such programs as OBE or Goals 2000 until they were presented with the truth. There are numerous books, videos, and cassette tapes you can loan or give to your friends and family in order to educate them on the important issues of our day.

3. Distribute the voting record of elected officials.

Many conservative and moderate political action groups now produce voting records that you can receive and distribute in your community. Most people are unaware of how their elected state and federal officials voted on the issues during their term.

Politicians rely on the fact that their constituents will have a short memory. If your elected official voted the wrong way on an issue, chances are you will have forgotten about it in a few weeks.

Voting records provide an excellent overview of whether or not your elected officials are representing your family, community, or state, versus voting for the special interest groups and his own political agenda.

Politicians hate voting records. All the more reason to get yourself a box full before the next election and distribute them far and wide. This kind of distribution has cost many elected officials their jobs.

4. Get involved in a campaign.

No matter how old or how young, anyone can get involved in the political campaign of his choice. Whether nailing down yard signs, stuffing envelopes, or working on a phone bank, you can be involved. Some of you have special gifts and abilities in leadership, administration, and organization and could be a real asset to a campaign in a major up-front way.

5. Write letters to the editor.

While I was in Seattle in November 1993, I read two letters written to the editor that were published in one of the Seattle papers discussing OBE and the "Parents as Teachers" program. Both editorials were very well written.

Thousands of people in the Seattle area are now more informed on Outcome-Based Education and the "Parents as Teachers" program because two informed individuals took the time to write a letter to their local newspaper editor.

6. Call radio talk shows.

As I am writing this chapter, I am listening to a local radio talk show hosted by a moderate broadcaster who takes numerous calls every day on all types of topics. This local talk show, on one of the Twin Cities largest radio stations, reaches many people.

The host of this show has had numerous guests and listeners, in studio and on the phone, discussing Outcome-Based Education and other such programs. In fact, it is the callers who alert the host to many important topics, like OBE, when they call in to express their concern.

Due to such calls, the topic of OBE and our failing educational system has been discussed many, many times. A few calls by informed individuals, who also provided this host with documented information, have successfully informed the masses of the truth about OBE.

I have found radio to be one of the most successful formats for getting the message out to the people of America. Over the past few years, I have been privileged to be a guest on over 200 radio talk shows. I was invited to be a guest on several of these programs because individuals like yourself gave my name, number — and sometimes my book — to their favorite local or national talk show host.

When I was on "The G. Gordon Liddy Show," which has 8-10 million listeners, nearly 7,000 people called and ordered an "issue brief" we offered on H.R. 6. After people received this issue brief, made copies of it and distributed it, untold numbers were informed, educated, and encouraged to call their Congressman and two U.S. Senators.

7. Get your favorite church, school, or organization to host a conference or seminar on education and other important topics.

As someone who travels the nation conducting seminars for groups, I know just how successful they can be. Over the past few years, I have been able to speak before many thousands, informing them on many issues that are confronting us today.

If you promote it, they will come.

8. Be documented in all you say and do.

In real-estate the key is location, location, location. When trying to gain support for our cause the key is documentation, documentation, documentation.

9. Be respectful and non-emotional, not angry.

Getting angry and emotional means you have lost control. You always want to maintain control so you can maintain your credibility.

10. Attend your local school board meetings.

You would be surprised how few people attend local school board meetings. With the local school board loosing all its power, not much takes place during their meetings — unless OBE is being discussed. If your local school board ever does regain power and local control, then please attend these meetings.

11. *Support organizations who are lobbying for and against the issues you think are important.*

Many organizations such as — Eagle Forum, Concerned Women For America, the Heritage Foundation, the Home School Legal Defense Fund, the Rutherford Institute, the American Center For Law and Justice — do a wonderful job in Washington D.C. working to protect your faith, family, and freedoms.

These organizations need your support, and you need their monthly newsletters and the other information they provide. (See *Resource List*.)

12. *Call and write your elected officials regularly on issues that concern you.*

One issue that needs your immediate attention is to insist that our lawmakers do away with Goals 2000 and repeal H.R. 6.

Your U.S. Congressman or Senators, however, may say they support the recent Health and Human Services Appropriations Subcommittee proposal that would cut all funding allowed for in Goals 2000: the Educate America Act. That sounds good, but such cuts would not mean the end of Goals 2000. Why? Because the real funding mechanism of Goals 2000 is H.R. 6, which allows for at least $62 billion in federal spending over the next five years.

Tell your Congressman and Senators that if they are serious about downsizing the federal government, returning local control, and doing away with Goals 2000, they must repeal H.R. 6. Any lawmaker who disagrees has not thoroughly studied the issue.

In addition, you need to contact your state representatives and insist they repeal any state laws requiring Outcome-Based Education graduation standards.

Don't back down because, after reading this book, you are probably more informed about current educational issues than your elected representatives. Go for it, and see what kind of response you get.

13. Educate the next generation.

Remember, "the philosophy of education in one generation will be the philosophy of government in the next." No matter where you send your child or children to school, the center of education must be the home.

Make sure your children are being educated in traditional history. It is so important that students understand the U.S. Constitution and Bill of Rights and what our founding fathers intended for this nation. Have them read the biographies of our Founding Fathers and/or watch videos on the lives of America's great leaders.

I would recommend that you and your family watch the video by David Barton titled, "America's Godly Heritage." If you want a real education in history and the Constitution, this video is a must. You will be shocked at how far our nation has drifted from its foundation.

Since there are only a few good public schools left, I believe the best way to educate the next generation is either in a private school or at home through a quality home-school program. I know there are many good conservative public school teachers, but intrusive legislation is increasingly preventing these teachers from doing their jobs as they would like.

Cal Thomas in a syndicated column which was published in the *Washington Times* on June 14, 1995 put it best when he said:

> If conservatives are serious about their disgust and their resolve to bring about change, they must stop sending their children to the once public, now government, schools. . . .
>
> As the secularization of our culture continues, one wonders why people with religious sensibilities continue to put up with it. If they separated themselves from the system that is trying to gut what remains of the foundational principles on which the country was built and put their children in private schools or taught them at home, not only would the students be

better off, it would force the government
schools to shape up or shut down.[4]

Our nation is now seeing the kind of product that the public school system is best known for producing. Allen Bloom, a
professor at the University of Chicago and author of the bestselling book, *The Closing of the American Mind,* wrote:

> There is one thing a professor can be absolutely
> certain of: Almost every student entering the
> University believes, or says he believes, that
> truth is relative. That anyone should regard the
> proposition as not self-evident astonishes them,
> as though they were calling into question 2 + 2
> = 4. Some are religious, some atheists, some are
> to the left, some are to the right, some intend to
> be scientists, some humanists or professionals
> or businessmen; some are poor, some are rich.
> They are unified in their relativism and in their
> allegiance to equality. The danger they have
> been taught to fear from absolutism is not error
> but intolerance. Relativism is necessary to
> openness; and this is virtue, the only virtue,
> which all primary education for more than fifty
> years has dedicated itself to inculcating.

As a former college professor, Allen Bloom met hundreds
of college freshmen every year who were fresh out of the government schools. If anyone can give an analysis of the kind of
product that public education has dedicated itself to creating
for the last 50 years, it would be Professor Bloom.

Do you want your child to become the person Dr. Bloom
describes? Someone who believes truth is relative and for
whom "openness" is his only virtue? God help us!

This book and my first book, *Cradle to College: An
Educational Abduction,* contain plenty of reasons why America's
parents must think seriously about making the needed sacrifices to get their offspring out of government schools.

14. Take your parenting responsibilities seriously.

All that is wrong in America today is not the fault of a failed educational system. It isn't even the increase of sex and violence on television or in the movies. Much of where America finds itself today is due to mothers and fathers who have not taken seriously their responsibility to be good parents and raise moral, virtuous, and responsible citizens.

Parents are the single greatest influence in a child's life. The question is — What kind of influence are they? Unfortunately many children today know their next door neighbors better than they know their own parents. For the past several years, poll after poll has shown that the average father spends less than five minutes per day talking to his child or children.

Our nation is feeling the effects of fathers who have dumped their responsibilities of parenting for the pursuit of a bigger house, a more expensive car, and the corner office.

Clebe McClary, an authentic American war hero, earned the Silver Star and Bronze Star as well as the loss of an eye and his left arm for his Vietnam battlefield valor. Despite being told he would never walk again, he determined to persevere and succeeded. An outstanding motivational speaker, Clebe McClary now travels the country speaking on the importance of family and particularly the importance of fathers leading by example.

Clebe makes it very clear that the reason he turned out to be the kind of young man that he became was the result of his father's involvement in his life. Clebe said, "My father had something that more men need today — a drug problem. My father drug me to church, he drug me to baseball practice, he drug me to school. My father was involved in my life."

Very few men ever retire saying, "I should have worked harder and spent more time at the office." Many men do retire and realize that it was really not worth all the sacrifice — the missed ball games, the missed recitals and school plays, the missed birthday parties. Most men retire saying, "I wish I had spent more time with my family."

Fathers, for the sake of our nation's future, please take your family seriously.

President Ronald Reagan was correct when he said, "Today more than ever, it is essential that . . . each of us remember that the strength of our family is vital to the strength of our nation."

15. *Pray for our nation and its leaders.*
Benjamin Franklin once said,

> I have lived, Sir, a long time, and the longer I live, the more convincing proofs I see of this truth that God governs in the affairs of men. And if a sparrow cannot fall to the ground without His notice, is it probable that an empire can rise without His aid?

Prayer has always been an intricate part of the righteous governing of our nation. Dr. D. James Kennedy in his sermon, "Church and State," made these observations:

> In reading over the Constitutions of all 50 of our states, I discovered something which some of you may not know: there is in all 50, without exception, an appeal or a prayer to the Almighty God of the universe. . . . Through all 50 state Constitutions, without exception, there runs this same appeal and reference to God who is the Creator of our liberties and the pre-server of our freedoms.[5]

As Christians, we are commanded to pray for those in positions of authority. If we don't pray, who will?

Time for Revolution

I have offered this list of things you can do because the most often asked question I receive is, "What can I do?" I do not want to simply tell you what is wrong with America, but what is also right with America and how you and I can make it better.

Part of making America better means stopping the agenda of America's agents of change. Why? Because their agenda is diametrically opposed to what most Americans desire.

If you doubt what I say, then remember November 1994. The Republicans in Congress told the public, through their "Contract with America," that they want to return power to the people, strengthen the American family, lessen the tax burden, and get our financial house in order. To this agenda, Americans said yes. Not one Republican Congressman or Senator was defeated, but many Democratic Congressmen and Senators did not return to Washington in January 1995.

The majority of Americans endorsed the "Contract with America" because the majority of Americans believe in faith, family, and freedoms.

A revolution began in America in November 1994, and it can continue. When I talk about a revolution, I mean the overthrowing of one form of government for another form of government. I am talking about returning to a form of government that governs from a moral foundation.

A revolution also involves a making a 180 degree turn in a completely *new* direction. When the American people embraced the "Contract with America" by electing a Republican majority to the U.S. House and Senate in 1994, they embraced a new direction. At the same time, however, American voters made it clear that they want a return to an *old* form of government — the constitutional form spelled out by our founding fathers in the U.S. Constitution.

The people of America did not embrace a new vision. The vision in the "Contract with America" was not new. The direction and vision embodied in the "Contract with America" is based on the vision the founding fathers of our nation conceived in 1776. This newly revived vision and direction proposed in the "Contract with America" will not be easily obtained or held onto, but at least the revolution has began.

I invite you to join the revolution if you have not already done so. Do not wait. It is time for all good men and women to come to the aid of our country.

The time for an American revolution is now!

Notes

[1] Peter Marshall and David Manuel, *The Glory of America*, (Bloomington, MN: Gargorg's Heart 'N Home, Inc., 1991), p.1.20.

[2] Carol Innerst, "Parents Rebel as Outcomes Replace Three R's," *The Washington Times*, Wednesday September 7, 1994.

[3] Dr. Dennis Cuddy, *Chronology of Education with Quotable Quotes*, (Highland City, FL: Pro Family Forum Inc, 1993), p. 39.

[4] Cal Thomas, "Graduating Without a Prayer," *Washington Times*, June 14, 1995.

[5] From the unabridged, printed sermon by D. James Kennedy, Ph.D., "Church and State." Tim LaHaye, *Faith of our Founding Fathers* (Brentwood, TN: Wolgemuth and Hyatt, Publishers, Inc., 1987), p. 93.

12

The Revolutionary's
Survival Guide

If you are going to start a revolution, you will need weapons to help you win the battle for your family, faith, and freedoms.

This chapter provides a list of *Terms and Definitions* to use during invasions on the home front — at school board meeting and letters to your newspaper editor.

The section on *Landmark Court Cases* will also give you needed ammunition to assault (not insult) your Congressman, Senators, and President with phone calls, letters, and faxes about important issues.

In order to keep the supply lines of information coming, I am including a *Resource List* of freedom-fighting organizations and how to contact them. You will also find a list of books, videos, and newsletters that will make sure you are getting a diet of truth.

To keep morale high and spirits up, there is a listing of where and when you can tune in to my radio program and also Michael Reagan's.

So get pumped up and battle-ready for the fight of your life. And be sure to write and let me know whenever you take the high ground away from the enemy.

God bless you as you begin to help reclaim our nation at risk.

Important Terms and Definitions

Benjamin Bloom: A psychologist, author, and humanist who is best known for being the father of higher order thinking skills, also known as the standards or outcomes that make up Outcome-Based Education. Often called the father of Outcome-Based Education, Bloom summed up his philosophy when he said, The highest form of intellect is when an individual no longer believes in right or wrong.

The Bureau of Apprenticeship and Training: An agency housed inside the Department of Labor that administers skill certificates recognized industry wide.

Certificate of Advanced Mastery: A certificate or diploma that students receive ideally at the age of 18 or the end of their senior year of high school. The Certificate of Advanced Mastery certifies that the student has obtained the needed skills and training to apply for a job in his chosen career major. A Certificate of Advanced Mastery is similar to a vocational certificate. This certificate is obtained after two years of job mentoring or job shadowing and community service work.

Certificate of Initial Mastery: An Outcome-Based Education diploma that students receive after they have met the state's federally approved Outcome-Based Education standards. A student ideally receives his certificate of initial mastery at age 16 or at the end of his tenth grade year. Without a Certificate of Initial Mastery a student cannot go on to receive a Certificate of Advanced Mastery.

Corporate Fascism: A philosophy or system of government that advocates or exercises dictatorship through the merging of state and business leadership*(American Heritage Dictionary)*.

John Dewey: An author and humanist best known for being one of the authors of the Humanist Manifesto. Often referred to as the father of modern education in America,

Dewey has been given this title despite the fact that he went to Russia in the 1930s to help establish the Karl Marx way of education and helped found the Socialist Society. He was also one of the founders of the National Education Association and became its honorary president in 1932. Among his many liberal beliefs, Dewey proclaimed that the purpose of school was not to educate children but to socialize them. Dewey also believed that high literacy was an obstacle to socialism.

Education Reform: A term liberals use when they don't want the public to know they are talking about implementing a liberal, socialistic, social engineering program such as Outcome-Based Education.

William Glasser: A psychologist, author and former Humanist of the Year and nationally recognized advocate and promoter of Outcome-Based Education. In his book, *Schools Without Failure,* Glasser writes, We have to let students know there are no right answers, and we have to let them see that there are many alternatives to certainty and right answers.

Goals 2000: Also known as the Educate America Act, Goals 2000 was originally unsuccessfully introduced as America 2000 during the Bush administration. According to the May 26, 1993 *New York Times,* as vice-chairman and then chairman of the National Governors Association, Bill Clinton played a leading role in forging the six ambitious goals for the year 2000. The national standards in Goals 2000 grew to eight under the Clinton Administration. Bill Clinton signed Goals 2000 into law in April 1994. Goals 2000 puts the federal government in the educational drivers seat and turns America's public schools into federal government-run schools.

H.R. 6: Also known as the Improving America's Schools Act of 1994, H.R. 6 is 1994 reauthorization of the Elementary and Secondary Education Act of 1965. This bill, which was established by Lyndon Johnson in 1965, must be reapproved by Congress every five years. ESEA has for years been the federal government's biggest bill for the funding of education in

America. In its original form, most of the funding in ESEA went to America's disadvantaged school children. However with the increase of the federal government's meddling in education, ESEA's billions now can go to any state that submits and has approved a state improvement plan (on OBE plan) as called for under Goals 2000. As the funding mechanism for Goals 2000, H.R. 6 will allow for at least $62 billion to be spent on education reform during its five year authorization (1994-1999).

Humanist Manifesto: A document written and signed in 1933 by eleven prominent college and university professors and other liberals who did not believe in God or the deity of God, but who believed that man is God. The signers also did not believe in the Bible, capitalism, traditional morality, or the traditional American culture. For the signers of the manifesto, humanism was their religion. Years later, the U.S. Supreme Court declared in footnotes in two different decisions that humanism does have a religious tone. Some humanists consider themselves religious humanists while others consider themselves secular humanists.

The National Education Association: The world's largest union and special interest group with 2.2 million American teachers on its roles. The NEA is one of America's most liberal, anti-family, anti-Christian special interest groups.

The National Education Standards and Improvement Council: NESIC is the equivalent of a twenty-member school board based in Washington, D.C. and was established via the federal legislation Goals 2000. The majority of the board's members are appointed by the President and must be professional teachers, meaning members of the National Education Association.

Outcome-Based Education: An educational reform program developed by psychologist Benjamin Bloom. OBE stresses standards or outcomes based on a politically correct, secular humanist world view. Traditional education is outcome-based, but Outcome-Based Education as developed by Benjamin Bloom is not based on traditional education but on lowering the standard so all students are equal. OBE is nothing less than the promotion of socialism.

SCANS Board: Housed inside the Department of Labor, the Secretaries Commission on Achieving Necessary Skills Board answers to the Secretary of Labor and is instrumental in establishing the national standards or outcomes that America's students must meet in order to receive their skill certificates.

Site-Based Management: A term used by the educational elite to deceive local educators into believing that they are developing and carrying out their own educational programs when in fact they are not.

B.F. Skinner: A behavioral psychologist who developed programmed learning also referred to as corrective thought control or coercive thought control. A very proud and well-known humanist, B.F. Skinner taught at Harvard University and was one of the first to promote the use of a machine for the purpose of remediation. Today, the Skinner philosophy has been enhanced by computers that can instantly correct wrong answers and responses.

Bill Spady: A modern-day psychologist best known for being one of today's most vocal supporters, advocates, and promoters of Outcome-Based Education.

Total Quality Management: A manufacturing model developed by William Deming in which the goal is to find out who your customer is and meet his needs. In education, Outcome-Based Education is often referred to as Total Quality Management in order to hide its true identity. Under TQM the child becomes a product or is more commonly called human resource. The customer is industry. The parent is the supplier of the human resource or human capital.

Whole-Language: A method used to try and teach individuals to read. Whole-language has become the alternative to traditional phonics. Whole-language is often referred to as a sight-based method for teaching individuals to read.

According to the national magazine, *The Executive Educator,* the two fundamental principles of whole-language are that children best learn to read precisely the same way they speak, and children should be empowered to invent the shapes of letters and the spellings of words.

Landmark Court Cases

The following is a list of court cases you need to know as you seek to defend your faith, family, and freedoms. (Special thanks the Citizens for Excellence in Education for compiling this list)

1. *Morrow v. Wood*, 35 Wis. 59, 17 Am. Rep. 47 471 (1874)
The schools cannot compel the child to pursue study that is forbidden by the parents.

2. *State Ex Rel Sheibley v. School District #1 of Dixon County Et AL.* 31 Neb. 552, 48 NW 393 (1891)
The right of the parent . . . to determine what studies his child shall pursue is paramount to that of trustees or teachers.

3. *Meyer v. Nebraska*, 262 U.S. 390 (1923); Yoder; Pierce
The individual citizen has the fundamental right to direct the upbringing of his own children.

4. *Pierce v. Society of Sisters*, 268 U.S. 510 (1924)
The court ruled that the state may not unreasonably interfere with the liberty of parents and guardians to direct the upbringing and education of children under their control.
A child is not the mere creature of the state.

5. *Hardwick v. Bd. of Trustees*, 205 p. 49 Cal. (1921)
The court commented that religious reasons were not the only basis for legitimate parental objection. It can also be a question of morals which may concern the conscience of those who are not affiliated with any particular religious sect. The court wrote that this involves:

> The right of parents to control their own children — to require them to live up to the teachings and the principles which are inculcated in them at home under the parental authority.
> Has the state the right to enact a law . . . the effect of which would be to alienate in a mea-

sure the children from parental authority? . . .
to answer . . . in the affirmative would be to
give sanction to a power over home life that
might result in denying parents their natural as
well as their constitutional right to govern
within the scope of just parental authority, their
own progeny.

6. *Prince v. Massachusetts*, 321 U.S. 158 (1944)
Parental rights of bringing up children cannot be interfered with, and there must be freedom from all substantial
arbitrary impositions and purposeless restraints.

7. *Van Allen v. McCleary*, 27 Mis. 2d 81; 211 NYS 2d 501
(1961)
Despite the compulsory school attendance laws, the parent
retains the right to direct the education of his child.

8. *Pie v. Ullman*, 367 U.S. 497 (1961)
Parental rights of bringing up children cannot be interfered
with, and there must be freedom from all substantial arbitrary
impositions and purposeless restraints. (Identical to *Prince v.
Massachusetts*.)

9. *Griswold v. Connecticut*, 381 U.S. 479, 486 (1965)
The state cannot interfere with the rights of a parent to
control his child's education.

10. *Finot v. Pasadena City Board of Education*, 58 Cal., Rptr.
520; 250 Cal. 2d 226 (1967)
The state cannot interfere with a parent's right to make
affirmative decisions concerning his child's disposition, particularly where spiritual, cultural or psychological factors are
involved.

11. *People Ex Rel. Vollmar v. Stanley*, 255 p. 610 Colo. (1927)
Children cannot be compelled to take instruction not
essential to good citizenship. The school board's control over
instruction does not mean that every child should be required

to take every subject which the board puts on the list.

12. *Dickens v. Emesto,* 37 A.D. 2d 102, 322 NYS 2d 581 (1971)
The state cannot interfere with a parent's right to make affirmative decisions concerning his child's disposition, particularly where spiritual, cultural or psychological factors are involved. (Identical to *Finot v. Pasadena.*)

13. *Vermont v. LaBarge,* 357 Atl. Rptr. 2d 121 (1976)
Compulsory school attendance must yield to First Amendment concerns.

14. *Wisconsin v. Yodar,* 406 U.S. (1972)
The state cannot assert the role of parents (patriae), over the parents' interest. The state's interest in universal education, however highly we rank it, is not totally free from a balancing process when it impinges on other fundamental rights and interests, such as those specifically protected by the Free Exercise Clause of the First Amendment and the traditional interest of parents with respect to the religious upbringing of their children.

15. *Minnesota v. Lundsten,* Beltrami County, MN (1980)
Compulsory attendance statutes cannot violate parents' First Amendment right to free exercise of religion and rights to privacy in family relations.

16. *Michigan v. Nobel,* Nos. S-791-0114-A, S-791-0115-A (57th O. Ct., City of Allegan, Michigan, Filed 12/12/79.)
State statutes must give way to the documented and sincere religious beliefs of the parents to educate their children.

17. *Kentucky v. Rudasill,* 589 SW 2d 877 (Oct. 9, 1979)
No one can be compelled to send his child to any school to which he may be conscientiously opposed.

18. *Ohio v. Whisner,* 47 Ohio st. 2d, 181 (1979)
State Department of Education minimum standards cannot

deprive parents of their traditional interest to direct the upbringing and education of their children by violating their First and Fourteenth Amendments rights to the U.S. Constitution.

19. *Valent v. New Jersey State Bd. of Education,* 274 A. 2d 832 N.J. (1971)
Reversed on procedural grounds 288 a. 2d 52 (N.J. 1972).
Concerned parents raised religious objections to their children being required to take a compulsory course entitled Human Sexuality. The school board's evidence indicated that 70% of the local citizens believed that sex education courses were necessary and beneficial for the students. The court noted that this was not an issue to be decided by majority vote. The judge wrote, "If majority vote were to govern in matters of religion and conscience, there would be no need for the First Amendment, which was adopted to protect the one percent who is sincere in a conscientious religious conviction. In conclusion, the court notes that: If educators are not careful about what they compel, parental discipline and respect will diminish as the great sovereign state forces its way into the home as a foster parent."

The following list of cases all ruled on The Ultimate Right of Parent to Govern or Control His Own Progeny. (Exact wording of the ruling follows list)

20. *Hardwick v. Bd. of Trustees of Fruitridge School District,* 54 Cal. App. 696 205 p 49 (1921)

21. *Trustees of Schools v. The People Ex Rel Markin Van Allen,* 87 111. 303 (1877)

22. *State v. Zobel,* 81 S.D. 260, 134 NW 2d 101 (1965)

23. *Shepherd v. State,* 306 p. 2d 346 (1957)

The parent has the ultimate constitutional right to govern or control his own progeny. . . . It would be revolutionary and possibly subversive to hold that any such overreaching powers exist in the state or any of its agencies.

24. From Parental Rights And Responsibilities, Joel S. Moskowitz, 50 *Washington Law Review* 623 (1975)

When the state chooses to override a parent's wish, the burden is on the state to establish that in order to function effectively as a citizen one must be versed in the subject to which the parent objects.

Resource List

Newsletters

Monthly Monitor, published by Michael Reagan, son of the former President, is America's most important newsletter. Mike has an in-depth understanding of current issues, contacts, and knowledge about issues, events, and people in Washington, and the unique ability to anticipate the next "big issue" to be debated in Congress.

In the *Monthly Monitor,* you get the actual truth — not somebody's spin on important issues — updates on bills before Congress, the history of issues, both past and present, in an easy-to-read and understand form.

If you have listened to Mike Reagan's talk show, you know his style — friendly, caring, unruffled. He has the unique ability to translate the dry, boring language of official Washington into an easy over-the-back-fence discussion of matters that affect you and your family every day.

Subscriptions: 1 yr: $34.95; 2 yr.: $59.95 Call 1-800-895-9898.

The Michael Reagan Talk Show is the most informative and pro-active of all the great conservative talk shows on the radio today. In addition to the *Monthly Monitor,* Michael now has launched The Reagan Information Interchange on the Internet's World Wide Web.

The Reagan Information Interchange is designed to be an "Information Mall" where the American people can quickly and easily find the information they need to make important public policy choices. The Interchange features a Congressional Bill Update, e-mail links to Members of Congress and much more. The Interchange also plays host to dozens of public policy organizations that want the public to have access to the same information that Washington insiders have.

To use the Reagan Information Interchange you should set your Web browser to: http://reagan.com

Organizations

Alliance Defense Fund
11811 North Tatum Blvd.
Suite P 184
Phoenix, AZ 85027
602-953-1200
Weekly updates available for $100 donation

American Family Policy Institute
Brannon Howse, President
P.O. Box 25062
St. Paul, MN 55125
(612) 739-4112
Order Line: 1-800-954-1122 Ext. 500

American Policy Center
14140-L Parke-Long Ct.
Chantilly, VA 22021
(703) 968-9768
Subscriptions available for monthly newsletter: *The Deweese Report*

Americans for Tax Reform
1301 Connecticut Ave. NW #444
Washington, D.C. 20036
(202) 785-0266

Christian Coalition
825 Greenbriar Circle #202
Chesapeake, VA 23320
(804) 424-2630

Citizens Against Government Waste
1301 Connecticut Ave. NW #400
Washington, D.C. 20036
(202) 467-5305

Congressional Quarterly
1414 22 Street NW
Washington, D.C. 20037
1-800-432-2250

Eagle Forum
316 Pennsylvania Ave. SE #203
Washington, D.C. 20003
(202) 544-0353

First American Monetary Consultants, Inc.
Larry Bates, President
5100 Popular Ave. Suite 3400
Memphis, TN 38137
1-800-325-0919

Heritage Foundation
5395 Emerson Way
Indianapolis, IN 46226
(317) 545-1000

National Right to Read
Bob Sweet, President
Jim Jacobson, Vice President
7379 Awsley Lane
The Plaines, VA 22171
1-800-468-8911

Plymouth Rock Foundation
P.O. Box 425
Marlborough, NH 03455
(603) 876-4685

Rutherford Institute
1445 East Rio Road
Charlottesville, VA 22901
(804) 978-3888

Books and Videos

Brannon Howse
Books:
• *Cradle to College*
(also titled, *An Educational Abduction)*
$10 plus shipping and handling.
• *Reclaiming a Nation at Risk*
$12.00 plus shipping and handling

Videos
• *Cradle to College,* Video
$20 plus shipping and handling
• *Certain Failure: Part I,* Video
(Explains H.R. 6 and Educational Technology)
$20 plus shipping and handling

To order call 1-800-954-1122 Ext. 500.
For quantity or case lot discounts, call 612-739-4112.

David Barton
Video
America's Godly Heritage
$19.95 plus shipping and handling

To order call: 817-441-6044

John Cummuta
Book and Video
Debt Free and Prosperous Living

For information and price, call 1-800-321-3465

The Brannon Howse Network

The following is a list of radio stations and times when Brannon Howse's 30 minute weekly radio program, *The American Family Policy Update*, can be heard. The schedule is subject to change. For further information, you may call The American Family Policy Institute at (612) 739-4112.

Alabama *Sunday 4:30 pm (CST)*
Enterprise 90.5
Selma 90.9
*Sheffield/WALKD 89.9
Arkansas *Sunday 4:30 pm (CST)*
Arkadelphia 91.9
Bentonville 88.1
Blytheville 91.5
Clarksville 89.9
Crossett 91.7
El Dorado 91.9
Forrest City 91.5
Jonesboro 90.5
Little Rock 103.7 *(day and time to be announced)*
Pine Bluff 91.1
Pocahontas 91.1
Warren 91.3
Colorado *Sunday 4:30 pm (CST)*
Trinidad 91.7
Georgia *Sunday 4:30 pm (CST)*
Cuthvert 89.3
Dublin 91.9
Griffin (WMVV) 90.7
Waycross 91.9
Illinois
Effingham 99.3
Flora 91.7
Mt. Vernon 91.3 *Sunday 4:30 pm (CST)*
Salem 91.3 *Sunday 4:30 pm (CST)*
Rockford (WFEN) 88.3 *Friday 12:30 pm (CST)*
Olney (WPTH) 88.1 *Saturday 2:30 pm (CST)*

Indiana *Sunday 4:30 pm (CST)*
Terre Haute 91.3
Salem 91.3
Iowa *Sunday 4:30 pm (CST)*
Fairfield 88.7
Ottumwa 88.1
Kansas
Great Bend 89.7 *Sunday 4:30 pm (CST)*
Hays 89.7 *Sunday 4:30 pm (CST)*
*Topeka (KBUZ) 90.3 *Sunday 4:30 pm (CST)*
*Wichita (KCFN) 91.1 *Sunday 4:30 pm (CST)*
Fort Scott (KVCY) 104.7 *Saturday 2:30 pm (CST)*
Kentucky *Sunday 4:30 pm (CST)*
Ashland 91.1
Campbellisville 91.7
Louisiana *Sunday 4:30 pm (CST)*
Alexandria 88.5
Jonesboro 89.7
Jonesville 91.9
Monroe 94.9
Ruston 88.3
Minnesota
Worthingon 88.1 *Sunday 4:30 pm (CST)*
Rochester (KFSI) 92.0 *Saturday 2:25 pm (CST)*
Winona (KFSI) 88.5 *Saturday 2:25 pm (CST)*
Mississippi *Sunday 4:30 pm (CST)*
Brookhaven 89.7
*Cleveland (WDFX) 98.3
Columbus 89.3
*Forest (WQST) 92.5
Hattiesburg 105.3
McComb 90.5
Natchez 91.1
Oxford 01.3
Starkville 88.9
*Tupelo (WAFR) 88.3
Vicksburg 93.3
West Point 98.9

Missouri *Sunday 4:30 pm (CST)*
Brookfield 91.5
Kennett 91.5
Memphis 91.5
Springfield (KAKU) 90.1
Nebraska
Hastings 91.7
New Mexico *Sunday 4:30 pm (CST)*
Clovis 91.1
Raton 90.1
North Carolina *Sunday 4:30 pm (CST)*
Beaufort 91.5
Black Mountain (WMIT)
Charlotte (WRCM) 91.9 (Rated by CCM as the eighth
largest contemporary Christian station in America)
New Bern 88.5
Sanford 88.7
North Dakota *Sunday 4:30 pm (CST)*
Jamestown 90.7
Willistown 91.7
South Dakota *Saturday 2:30 pm (CST)*
Gregory (KVCX) 101.5 FM
Ohio *Sunday 4:30 pm (CST)*
Martins Ferry 91.1
Shelby 89.9
Steubenville 88.9
Oklahoma *Sunday 4:30 pm (CST)*
ADA 88.7
Ardmore 91.9
Idabel 91.9
Norman 89.3
Peteau 91.7
Stillwater 89.7
Tennessee
Bristol 90.5 *Sunday 4:30 pm (CST)*
*Jackson (WAMP) 88. *Sunday 4:30 pm (CST)*
Lawrenceburg 89.9 *Sunday 4:30 pm (CST)*
Shelbyville 91.3 *Sunday 4:30 pm (CST)*
Tullahoma 88.5 *Sunday 4:30 pm (CST)*

*Chattanooga (WDYN) 89.7 *Saturday 3:30 pm (EST)* 100,000 Watts.
Texas *Sunday 4:30 pm (CST)*
Abilene 91.3
Amarillo 90.7
Borger 91.5
Brownfield 90.7
Crockett 91.9
Dalhart 91.7
Dumas 91.7
Hereford 90.7
Lamesa 91.3
Levelland 91.9
Pampa 90.9
Pecos 91.3
Plainview 90.7
Victoria 88.5
Utah *Sunday 4:30 pm (CST)*
St. George 88.7
Virginia *Sunday 4:30 pm (CST)*
Bristol 90.5
Washington *Sunday 4:30 pm (CST)*
Sunnyside 91.1
Wisconsin
*Tohma (WVCX) 98.9 *Saturday 2:30 pm (CST)*
La Crosse (KFSI) 91.9 *Saturday 2:25 pm (CST)*
*Milwaukee (WVCY) 107.7 *Saturday 2:30 pm (CST)*
Oshkosh AM
Lancaster (WJTY) 88.1 *Sunday 2:25 pm (CST)*

All stations are FM unless stated otherwise. All times are based on Central Standard Time.
* Indicates 100,000 watt station.

THE MICHAEL REAGAN NETWORK

As the education reporter for the Michael Reagan show,
Brannon Howse takes to the airwaves many times each year to
inform Mr. Reagan's listeners of the latest attacks on educational freedom and parental authority and to give them pro-
active ways to be involved in the battle for faith, family, and
freedoms.

In April and August 1995, Brannon was asked by Michael
to sit in as host of the show in his absence. The Michael
Reagan Show is now the nation's third largest nationally syndicated radio talk show, and the nation's largest nationally
syndicated night-time talk show.

Take note of the Michael Reagan Network schedule below
and tune in today!

Alaska
Anchorage KENI-550 6-9 pm
Alabama
Tuscaloosa WTNW-1230 9-mid
Huntsville WTKI-1450 9-11 am
Arkansas
Little Rock KSYG-103.7 8- 11 pm
Arizona
Flagstaff KVNA-690 7-10 pm
Phoenix   KXAM-1310 3-5 pm
California
Alturas KCNO-570 6-9 pm
Bakersfield KERN-1450 7-10 pm
Burney KAVA-1450 6-9 pm
Fresno KMJ-580   6-9 pm
Modesto KFIV-1360 6-9 pm
Palm Springs KPSL-1010 7-9 pm
San Diego KOGO-1590 6-9 pm
San Francisco KSFO-560 6-9 pm
Santa Barbara KGLW-1340 6-9 pm
Colorado
Denver KTLK-760 7-10 pm

Eugene KPNW-1120 6-9 pm
Grand Junction KNZZ-1100 7-10 pm
Connecticut
Hartford/New Haven WAVZ-1300 10-mid
Waterbury WWCO-1240 9-mid
Washington D.C.
WMAL-630 2-5 am
Florida
Bradenton WWPR-1490 9-mid
Ft. Meyers WINK-1240 10-mid
W. Palm Beach WBTZ-1290 10-mid
Tampa WWPR-1490 9-mid
Tampa WLFA-970 1-4 am
Georgia
Albany WALG-1590 9-mid
Macon WMAZ-940 9-mid
Hawaii
Honolulu KHVH-830 7-10pm
Iowa
Des Moines WHO-1040 10pm-1 am
Idaho
Boise KXFD-580 7-10 pm
Idaho Falls KID-590 7-10 pm
Illinois
Fairfield WFIW-1390 9-mid
Peoria WTAZ-102.3 9-mid
Rockford WROK-1440 9-mid
Spring Valley WAIV-103.3 8-11 pm
Indiana
Ft. Wayne WOWO-1190 10-mid
Lafayette WASK-1450 11-noon
Kansas
Wichita KNEW-1450 7-10 pm
Wichita KNSS-1240 8-11 pm
Kentucky
Lexington WVLK-590 10-mid
Louisville WWKY-790 10-1 am
Louisiana
Baton Rouge WJBO-1150-2-5 pm

Massachusetts
New Bedford WSAR-1480 10-mid
Maine
Bangor WSNV 10-1 am
Michigan
Detroit WXYT-1270 9-12 mid
Flint   WFNT-1470 8-11 pm
Petosky WJML-1110 1-3 pm
Missouri
Kansas City KCMO-810 9-11pm
Montana
Billings KBLG-910 7-10 pm
Bozeman KMMS-1450 7-9 pm
Hardin   KKUL-1230 7-10 pm
Helena   KBLL-1240 10-1 am
Missoula KGVO-1290 7-10 pm
Whitefish KJJR-   7-10 pm
North Carolina
Wilmington WMFD-630 9-mid
North Dakota
Grand Forks KNCC-1590 9-11 pm
Nebraska
Grand Island KMJJ-750 10-mid
Omaha KFAB-1110 8-10 pm
New Mexico
Albuquerque KKOB-770 8-10 pm
Nevada
Reno KOH-780 7-9 pm
New York
Albany WGY-910 2-5 am
Elmira/Watertown WENY-1230 10-1 am
Glens Falls WWSC-1450 1-3 pm
Middletown WALL-1340 9-mid
Ohio
Akron (syracuse) WNIR-101.1 3-5:30 am
Lima WIMA-1150 9-mid
Dayton WMVR-1080 9-11pm
Youngstown WKBN-570 10-mid

Oklahoma
Blackwell KOKB-1580 8-9 pm
Oklahoma City WKY-930 8-11 pm
Oregon
Eugene KPNW-1120 6-9 pm
Medford KCMX-580 6-9 pm
Portland KOTK-620 6-9 pm
South Carolina
Florence WPDT-105.1 9-mid
Greenville WFBC-1330 9-12 noon
Tennessee
Chattanooga WBDX-102.7 9-mid
Texas
Amarillo KPUR-1440 8-11 pm
Dallas   KLIF-570 8-10 pm
El Paso KTSM-1380 1-4 pm
Houston KPRC-950 9-mid
Texarkana KTWN-940 9-mid
Utah
Blanding KUTA-790 7-9 pm
Salt Lake City KCNR-1320 7-10 pm
St. George KDXU-890-7-10 pm
Washington
Tri-Cities KONA-980-6-9 pm
Seattle   KVI-570 6-9 pm
Spokane   KGA-1510 6-9 pm
Central Washington KULE-730 6-9 pm
Wenatchee KPQ-560 6-9 pm
Yakima   KUTI-980 6-9 pm
Wisconsin
Madison WTSO-1070 9-11 pm
Milwaukee WISN-1130 8-11 pm
Wausau   WXCO-1230 10-mid
West Virginia
Clarksburg WHAR-1340 9-mid